ON
THE
UNIT

ERIC BISECA, N.D.

ON
THE
UNIT

A Personal Narrative of
Meditation, Trauma and Juvenile Justice

atmosphere press

To the teachers and parents
of tomorrow...

◆ TABLE OF CONTENTS ◆

PART 1: Inner Technology

PART 2: Sacred Sociology

FOREWORD
by Dr. Sheena Sood

In January of 2020, I started teaching a weekly trauma-informed mindfulness and yoga session in the young women's unit at the Philadelphia Juvenile Justice Services Center (PJJSC). I am a yoga practitioner, a sociology professor, and a Philadelphia-based activist who is committed to abolitionist politics. Although I believe in fighting for a world where prisons, police, and border walls do not exist, I made the decision to teach yoga inside an institution that cages youth because penitentiaries are an unfortunate reality of our present society. I also believed that although youth and adults in the carceral system are discouraged from feeling a sense of connection with their bodies, their health, and overall humanity, they have the right to (re)connect to a quality of oneness within themselves. I offered yoga through a decolonial spiritual framework in hopes that incarcerated youth and adults would be able to find a momentary sense of awareness of their own humanity and capacity for love and transformation. My weekly yoga class was abruptly halted in March 2020 due to the COVID-19 pandemic.

Since then, I have often thought about the youth in the PJJSC, and more generally about the incarcerated population in the U.S. prison system, —our caged members of society whose health and wellness are so easily deprioritized during public health emergencies due to the blatant structural violence and racism of mass incarceration.

When Eric asked me about writing a foreword for his text, we had only met once, and it was coincidentally a "1-minute" encounter. A mutual friend who connected us shared about Eric's history as a teacher in the youth prison, but when we connected, we did not get a chance to discuss his experiences as a healer and educator in the PJJSC. We did not get to talk about his experiences as a white teacher in racist and colonial prison system; nor did we get to talk about the philosophy and methodology of decolonizing yoga. Hence, when Eric shared that his manuscript shared about his experiences as a trauma-informed educator and mindfulness teacher at the same youth prison where I spent a couple months teaching yoga, I knew I wanted to put my eyes on this text. I can now say after reading the text that I am so deeply grateful I said yes, for I have benefited tremendously from its wisdom.

Eric has developed such a thoughtful, humbling, and insightful pedagogical praxis of *beingness,* or the "one-minute moment," —a curriculum that educators across public school systems can find useful in their classrooms. We need more texts that are unafraid in their willingness to integrate spirituality with an education for liberation framework. *On the Unit* is such a text. Biseca's strategy of the "1-minute moment" strives to help youth in situations of material captivity find a dose of inner freedom to heighten their awareness and connection to a higher consciousness. So often, educators spend countless hours trying to instill discipline, memorization, knowledge and skills into their students' minds without considering ways we can bring them into deeper presence and healing. The "one-minute meditation" mitigates the effect of hierarchical methods of teaching by using observation, breath work, and focused concentration to offer young people a conscious practice of self-awareness. *On the Unit* is an autoethnographic entry point to the interconnect-edness of structural violence and intergenerational trauma, and the impact that a carceral state has on our education system and its youth. In this text, Eric seamlessly weaves together themes of resilience, grounded self-reflection, and a philosophy of *beingness* while constantly reminding the reader of the ever persistent violence of prisons. My only caution to readers and educators is to consider your own positionality with regard to structures of race, class, gender, and social categories of oppression and privilege should you choose to incorporate this curricula in your classrooms.

Until the abolition of prisons, police, and penal systems becomes a reality, educators have a duty and an obligation to consider how we can build more liberatory containers of healing and resistance in our classrooms and the world we inhabit. As racial capitalism, settler colonialism and global patriarchy continue to exacerbate suffering, class warfare, and ecological devastation in the U.S., our education and carceral systems continue to indoctrinate our youth into reproducing oppressive conditions. Our youth are being raised in an education system that is characterized by oppression and fear —a system where they are discouraged from being true to their passion and purpose because the system benefits from their miseducation and banks on them being disconnected from a higher consciousness. But now is the time for educators to encourage our youth to resist the status quo in hopes that they will chase their most liberating, and most creative dreams. Eric Biseca's *On the Unit* is a testament to what the late black feminist educator, author, and cultural critic Bell Hooks identifies as an approach to "education as the practice of freedom" —of teacher as healer. Honestly, there are so many healer educators with courageous hearts showing us the pathway of education as freedom. We need all of you to be sharing your tips and tools in the way that Eric has so vulnerably shared in this text. Onward toward freedom!

—Sheena Sood, PhD

STATEMENT OF LIABILITY

This work is in no way slanderous or critical of the School District of Philadelphia or any of its employees, nor is it to the Philadelphia Department of Human Services or any of its employees. The references made in this work provide written and oral insights of former students, and to protect their privacy, only their initials are referenced. The purpose of this book, as you will read, is by no means an attempt to exploit students or their educational experience, but to unearth their conscious experience and struggles in demonstrating the need for close examination of our institutions and the need for change in how we approach trauma-related anxiety in schools. My critique, as you will read, is that of the education system and general practices associated with its theoretical and institutional framework. This is more than a critique, however, it is a manual, a reference and a story of a journey to discovery—a tragedy and triumph. It can be used by educators, parents, seekers and professionals alike. Finally, none of the strategies suggested in this book are substitutes for medical treatment and or medical advice. I am not a medical doctor, nor do I have competing interests, external funding or represent the interests of any medical industry, corporation or organization.

PREFACE

These writings and reflections were born out of a raging epidemic of teen violence in the city of Philadelphia, a season of explosive racial unrest, as well as the all-too-familiar Covid-19 pandemic in the years 2017-2022. At the Juvenile Justice Service Center, where I carried out my duties as a trauma-informed public school teacher, I developed what could be interpreted as a "war-time" intervention platform to better serve my students and what I saw as their immediate needs. My pedagogy and lessons gradually transformed into an "intervention" based format that better allowed me to address issues dealing with trauma-related anxiety and crisis management. I did not decipher at the beginning of this work whether the "mindful" practices that I employed were preventative or therapeutic, but answers appeared as the work progressed. These writings provide an in-depth reflection and slice of qualitative research done with young people coping with the trauma and other forms of anxiety accrued in their challenging social circumstances and deeply complex lives. It is my hope that what is compiled here demonstrates the need for conscious practice within or in addition to an alternative approach to educating hyper-traumatized and traumatized youth (ages 13-20). Juvenile justice is a complicated subject tied closely into our ever changing political climate and societal framework.

Immediately upon starting at the center, I saw the need for a trauma-informed approach. Over a 4.5 year period, I developed a curriculum and pedagogy that integrated lessons into a personalized and "spiritualized" form of learning and healing that I call *Beingness*. Conceived organically through trial and error, the beingness platform integrated meditative techniques and social-emotional oriented lessons that reflected the need for self-awareness, empathy, self-efficacy and spiritual responsibility with added dimensions addressing identity. Breakthrough experiences in the classroom molded these techniques that both uncovered trauma and provided a new pathway upon which healing occurs so that true learning could take place. **While meditation and mindfulness-based activities proved nearly ineffective in the group setting of mostly traumatized juvenile delinquents in the city of Philadelphia, the pedagogy of *beingness*, grounded in a what we later came to call "the one-minute moment," proved to have a direct influence on the classroom and many individual student residents by producing a trigger-free environment, the will to learn and discover and a new identity for some of them.** It greatly influenced participation as well. It is my hope that this pedagogy and technique can be used in schools, summer camps and detention centers around the country for a generation of young people facing unprecedented levels of violence, anxiety related issues and social dilemmas. This memoir begins with my philosophy of wellness and then approaches my work through a "spiritual," sociological and academic framework, and yet is endowed with the rich experiences and voices of incarcerated youth. The chapters examine stories and data through the sociological constructs of race, gender, and religion within the context of trauma. This is the story of what I learned, what my students learned, and how we can all benefit from a change in our approach to juvenile justice, trauma-informed education and mindful practice...As a public school teacher, I approached this memoir with respect for school protocol while grounding myself in the values of holistic wellness. As an emerging wellness practitioner, I focused on the need for healing so that learning could occur. I do not condone criminal behavior and despite my sympathetic tone on occasion, the memoir is in no way excusing the acts of criminality by the young people that I taught and interacted with. It was always my empathy for them that truly inspired them—never my sympathy. So, let us commence with this experience, beginning with respect and gratitude for all those who helped me along the way, including my students, in the hopes of creating a more joyful world for all whose stories are intertwined in these pages.

◆ PART 1 ◆

INNER TECHNOLOGY

◆ CHAPTER 1 ◆

A PHILOSOPHY OF
WELLNESS AND BEINGNESS

The Difference Between Knowledge and Information

Daoists are forever making inferences to a cup of tea to explain life's riddles. My tea metaphor is this: Our intelligence is the cup itself, the "potential" to retain. The tea bag or herbs represent our experiences, the sum of sensory information (tactile, visual, auditory, gustatory, olfactory and mental). The hot water, symbolizing the mind and its desire to learn or absorb, is added to the tea, resulting in attained knowledge, or the *taste*. "Education" is merely the exterior design or shape of the cup. Just as the outer cup presents a certain style or appropriation, our education is very much designed or formatted to reflect a surface-level fitting. It is the magic fusion of the herbs with the heated water that creates the lasting result and impression-adding to the uniqueness of the individual's experience by expanding their awareness. **If we apply this tasty metaphor, it becomes clear that education, knowledge and information all have different roles and significance in the context of learning.** Of course, we in this digital era are exposed to abhorrent amounts of information to the point that we mindlessly consume it. It is either then reinterpreted or regurgitated in another form, but most of it is disregarded. We spend many hours of the day discerning which data is worth recalling. Our senses barrage us and our mind has little time to observe or internalize what we experience. The consumption of information not only informs, entertains, inspires and even pays us, it has become (or maybe always was) the modus operandi of our education system. As information becomes more accessible and more attractive through channels other than teachers, we are being forced to take a hard look at what children are actually "learning" and how it is serving them. *Are they learning to hold the fancy teacup or are they actually drinking tea?* Conflict theorists and others would argue that the education system was put in place perhaps as a "molding" or "programming" apparatus reflecting economic interests of the ruling classes, Others would argue that it provides a foundation upon which young people are socialized and society's values are propagated. Regardless of what education's purpose and outcomes are, studies have shown that it has little bearing on our happiness, success, and, I would add, *wellness* at any point in our lives. What is it missing? Perhaps many things, but let me first say—the emphasis on *knowledge*. True knowledge is tied intricately to *the self*. It spawns self-awareness and it reflects a lasting impression of an experience. Knowledge that brings self-awareness comes in small doses in life and even smaller in our schooling, generally speaking. It is this awareness-based knowledge that remains with us after an experience.. I might have studied the layers of the atmosphere in science class, but what part of that study created a lasting impression? How did it add to the conscious experience of my life or the collective consciousness of human beings? Some would say, "The point is not to add to the conscious experience, the point is to learn the information. I would say that we don't learn much from exposure to logos-based "information" unless it changes us. It is the tea, the impression left in our being, that inspires *pathos*, or emotional response. The potential of that experience to create a new awareness is the greatest of treasures in this universe of infinite knowledge. It is experiential knowledge that creates us, continuously molds us. That which left an imprint in our "emotional body" and impacted our perception of ourselves or the world remains with us at the moment of and after death. Information comes and goes. Knowledge, as the ancients believed, remains with us forever. If education proposes an agenda and programs our perception in a certain way, it is knowledge that can allow us to transcend such programming. Self-awareness gained is the gateway to the sixth sense, the mind's eye and beyond. When I came to realize this through my own impressions as a young student of mysteries, I realized that I had to become my own master. As a teacher, I saw that my own self-awareness was instrumental to capturing the interest of others—no matter what I was teaching. When my students were introduced to activities promoting self-awareness such as becoming conscious of the breath, a certain authenticity prevailed upon them. They experienced the difference between attaining knowledge and acquiring information ...Their authenticity enabled them to discern and discard useless information. We can all learn to make use of information instead of just consuming it, to attain knowledge so that it contributes to a greater level of consciousness.

A Brief Philosophy of Learning and Beingness

One cold south Philadelphia morning (insert *Rocky* music if preferred), I sat on the edge of my bed after yet another sleepless night, and pondered quitting my job. I was mentally and physically exhausted. The 1st year of working in a juvenile prison had worn me out. Or should I say, I wore myself out while doing it. That morning, in the middle of the resignation email to my admin team marked a low point in a long journey. Before pressing the "send" button, I called my mother and explained to her that I'd rather go homeless than work another day in the prison. She and my aunty, whom I stayed with at the time, both responded with the same basic sentence. "Get your ass up and go to work." I decided to take a few days off and ponder the decision. They couldn't understand, nobody could, what it was like for me. After 24 hours of rest, I realized what I had to do. I rose from my slumber the next morning around 4:40am and took a cold shower, rubbed sesame oil on my body and sat on 3 folded rugs to begin the practice of *Sadhana*, which included intense breathwork and posture. This ancient practice of the Yogic tradition that utilizes breath and muscle control to strengthen the body and mind begins with a cold shower and ends with a 10 minute nap. It was Sadhana that sent a breath of life into my existence. It forced me to go inward in order to expand outward. My higher self demanded drastic measures, and so I had to get down to rise up. It was time to align myself with the rhythms of life, the cosmos and beyond. Although my role in the prison had my back against the wall, it wasn't time for me to walk out the door. It was time for me to master myself so that I could be the person I needed to be. I supplement this seated practice with training in the movements of the Afro-Brazilian art of *Capoeira Angola*. Since that dismal morning, I have hardly missed a day of this routine, and my warrior spirit, my compassion, my self-awareness and my ability to harmonize with all that surrounds me has heightened. I guess you could say I haven't had a good ol' fashioned American morning with a side of bacon in a while, but I don't regret it.

I try to never look back, unless it elevates me upward and onward. Without this morning routine and training in these spirit sciences, I would probably not have been able to write this book—I certainly would not be able to maintain the mental focus that I needed to teach in the juvenile justice center and education system before and during the Covid-19 pandemic. It is the culminating moment of a long journey, and it has added the qualities that define my identity. For the first time, I have *innerstood* the rewards of perseverance, self-love, and the miracle of creation. Without performing the intricacies of my morning *Sadhana*, I would not have been able to heal the aspects of myself that were unintegrated with consciousness— the parts of myself that were divided. Without the daily morning gratitude toward my higher self and the Creator, I would be moving forward with no reference point—like an uncharted ship in the night. So I would say, emphatically, that praising, healing and learning are intertwined in *Sadhana* like a caduceus creating the thread of expanded individual consciousness. And like the 3 threads of hair in a French braid, they are part of a larger network of hair on the head, that larger network representing our collective human consciousness. It is our *collective consciousness*, a term first coined by Carl Jung, that allows us to bond with others through empathy and archetypal memory. Beyond that, we are each waves in the ocean of cosmic, universal consciousness, having a human experience. These 3 levels of consciousness—individual, collective and universal were essential venues in reaching the young minds in my classroom. Many times, my students may not have been able to bond amongst themselves or with me on the surface, but they would automatically bond with the things of collective consciousness—like the seasons, animals, emotions, and definitely the act of collective conscious breathing... We are all a miniscule but profound aspect of consciousness— and the things of consciousness are embedded in our existence. Consciousness is the summation of every number in the universe and every element known and unknown. It is earth, air, fire, water and aether. It is the single governing force of the Mind. As sure as we can imagine a butterfly with our eyes closed, consciousness is found within us. After all, we are conscious beings having a human experience. Despite the complexity of that human experience, I'd like to continue to focus for now upon one essential phenomenon that alters consciousness—the experience of *learning*.

After instating my morning routine, many revelations about myself and my work began to come into fruition. For one, I began to become aware of what my students were truly *learning* in my classroom and what they were not. I was responsible for preparing them for the real world and I gave this great consideration. For months, I pondered the question, why were they not responding to me the way I needed them to? Why were they not as interested as they could be? I reflected on myself and my own practice. I began with the element of fire. The fire of concentration.

The "Fire" of Concentration

Like most of us, the majority of my students were not trained to be able to focus their attention upon something for a long period of time unless it could be tracked or in some way sensually stimulating. This affected their ability to be studious or introspective. In the 8 fold path of Raja Yoga, which includes pranayama and meditation, one must learn, above all, to acquire *dharana*, or focus. Focus is a property of the element of fire. Metaphysically, fire is the element of direction and will intention. The fire of focus comes with the focused intention of the will and the fine-tuned power of precision from the mind. There were many hindrances, of course, to my students being able to concentrate—certainly their past and present traumas and existence in a state of survival were not conducive to concentration. More importantly, few were ever taught how to concentrate. This is why meditation in the classroom, from the onset, was a struggle. It was an advanced form of focus. It was like asking young people who had just learned how to use a lighter to make a fire in a dark, cold forest. I knew meditating before class began would be beneficial for them, but it soon became apparent that this had to be a special meditation. It had to be accessible. I had to add something to the very airy and obsolete practice into something that provided them with the presence, the focus, the fire of spirit. This special meditation would become known as the *1-minute moment.*

Making such a change was not a one step process. I was aware that my role as an English teacher in an underserved community carried an innate colonialist effect and implementing modes of discipline could be received as aggressive. This certainly proved true on many occasions until the *1-minute moment* was understood and implemented thoroughly. Our educational framework places value on rote knowledge, critical thinking and recollection-based learning models to prepare young people for a career reflecting their socio-economic reality. I was never satisfied with this model. To me, there was no real "training" that endowed students with the tools to think critically or introspectively—to learn first through the ability to focus. They certainly were not trained to concentrate—neither was I. It took many years of martial arts, life changing experiences and of course, the practice of Vipassana meditation to heighten my ability to focus. Even now, I falter on occasion. Our culture emphasizes efficiency, but does not rear us with the ability to focus. In schools in western China and Tibet, 9-year-olds adhere to a strict morning routine of exercises involving repetitive affirmations while assuming stretch poses, reciting and completing precise physical tasks hours before breakfast.

Although I wanted to give these young people in Philadelphia the literary and writing tools they needed to make academic progress, I had to make discipline and focus an expectation. As Jocko Willink said, "It is discipline that gives you freedom." I used the "fuel of concentration" to implement the 1-minute moment into a pre-class ritual. That fuel was repetition. To me, the deepest level of learning occurs when we have created meaning of an experience from our cognitions to our spirit, that which aligns us with consciousness. This occurs with repetition, which establishes neural pathways in the brain to strengthen behavior. Like a beaten pathway in the woods, repetition stamps out an embedded "2nd nature" into the act that we learn to repeat. Whether the act is chanting, breathing or sitting still, repetition strengthens neurotransmission and memory in our body, creating cellular awareness, bringing tremendous synchronicity between the body and mind. The act that is embedded into our consciousness is embedded into our heart. So when we learn something, it remains not only in our mind, but in the home of spiritual and personal power.

Of course, the words *discipline* and *repetition* both have negative connotations, but as I saw the power of focus training manifest, I cared less about offending people. By year 3, massive changes were happening around us at the center and I realized that the times were calling for revolutionary practices, rebellious acts in the classroom. During this period of social unrest, community violence and pandemic, I affirmed for myself that they needed life skills, coping mechanisms, self-awareness and discipline more than what the traditional learning model offered. I was sure my attempt to decolonize was just as thorough. Despite the many roles I had as their teacher, instilling discipline was the one I prioritized. I reflected much on the significance of this responsibility. It was the 1st step toward showing them the path to authenticity. It was their first tool in a lifelong job of learning. The 1-minute moment would introduce them to an act of focus that would specifically alter the chemical content of their brain, activate their parasympathetic nervous system and prefrontal cortex and bring balance to their Hypo-pituitary axis, the governor of their emotions. Most importantly, it would channel their spiritual fire and create meaning from information. By igniting their focus, they were able to attain true knowledge.

The "Waters" of Observation

If one reads online that bees are dying from DDT pesticides, have they learned something or acquired a piece of information? If one sees a bird that they had never seen before flying above, are they acquiring a piece of information or solely experiencing something through the senses? We seem to have forgotten that acquiring information is not the same as learning something. The legendary martial art rule of thumb affirms that to truly *learn* something, we must have *done* it 10K times. Along the same traditional thinking, I can feed a hungry person vegetable stew, but if I teach them to garden, they can eat for a lifetime.

"It is difficult for man to establish a control over his mind, for he has to discover how it works, how it deceives him and by which methods it can be subdued. As long as the mind restlessly wonders about amidst objects, ever fluctuating, excited, agitated and uncontrolled, the true joy of self cannot be realized and enjoyed...If he has subjugated the mind, he may be said to be, in his subjective freedom and power, the emperor of emperors." Swami Sivananda, *"Meditation and Mantras"*

Next in the sequence of adapting my teaching so that my students could learn was that of incorporating an ability to observe. When we observe, of course, we 1st utilize our senses. A quality of observation, however, occurs beyond this point when we observe by engaging our consciousness. The ability to observe from this place of consciousness, some would call it "the self," requires a control of the mind and the emotions. It involves the objective ability to separate oneself from that which is being observed. Despite the reality of a subjective experience, the mind is able to detach from the self and the body, for that matter. This advanced ability to observe uses the fire of discipline, but reflects the quality of water. Water is the only transparent element, and it reflects back what observes it. Water reminds us that observation requires a quality of stillness, non-attachment and transparency. It is a dance of the senses and a fluidity of the mind that allows us to internalize from observing. By observing from a place of consciousness, we can freely interact with the world and not attach to it. We can mindfully observe our emotions without becoming them. We can observe our thoughts without acting. Clear waters reveal the refined mind of the objective observer. Riding a roller coaster is a raw, unadulterated experience that takes form, shape and triggers emotional responses, yet, it is an experience of the mind. When it is not observed from consciousness, It happens in a complete blur to the point where nothing is remembered. An experience provides clarity when it can be fully observed with clarity. Though this advanced practice of observation was not attainable or understood by most of my students, many did grasp the ability to observe their own thoughts and emotions.

By experiencing life through our physical senses and mental capacities, we acquire information. By experiencing life while observing those senses and capacities, we learn. The ability to observe can truly blossom after learning to focus. I surmise that an advanced state of *beingness* occurs when we can observe our thoughts, our actions, our emotions from a "higher" self. It is this self, the master identity, that observes and then embodies the memory of experience, creating a new part of us. Exercises that require the mind's total attention as well as exercises requiring the skill of observation allow us to develop this higher self vantage point. If I have to sit in a certain pose for 1 hour per day, I eventually stop becoming distracted by the discomfort in it and begin observing my discomfort while I endure. I am observing from a place of consciousness. Several of our classroom activities involved the students observing an aspect of themselves and then identifying with it as an aspect of consciousness. As I will explain, the 1-minute moment provided the repetition and focus that awakened the higher self. Conscious breathing allowed the residents to dabble with true observation and apply it to their learning experience. Sometimes they would describe the difference between their thoughts during meditation and their thoughts during regular class. Another associated exercise was a writing lesson reflecting the principle of *beingness*, where instead of describing a river or how they feel when they see a river, they describe themselves *as a river*...Or, they describe themselves in the river from the perspective of someone or something else. Though this seems like a high level thinking activity, young people usually enjoy the challenge and take to it right away. Instead of asking them how they were feeling on a winter day, I asked them how they *were* winter on a blustery day in December. We would first compile a list of characteristics of winter, then, respond. The following student's wrote these responses:

"I am winter because I am dark, I am cold. I make people chilly." E.G, 2019

"I am winter because I am hot chocolate. I am waiting for spring and the Sun." G.G, 2019

Observation as a discipline is fruitful and potent. It can be utilized to create *responsibility*, or the ability to *respond* to the world, not react to it. By observing our own emotions or the emotions of others, we can separate from them without identifying with them. We can act intentionally instead of impulsively or aggressively. By observing our actions as an addict, for example, we can isolate that which is outside of us manipulating our behavior. We can see that the addiction may come from something we feel that we lack within ourselves. We can observe the source of that deficiency by articulating the experience of our thoughts and emotions. We can soon see that addictive behavior is not who we are.

The "Air" of the Breath

A final elemental piece that better allowed my students to learn was the workings of the breath. No, I didn't have them breath consciously while they were reading and we didn't take deep breaths before every class discussion, but we managed to implement a regular synchronized breathing exercise at the beginning of class. That practice, as I will later explain, stimulated the Vagus nerve, the central cranial nerve that governs emotional response and regulates the nervous system. Attaching the breath to any activity is transformative. It brings an undeniable experience of flow and ease. One reason for this is that the breath is the link between the body, mind and auric fields, and as I will explain, breathing in certain patterns creates alignment in these parts of our being. And so it was the breath that was the final piece of the puzzle for establishing a truly restorative experience for traumatized youth in the center. It became a portal in which learning and observation could take place.

One could argue that the sole purpose of life is to learn.

Not only is trauma and or anxiety an obstacle to learning, but lack of training in concentration, observation and conscious breathing. With these practices, that which hinders learning is transcended. The blockage in consciousness is removed. When my students were able to concentrate and observe from a place of consciousness, they then began to identify with the things of the self—the cosmos, nature, archetypal knowledge and emotional experiences that made them human beings. They began to discover something that faded in their childhood at some point—the joy of learning.

In these next few sections, we will examine how observing, breathing and learning are all interconnected aspects of an "inner" technology. This innate technology that only needs activated through practice can bring us expanded consciousness, or the state of *beingness*. The dance of beingness, I would surmise, is the key to a life of balance, of wellness, of joy.

From Mindfulness to Beingness

In line with our "teacup" references, a wise, tea drinking man once said, one must have an empty cup 1st in order for it to be filled. As stated, the emptying of our individual "cups" in the classroom was initiated 1st from the discipline of a daily conscious breathing activity called the *1-minute moment*. This very calculated quasi-ritual allowed them to move beyond the egoic and incarcerated self to a state of interconnectedness with each other, myself and consciousness that released them from survival mode. It was from this vantage point that instruction took place and integrated them with aspects of consciousness. This integration took place more through their *identity* with consciousness (which I call *beingness*) than through their awareness of the present moment (which one might call *mindfulness*). It took place through their ability to observe and respond accordingly.

Each student learns differently because each has their own relationship with conscious experience. Most of my students were traumatized. For them, there was only immediate *experience* because *observation* brought great pain and angst. For the most part, they were not unable, but unwilling to step outside of themselves. Nobody guided them through such a process and the world of mainly visual and auditory experiences was one that fed their greatest desires. Theirs was a conscious state in search of pleasure, of stimulation, in a world of scarcity and chaos. Therefore, they struggled with being responsible or disciplined students because they couldn't see themselves as such. They struggled with learning because they lived in a constant state of fear. They struggled with allowing their true self to emerge because the outer shell, the societal identity that protected them on all levels in this world, could not be cracked. They allowed themselves to be distracted because they didn't want to miss an opportunity for pleasure. This is why a disciplined practice and the identification with consciousness became crucial components.

The breathwork and conscious movements of my morning practice are my guides, my tools and my salvation. We are living in a time when the breath has been at the core of some of the most pivotal political and social events in the history of the United States. The era of Covid-19 began with images of thousands packed hospitals gasping for air on ventilators, as the virus spread throughout the globe in a few devastating initial waves, causing the deaths of millions. Still, today, we navigate through the twists and turns of a socially divisive public health crisis that has changed the life of nearly everyone in America. As if the Coronavirus hadn't reeked enough havoc by the summer of 2020, an explosive era of racial unrest soon swept across the U.S like wildfire, redefining a new era of civil rights. The protests were, of course, triggered by the Minnesota police killing of an unarmed suspect, (one of hundreds of unarmed black men killed by police), who was horrifically executed by suffocation in front of the eyes of the nation. One hot summer day in Philadelphia, as in other parts of the country, we chose a day to kneel in protest in front of the district administrative offices for over 8 minutes, the duration of time Floyd struggled to breath. During those 8 minutes, and for the past 20 years, I've studied, experimented with and practiced conscious breathing, movement and meditation. I've come to realize that the ability to become aware of the breath is not only a key to living a meaningful life, but the key to recognizing who we truly are. By now, in this era defined by breath *being taken away*, we've all had a great opportunity to think about, and perhaps realize, just how sacred, subtle and significant the act of breathing really is. Before delving into the breath, let us look at the context of our breath, our life and our individual consciousness. Let's begin with our relationship to society and time.

Controlling Anxiety by Controlling Time

Some say that time is always on our side. Others believe that time is the enemy. My traumatized students struggled with focus and initially, observing their breath because of their trauma, which, in an ultimate sense, was due to their fractured consciousness and sense of *time*. Time was not a friend to them. They gave all of their attention to the past and the future and neither dimension gave them anything back. They waited on time for their hearing, their court date, and their arrival back home. He or she existed in a mental "waiting space" that resisted, and even despised the present moment. That present moment, where the eternal exists, where consciousness resides, was a strange and almost unknown dimension to them. In filling their present moment with distractions (videos, social media, info-consumption), how would they ever come to realize that this was depriving them of true awareness of consciousness? Were they in a state of mind that should even care? These processed delinquents, representative of the next generation around the globe, are products of an era, a worldwide culture that uses time as a great equalizer and variable that informs all phenomena. They were encultured to worry about doing things "on time" and having the resources to make things happen—efficiently. They made desperate attempts to acquire money in a society where time and money are sure bedfellows. Caught in the bottom rings of a time-allotted hierarchical culture that chases both time and the almighty dollar, young people everywhere, but especially the marginalized, are forced to consume, then indulge within a regular schedule of work or hustle. Maybe we cannot change the tide of global culture or the "quickening" mode that it seems to invite, but we can certainly begin to examine our collective anxiety as a byproduct of this culture. One thing is certain, a culture where time is a variable of scarcity will puncture its own existence. The truth is that time only exists in the manner that we individually, and collectively, decide.

With discipline and responsibility, we all can control time and reconfigure our reality. Of course, my students' perception of time was, indeed, accurate—it is a kind of enemy. I don't feel the need nor do I have the background to dive into quantum physics to support the statement that time is a dimension of this universe and man has constructed time to serve "his" needs. I would not go further as to say that living as 3-D beings, (length, depth, breadth) limits our consciousness to the time dimension and severs the flow of infinite, universal consciousness into our being. Seekers and students of the great mysteries know that we can access universal consciousness, but we must leave the realm of time and space, which most of us don't exactly have on our bucket list for now. So, yes, we must deal with time. Can we, however, utilize some of our supreme innate abilities to attain the quality of mind to manipulate time so that it serves us? Yes, but we must respond differently to the world around us and most importantly, change the world *within* us. Not easy, but doable. Despite time being their enemy, I asked my students one day, does time really exist? They pondered, some said yes, some said no. Some said both. They were all correct.

In the youth prison, miraculously, I spent much of my and my students' time cultivating a culture of *beingness* by, ironically, observing constructs such as time. We examined our relationship with time. We discovered that the root of anxiety is the conscious obsession with the past and future, two dimensions of linear time. After a fair amount of meditation, many of my students began to realize that are concept of time begins with how we are taught "history," a series of sequential events reflecting a cause and effect phenomenon. We are rarely taught about what time truly is, only that it keeps moving and the rest is history. We are not shown the wheel of life, which reveals the essential motion of time—a circle. Like the seasons, the Yugic cycles of time and the cycles of the elements—earth, water, air and fire, time in its original form is only a circle, reflecting changes of one ever present reality. When my students made the connection to this circle of time, they made a similar connection to the circle of life. When one sees that all of linear time is connected in a cycle, then one can see that all of life itself is connected in the same fashion. There is only oneness and there is only constant change within that oneness...

One who is anxious is always reacting to the present by worrying about the future. If we are human beings, in the present sense, we can at least consider a concept of timelessness. In the truest sense, *beingness* is timelessness. A *being* responds to the world instead of reacting. To react means to try and redo what has been done or do something instead of what has been done. We are human beings, not human doings. You could react to this philosophy by rolling your eyes or you could respond to it by continuing to read! So, the word *respond* shares the root word with *ponder*. To *ponder* is to pause and think. *Responding* to the world, as opposed to reacting, is a transcended and disciplined course of action, involving control of the mind and emotions. Before you skip the rest of this section because you don't have time, consider the prospect of a future where time becomes less of a factor. When we create more moments in the awareness of the present, we eliminate the effects of time on our lives and create opportunities for true learning, true healing and unimaginable abundance.

Most of our children grow up in a world "on the fly." They learn that hurrying helps get more done, and getting more things done assures success. The resulting competitive edge to acquire academic degrees, certificates, training and skills that we are to utilize ultimately deludes us to think we have a greater chance at success because we can compete. Life has become a sacrifice of sanity for success with the endless pursuit of credentials and beating everyone else out of the way to arrive first—and the universe doesn't reward haste with any permanent abundance. We have become completely electric, void of the force of magnetism, completely masculine, void of the feminine, and action-oriented, void of stillness. We are moving because time is moving. "It is the empty pot that makes it useful," is a concept from ancient *Tao Te Ching*. We have yet to discover how stillness can attract the very things that we chase. The true revolution will be one of timelessness, and *beingness*.

This critical view of the time construct does not need to

limit our interactions with people around us, but we can use it to collectively transcend our entanglement with time. While spending time in solitude or in nature helps us attune to universal consciousness, those in our lives, and sometimes strangers, around us, can certainly help trigger an inner transformation. Undoubtedly, talking to someone without angst can open up many healing channels and generate a spiritual act of rebellion. Conversation is meditation, and having the courage to approach someone and say, "I'm not worried about time" or, "Let's not be in a hurry," can move mountains. Dissociating with time does not mean dissociation with reality and dissociating with society does not mean dissociating with others. Relegating our precious time to return to daily practice is, however, a way that we can become more self-reliant in a world that cannot always be there to listen or provide for us. The inner voice is something/someone that is always with us. Time invested in nullifying the effects of time is time well spent.

The Societal Identity

In addition to the 1-minute moment, what could I *teach* the young people in a cold and desolate prison setting? How could they begin to utilize their concentration and ability to observe? Is knowledge not gained through real-world experience? From my decades as a student, whether it'd been from martial arts or at the post-graduate level, I've come to realize that a teacher must instill techniques for eliminating distractions that hinder learning in a pupil, including the distraction of their own ego. The ability to focus is crucial in creating self-awareness. Self-awareness, or the ability to recognize consciousness within your being, has the power to birth a new identity—one that values life, learning and knowledge. Conscious breathing and observation-based activities served us by eliminating a large chunk of the "incarcerated" individual by instilling a sense of discipline and responsibility, but their learning was markedly enhanced when I was able to alter the curriculum so that it provided them with a foundation for a new identity and interest in learning. 1st, they had to understand that which stood in the way of their new self—the societal identity.

I surmised over time that if I truly reached these young people in the prison, I had to not only help them see the value of learning, but allow them to *identify with consciousness.* They were not different from most of us. Most of them had created an identity through materialism, status, and relationships with others based on how those others perceive them. There is much to be explored here, but for now, let's just refer to this outgrowth of the ego as our *societal identity.* It is the frame of mind that keeps young people distracted and keeps us all divided—among each other and within ourselves. For example, instead of acquiring an inner focus, learning about the self and exploring their unique gifts, many suburban and urban youth grow up wanting to play roles that are glorified in the media culture—a fast paced, overstimulating array of prepackaged characters that promote consumerism and material wealth. Although there is a great deal of conscious and colorful new awareness in pockets of the younger generation, more and more, most are distracted at a young age with the immediately gratifying, pleasure-seeking life, and their mind becomes insatiable because they cannot control its desires. They are not exposed to the path that leads them to greatest pleasure—self-awareness and an identity with consciousness. They are not trained to concentrate or control the mind, so it often creates an internal adversary, which leads to forms of depression or anxiety. There is separation in their body and mind, reinforced by an easily divided attention. In addition, they are not exposed to the things of timelessness and the collective consciousness.

Just as dreams and aspirations are necessary, a societal identity is perfectly important to cultivate, when it can be paired with a balanced perception of reality. That reality includes available opportunities and avenues of personal growth. Societal identity wants to be liked and popular. Its main vehicle today, social media, promotes the ego like no other modern day mechanism. The ego wants to be free to explore all the pleasures of life, yet it does not realize that self-awareness provides true freedom, which is freedom from desire. To discipline the ego is to cut deeper into the societal identity, to strengthen the self. Gadgets and devices fuel an unconscious and fragmented mind, one that allows the ego to be distracted easily by the possibility of a new pleasure or experience. When we become the master of ourselves, our basic desires do not interfere. Let's face it, however, this is America and America is not Tibet. The justice center was not an Ashram and I am not a monk. I was aware that we all feed the egoic, societal identity, but I tried to show my students that there was another way. To add a dimension of the self through a disciplined practice, one that facilitates awareness of *consciousness,* brings us a tremendous sense of freedom, power, authenticity, connectivity and wisdom. By diverting my students away from the lure of societal identity, the space to explore their true identity was created. The distractions were always there, but they were quelled through the use of conscious breathing. A curriculum of *authenticity* was emerging.

I have realized one profound truth as a teacher and one who has had the opportunity to spend thousands of hours with young people. They desire authenticity. Ultimately, I am not one who seeks enlightenment nor can I expect another to follow any spiritual path, but, I can only say that I've come to *innerstand* the power of my own authenticity. As a teacher, being *authentic* through my identity with consciousness was the best lesson plan I could produce. This pedagogical foundation has remained with me in even the bleakest of circumstances and proved to anchor my philosophy throughout my time in the center. As you will read, these revelations arrived when I began to introduce concepts that I felt de-emphasized the societal ego through a curriculum grounded in authenticity, or learning through *archetypes, intra-communication, emotional intelligence* and the discipline of *conscious breathing.* Learning was enhanced through concentration, observation and breathwork, but identity was forged through these themes. Granted, most of my students may not have discovered their full authenticity, but most were able to grasp or identify with one of the levels of consciousness (individual, collective or universal). I did witness the powerful shift in their ability to retain information as their identity merged with collective consciousness. As they participated in the *1-minute moment* and the curriculum of authenticity I was inspired to see some of them taste the fruits of a new form of being and knowing.

On the horizon is a new earth. For many, it will be a new way of being. For those that choose to observe their experiences and not identify with them, they will find it easy to leave the constraints of time. For those who cling to their experiences, they will also cling to time. Ironically, by going into the darkness, the "inner cave" as Joseph Campbell referred to it, we are forced to find our way out of it—in that dilemma, we release what we fear and find an eternal part of ourselves. In this era where there is much darkness and despair on the planet, we are witnessing our collective dilemma. We are rebirthing a species. Out of the division comes integration and out of the separation comes oneness. We are experiencing (and hopefully observing) one of the greatest awakenings of mankind and the dawn of a completely new age. One of our tests will be through our ability to access consciousness—and to eventually transcend time itself. This is where concentration, observation and authentication crescendo into a marvelously fully human way of being. They serve to nullify the effects of time and to create the ultimate preparation for the future—full consciousness of the present.

Our being and bodily systems within it contain the answers to all of life's mysteries. The pace and patterns by which our body functions and our brain secretes hormones, processes and stores information, regulates our nervous system is still and will always be governed by the same laws that rule upon the sun, the moon and rest of the cosmos. We are the cosmos, the planets, the constellations. Nothing happens in the cosmic realm that does not influence or affect us. We are inextricably connected. As in the body, nothing in nature happens suddenly, without warning or process. Therefore, neither should our actions. By regulating our breath, our actions and movements, we rekindle our true nature, which is one of rhythm, the conscious, balanced, acting of time.

So let us move out of the quantum realm of time and space and simply look at ourselves. This is the fundamental and 1st principle of spirit science. Harkening back to Hindu ideology, Yashoda, the mother of Vishnu opened the infant's mouth to see if he had eaten dirt—she peered inside to find, miraculously, that it was an opening to the whole of the universe and beyond. A metaphor for all that is within us. In the study of self, we discover the secrets of the entire creation. This was known by marvelous pyramid-building geniuses of the ancient mystery schools in Egypt... The one axiom that they held sacred was written on the lintel above their temple walls— "Know Thyself."

◆

My Study of Well-Being

"Wellness" in the 80's was having a cabinet full of food, a six pack in the fridge and a high school football game to watch on Friday night. Self-care was virtually unheard of unless it was lifting weights—especially in the rust belt and blue collar neighborhoods that I came of age within. Thanks to my father who was a school teacher and mother who was a master in the kitchen, we ate at least one good cooked meal per day, but many of the neighborhood kids survived and thrived on "corner store" snacks in an era when more GMO, preservative and additive altered food was the norm. Exercise was a thing we did when playing sports and, of course, the sound *Yoga* could have been mistaken either for a street greeting or a reference to the Jedi master from *Star Wars*.

It was around my 21st birthday one fateful night that led to "wellness" being placed at the forefront of my life. While walking home from my girlfriend's house, I was accosted and beaten in the street by a few men who, from what I can remember, didn't like something about me. Fortunately, after briefly losing consciousness, I was taken to the hospital by some caring neighbors. Not so fortunately, after an MRI and subsequent tests, I was diagnosed with a tumor in my pituitary gland (*Adenoma limbic encephalitis*). Ironically however, it was the best beating I could have ever taken. I tell my students that we never know why the bad things in our lives happen to us, and that's why we shouldn't view them as "bad things." After getting the news that the pituitary needed to be monitored and the growth contained from metastasizing, I received the regimen of prescriptions that (theoretically) would keep things stable. The blessing was that it was detected at an early stage. Still, my mind adopted a sense of urgency and I didn't feel right taking the prescribed meds for an extended period of time. Ignoring the growth seemed foolish. I was not one to be depressed, but was still emotionally distraught, hurt and confused—most of all, I became anxious. To quell the anxiety, I dosed more heavily on marijuana and alcohol, and for years, they became two familiar, but toxic friends; At one point I decided to go back to the boxing gym—to fight my way through it. I was reacting to the possibility of my own early death and having no knowledge of consciousness, I allowed destructive thoughts to uproot my sense of stability. Despite my flawed choices of self-care, I was saved by an angel once again, an elder at the boxing gym, who instructed me not to come back. "What the hell are you doing here?...Go learn to do meditation or Tai Chi—something that won't knock your head around..." Meditation? Hmm. I had heard of it.

The next day, I checked out some books from the library (imagine that!) delving into meditation and martial arts from around the world. *Vipassana, Qi Gong, Tai Chi, Yoga.* My studies expanded and quickly turned into a rudimentary exploratory practice as I began a regimen of meditation and martial arts that has remained with me consistently for the past 25 years. Before these modalities introduced me to my emerging consciousness, I was unaware of the universe inside of me. Before Vipassana meditation, I was able to retain information and internalize things of importance, but I was not able to *observe* things or observe myself. Before meditation and *Pranayama* (energizing through breath control), my outer reality guided my actions, instead of the inverse. Like many of my own students whose stories I share with you in this book, I was young, easily depleted and had anxiety on a daily basis. Like many of them, I wasn't diagnosed with anxiety, but it was impacting my waking reality. Now, as a sovereign man, my inner world guides my life and my outer reality is much more manageable and meaningful. I can say that instead of anxiety, there is authenticity. Instead of exhaustion, there is boundless energy and inspiration. Instead of reaction, there is responsibility. This is the power of conscious breathing, the path of meditation and the understanding of *beingness*. With the help of proper nutrition and movement (*Capoeira Angola* and *Yoga*), I can say that my morning practice has become a series of fruitful, conscious reflections of "biogeometry," or the aligning of my physiology with the geometry of the universe. I practice and observe my movements with tremendous vitality and clarity, at 42, I feel better than when I was 24. A daily practice creates a space of expansiveness and integration, whether meditating or moving with the fury of fire and or the fluidity of water. I feel the elements living within me. I revel in the opportunities for growth and greater joy and have realized that the darkness within my own being and healing journey incorporating that darkness into my light has been my salvation. It allowed me to see myself as a whole being—not a being of only goodness or only malice, of light or shadow, but of my own authentic combination of it all. This is my foundation for my approach to wellness—authenticity.

Of course, there are endless factors that contribute to one's wellbeing. Everything from our feelings about the career or work that we do, to our white blood cell count, to how much butter we put on our toast are part of the spectrum that encompasses our *wellness*. Parts of our lives are either in alignment with our own healing journey, or not in alignment. At the end of the day, even our imbalances are aligning us with what we need to learn. By identifying and embracing our imbalances, we learn to make ourselves whole—we learn to create balance by integrating all aspects of self. Many of my students were able to experience a taste of *beingness* by embracing themselves as they were, that is exploring into their authentic identity, one that embraced them into the collective consciousness. This is not as easy as it sounds—especially for those dealing with the many forms of trauma.

Traumatized or not, we are all more than mind, body and spirit; our potential to access channels of healing and growth is endless. By seeing ourselves as words within the poetry that is nature, we can begin to recognize the totality of just who we are. We are able to experience the great spirit science of consciousness and find the many aspects of ourselves that make us who we are. We are a unique combination of the snapshot of the cosmos at our birth, the zodiac, which reveals our potentials and tendencies. We are the 4 seasons in different hues and combinations, the 5 elements, the 7 Chakras, the 14 meridians of Qi, the masculine, the feminine, the 72,000 nadis or nerve endings throughout the human body that conduct electro-magnetic life force. Infinity is our essence. When do we finally become 1 complete and whole being? I'm not sure about that, but I'm pretty sure that is not simply a matter of searching google or following our YouTube heroes. It does take large spoonfuls of discipline and self-awareness. By honoring our own experiences and the knowledge gained from them a certain *spiritual responsibility* is established. The result of cultivating such a responsibility is an internal driving ethical character that automatically begins to guide us. When we take responsibility, we are ready to look at reality. We are ready to shed our ego by becoming our higher self, by becoming *love*.. Believing in love or the higher self may not be important, but assuming responsibility for loving ourselves is crucial. By sharpening the mind and training the body, releasing the fear, opening the heart, a commitment to spiritual responsibility brings us from a lower, survival state, to a thriving state. It allows us to remember who we truly are and how each one of us is on a different leg of this grand archetypal journey. Once we commit to spiritual responsibility, nothing, no condition, no ailment can stop us from embracing and becoming our authentic self—nothing can stop us from merging with Consciousness.

Observation Meditation

Begin a conscious breathing routine and learn to *observe* by following the guided meditation below. Don't worry about addressing issues or letting imbalances arise, just cultivate the ability to observe..

First, be seated in a comfortable easy pose of half lotus or sitting upright in a chair. Be sure no matter where you are seated, that your spine is straight, but your muscles are at ease. There is no tension in your body as you let your hands sit softly face down in your lap with elbows naturally aligned with the torso. Glance at the space around you, observe what it looks like, sounds like, smells like. Close the eyes and begin slowly breathing through the nose down to the belly. Follow the inhale and exhale as you slow the breath, keeping the pace rhythmic and deep. The belly slightly expands on the inhale, contracts on the exhale. Observe the subtle sounds of the breath. Soften it so that the breath becomes noiseless. Notice any thoughts still passing through your mind. Don't analyze them. As you observe, identify only with the cool, healing breath coming into the body and warm, cleansing breath that leaves it. Notice how satisfying it is. Allow yourself to be yourself and just observe it all until nothing else comes up. This is when meditation begins...

The Biofields, the Source of Breath

The breath has been likened to a "bridge" linking the physical with the non-physical world. I would go further to say that it is the link between mind and body. What other function do we possess that is both voluntary and involuntary? In this matter, the breath also becomes the link between the sympathetic and parasympathetic nervous system. As we delve further into understanding the dimensions of breathing beyond the simple act of inhaling and exhaling, we must first understand the energetic realms that facilitate the breathing process. How are these realms or dimensions defined and how exactly does the breath link them?

Instead of focusing on the physiological process of breathing, let's begin our focus on the meta-physical, which is the realm in which all things physical, manifest. Let's very briefly take a look at a deeper layer of our existence and leave our preconceptions at the door. Let's respect ancient or esoteric wisdom as well as conventional scientific discovery.. An exciting new branch of science called "Biofield science," within the realm of quantum physics, seeks to establish proof that energetic fields beyond the human body are in existence. Biofield science, along with a broader field known as *Auraology* is allowing us to move beyond the limitations of molecular biology into the stratum of a human consciousness—the unseen world. These "intra-personal" fields that interact and represent spiritual, mental, emotional and physical dimensions of an individual have origins defined as: "...of energy and information, both putative and subtle, that regulates the hemodynamic function of living organisms and may play a substantial role in understanding and guiding health processes."

The fields, or sheaths beyond the immediate vessel of the human body are part of a larger, interconnected stratum of awareness and energy. According to the ancient Vedic and other traditions, these stratums hold distinctive "energy bodies." Each field, layered in sheaths, can be considered an informative entity responsible for a certain domain of our existence. They emanate frequencies that become gradually less dense the further the distance away from the physical body. It's important to note that these sheaths are completely translucent and allow electromagnetic information and energy to travel to and from the physical body and (see image 1). All sheaths contain dynamic frequencies that we interpret as information—the most physical being experienced by the "5 senses" of the physical body. The sheaths beyond the body include astral, mental(causal), celestial, astral, mental, emotional and ethereal layers of consciousness. These outer layers most likely explain why certain x-ray technology can detect various colors representing different degrees of light in a human body according to emotion. Dr. George Georgiou writes "These fields have rich textures, uncommon shapes, intricate weavings, and assorted colors that distinguish each of them...and our energy and awareness is constantly shifting within their realms.."

The breath is actually drawn in from these levels until it molecularly transforms into oxygen. Like breathing, all experiences are 1st introduced to the mind, which is omnipresent throughout all of the fields. Emotions, for example, are experienced after thoughts, reinforcing the premise that the mental field is a sheath outside of the emotional field. Although they are fully integrated and dependent, these fields act independently as well. Our emotional "field" literally "lights up" in different parts of the physical body in various degrees depending how we feel (see image 2). The outer astral layers, for obvious reasons, are much more difficult to observe—unless one fine-tunes their subtle awareness in the practice of meditation and or *Pranayama* ("breath energy"). Such practices create added layers of conscious sensitivity, intuition and expand/extend our individual consciousness beyond the physical, mental and emotional realms with practice. Regardless, the interplay of these "auric" fields and how they define our waking (and non-waking) reality cannot be understated. They are considered to be energy sources or *Chakras*, and distinctly connected to each of the 7 well known spheres that align with the spine. The 7 "outer" Chakras, of course, are rarely recognized, but hold within them realms of consciousness that connect us with an incomprehensible source of knowledge and energy. So in actuality, there are 15 Chakras, including the sheath-like auric fields that correlate with cone shaped wheels extending behind and in front of the torso. The recognition of these bio-fields allows us to view human beings as much more than protoplasmic material with a brain, but as a potential channel of earthly and cosmically informed intelligence. It is important to note that traditional medical models rooted in molecular biology take a "reductionist" perspective that examines the part instead of the whole and views the human body as a disconnected entity from the mind. We will examine a refuting of this more later in this chapter. Ultimately, the Bio-scientific perspective, a multi—dimensional and holistic view, allows us to see that the nervous system is intricately tied to the astral body, the emotional body, and so on. As stated, it is the breath that creates interconnectivity throughout these systems. So, any function of the physical body, whether it be the limbic system or the digestive system, is an experience of the outer bodies as well. So, it is essential that we view the act of conscious breathing, not only as an act of the respiratory system, but an act of the entire auric energy body. Breathing integrates the auric fields and is interconnected with mental and emotional processes. Hence, a disturbance in the breath, short breathing or disjointed breathing, can be traced to imbalances in the auric fields. These imbalances often show up as "stuck energy," miasmic "clouds" or simply misaligned flow of Qi in the meridians or chakras. What is important to recognize for our purposes is that each field contains within it, an indicator of mind, body and yes, breath.

The 7 Layers of Our Aura

- The Ketheric Template
- The Celestial Body
- The Etheric Template
- The Astral Body
- The Mental Body
- The Emotional Body
- The Etheric Layer

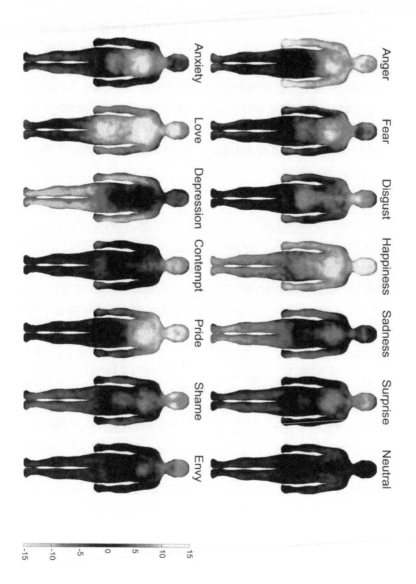

The Breath and Consciousness

It was always a challenge for me to speak about the divine properties of the breath without using the term "God" with my students. It can, however, be done. Without diving into the mysteries of human existence, let's certify that the breath is a life-giving energy conduit linking directly from an abundant universal source. We will call that source, *Consciousness*. The phenomenon of acquiring this energy conduit in the form of "air" to utilize and attain life force energy is nothing short of a miraculous process.

Inhaling and exhaling simulates the expansion and contraction of the universe and by the same token, is the most gratifying, immediate and urgent form of sustenance known to life on earth. Few things are more paradoxical than the mundane act of breathing. We take for granted, yet it holds within it the precious life-giving properties that can heal us and bring us closer to unimaginable wisdom. Some of my students had never taken a conscious breath in their life. What is it like to take a completely inhibited fully conscious breath of fresh air after holding our breath for some time? It is bliss. A wise man (Joseph Campbell) once said, "Follow your bliss."

The simple, yet complex process that defines the essence of being alive, must be the most overlooked form of healing and regeneration known to man. According to Dr. Singh Khalsa, more than ¾ of all Americans do not get enough oxygen to sustain normal levels of health. We breathe unconsciously to survive, but breathe consciously to thrive, yet we are barely breathing. What we have to realize first is that by simply attaching meaning to our breath or regulating it, we are heightening the awareness of our existence at all levels— that is, all of the energetic/auric fields. By breathing consciously, we're, indeed, integrating the "two worlds," the physical and non-physical, represented by our western concept of the mind and body. "The breath of God" within us has the capacity to directly provide an awareness of the absolute power of the present moment, the manifestation of eternity.

Breathing consciously requires a conscious adjustment of the physical body as well. A true deep breath does not go into the chest, it circumvents the lower lungs and pushes down the diaphragm. This causes the belly to slightly expand (on the inhale) and contract (on the exhale). I would also remind the youth daily, a true deep breath is quiet and slow. Not even you should hear it. The master's breath is slow, deep, low and quiet.

While conscious, diaphragmatic breathing results in greater levels of awareness, it also results in the *activation* of oxygen that is being taken in so that it becomes more than oxygen, it becomes life force, or what the ancient vedic masters called "Prana." Prana is an ever-present subtle life force that manifests through electromagnetic light and oxygen. By attaching our quality of mind and awareness to the air that we take in, that air becomes the high-frequency elixir that is Prana, the original creative power of the universe that flows in us and around us. Subsequently, in this access of Prana through conscious breathing, we are not *searching* for bliss or relaxation or life force, but we are removing the barriers or anxiety that keep us from our true state, where bliss is our true essence. In our silence, in our stillness, we allow for something greater to take control. The key is attaching meaning to the breath to gain an *awareness* of it. When something is meaningful to us, we become more aware of it. When we focus on something, we give it power. Similar to presenting a lesson to my students, I justified the meaning of our objective to them so they just weren't following me, but connecting to the significance of what we were doing as relevant. When our conscious breath becomes more relevant, its healing power increases. The full scope of conscious breathing consists of first noticing the path of the breath from the nose to the navel, and then extending that awareness to various parts of our body or Chakras. We can also regulate the breath, creating a different kind of awareness gained from rhythm, which involves counted breathing patterns that influence various bodily functions, helping us balance and heal our entire being. All of this can be considered mindful (or mindless) exercise, but attaching meaning to it enhances its function. The regulation of the breath was the tool that I used with my students because it was the best for those with extreme anxiety. Also, it aligned with the contextual limitations of the detention center. Through the auric fields, the breath allows us to directly intervene with our emotions as well. Hence, breathing consciously is truly the first step to gaining control over your own mind and body. It then can be applied to anything that you want to do well-cooking, dancing, surfing or even just conversing with others.

Breath and Bodily Systems

If we were a computer, our auric fields would be our Wi-Fi router and our mind would be the signal. Our breath, our browser. The energetic waves that we attracted to that system would serve as *Prana*. The intake of Prana through the breath contributes to the energy frequencies of our Chakras, our organs and even our thoughts, and it also is responsible for regulating all of our body's physical functions. There are specific channels or meridians (aligning with the spine) that serve as "highways" carrying subtle energy throughout a persons' auric and physical being. When those meridians are blocked, imbalances show up in our mental and physical health. By breathing consciously, we help keep those channels open. As the air travels through the respiratory system and energy travels up and down the vagus nerve or hypo-pituitary-adrenal axis, or HPA (In Sanskrit, *Shashona*), life force travels to the other meridians and the thousands of Nadi's or nerve endings activate as energy conduits. The 3 types of energies—electric, electromagnetic and subtle, are all found throughout the physical and auric body. Ultimately, it is electromagnetic (light) energy that brings balance to the body and being.

The simultaneous connection to the emotional body is a reminder that the flow of Prana is the energetic "river system" of the universe and all of our auric fields are linked through that flow. In other words, just as our emotions are experienced within our body and our mind, so is our conscious breath. Let's tie the emotions and breath together through the few things that begin to immediately happen, anatomically, once we begin breathing consciously. First and foremost, the brain begins triggering the secretion of neurotransmitters and hormones in various areas of the body's endocrine system (network of glands). This production happens because of the ability of the PNS (parasympathetic nervous system) to interpret brain signals/messages (through synapses) and the HPA cortex (hypo-pituitary adrenal), which is the intercon-nected "axis" of energy that links the pituitary gland and Hypothalamus in the brain with the rest of the endocrine system (this is also known as the brain-gut axis). It governs the immune system, metabolism and other vital bodily functions, synchronizing the connections between mind and body—specifically brain and gut. This is one reason why breathing down to the diaphragm for optimal health makes sense. Although the diaphragm does not actually collect air, it is a muscle that allows the lower lungs to fill and push out the belly to expand on an inhalation. During this slow and deep breathing, we are bringing "consciousness" to our receptors that link our gut and endocrine/adrenal system with our brain. That triggers the release of a regulated dose of "healing" peptides, neurotransmitters and hormones in the pituitary gland, specifically, Serotonin, which has a calming effect on the body. So, we can literally breathe emotional contentment into areas of our body by directing our mind to be conscious in those areas while we breathe. As our hormonal secretions allow us to alter our energy body, we experience more blissful feelings and our emotions become an outgrowth of this alignment. All of this shaping, which occurs down to the cellular level, begins with the PNS and HPA cortex stimulating the production of balancing hormones. Amazingly, it also slows the heart rate and activates our pancreas to produce enzymes for digestion, while regulating oxygen intake into the blood. The back of the brain (used for higher level thinking) is also activated, as opposed to the lower brain (activated when we are in survival mode). When we are unconscious of our breath and responding only to external stimuli that we perceive from the senses, we are more likely to generate an hyper-emotional state of limited awareness and low vibrational frequency. This state stimulates the sympathetic nervous system which is activated with the production of the hormones of adrenaline and cortisol. If adrenaline and cortisol are produced too much on a regular basis, they can wear down the body, simultaneously causing inflammation and hyperactivity in the brain. In cases of trauma-related disorders, the effect has been a conditioning or programming of high-alert, fight or flight responses to many times harmless external stimuli—that, perhaps, represent something that previously hurt us. Those with trauma related anxiety breath unconsciously, rapidly and are always in a state of "false alarm," leaving them to feel emotions of frustration and desperation. Mooji reminds us that "If you are living in fear, then you are living in exile of yourself."

The Vagus Nerve and HPA

We've all been reminded that emotions are innately connected to our gut. Perhaps you've had "butterflies" in your stomach? This is because of the system that directly links the brain with the core, or stomach, called the Hypo-Pituitary Adrenal Axis, or HPA. A final, crucial part of conscious breathing to influence our emotions is the "awakening" of the vagus nerve, the governing component of the parasympathetic nervous system and physical aspect of the HPA. I call it the "bike trail" of the spinal cord. This main meridian pathway of the body and largest cranial nerve is a regulator for the whole network that manages an array of critical bodily functions, including control of mood, immune response, digestion, and heart rate. Additionally, it is the main thoroughfare for the signals between the brain and the branch of nerves that spread open at the base of the sternum. This is why ancient traditions identified particular emotions associated with various organs in this area—the liver-anger, the kidneys-guilt, the heart-sadness and worrying-the pancreas. Both the HPA and the Vagus nerve seem to be responsible for motor and sensory information and the responding emotional and cognitive areas of the brain that create all the major peripheral intestinal functions.

The vagus nerve is activated through deep, slow, conscious breathing. An insightful study of contemplative activities and the vagus nerve published in *Frontiers of Neuroscience* describes the strong correlation between breath regulation and vagus nerve stimulation: "This could explain the physical and mental benefits of contemplative activities through changes.... in respiratory vagal nerve stimulation (rVNS).

The study goes on further to report that metacognition or "awareness actually begins in the body—specifically the vagus nerve.

"Metacognition and cognitive enhancement starts in the

body: somatosensory exercises are in their view early versions of the techniques involved in attention, meta-awareness and metacognition. This being the case, body awareness could be involved in producing effects on emotional and cognitive levels."

This verifies that it is highly likely that conscious breathing is the start of a total mental and physiological shift that is first anatomically apparent in the vagus nerve. Breathing consciously creates an automatic shift that brings the body back into a state of rest and repair instead of fight or flight. "The breath is our first weapon against the sympathetic (nervous system) overload," says Dr. Singh Khalsa, a foremost yogi, yogic researcher and medical doctor. Our systems and organs experience a powerful oxidizing, anti-inflammatory effect along with cellular growth, two of many acts of reparation.

Conscious Breathing and the Mind

To add, the famous "Pert" molecules that were identified by the late Dr. Candace Pert in "Molecules of Emotion." Pert, also a neuroscientist, found that the biomolecular basis for our emotions can be found in actual peptides called "ligands" that are found throughout the body, not just in the brain. The ligands have receptors that send messages directly to the brain and can influence all systems of movement in the body simultaneously. She illustrates the effects of conscious breathing in simple terms: "Simply bringing awareness to the process of breathing initiates the release of peptide molecules from the hindbrain to regulate breathing while unifying all systems." Her extensive work has brought riveting conclusions. Mainly that "the brain is the receiver, not the source...and your mind is in every cell of your body." So, when the whole body "experiences" consciousness through breath control, the vagus and the brain appear to produce the fruits of this consciousness—the hormonal release, the oxygenated blood, the production of enzymes, the list goes on...that nourishment which comes back to the body full circle.

Conscious breathing also creates something Dr. Areille Schwartz calls "neuroception" a form of knowing yourself better and being able to control your response to things in your external environment. She writes:

"Conscious breathing can help you to perceive changes that indicate you are reacting to stress... I invite you to recognize that each nervous system state gives you access to different emotions and sensations...Once you increase your perception of these sensations, you can then begin to discern whether the autonomic response you are having is a reflection of an area in your present-day life that is leading you to feel unsafe...sometimes these nervous system states are connected to memories of difficult times in the past...you can consciously let go of unnecessary defensive reactions by finding a posture that helps you release emotional tension or you might connect to your breath in a way that helps calm down your nervous system."

This state of awareness clearly extends to our emotions rooted in unfounded fears—which begin with the senses. Our sensory abilities are directly linked to the brain through *dendrites* that receive messages through the axons of our nerves. The senses are the first encounter with the outside world that activates a sort of alert, protection or pleasure source. Thoughts are products of the perception of our senses or the stimuli that interact with our nervous system. We can liken explosive anger to mounting frustration and see that such a constantly "frustrated" state of mind is a response to a continuously defeating sensual situation. That situation is being incapable of managing sensual intake and keeping calm or balanced. One can imagine that a multitude of defeating situations, where the repeated response to external stimuli is exhausting, causes a lack of efficacy, or frustration. Emotions can build on top of one another and evolve into very complex "limbic takeovers." We respond to our own negative emotions by creating greater frustration and more ways to express it. We become hostages of our own unnecessary reactions. Goethe was ahead of his time when saying, "Never let the things that matter least get in the way of the things that matter most."

Our body and mind are here among other things, to protect us. We overreact to the stresses of life because we fear for our well-being. There are so many layers of protection that can be created by the mind that we can find ourselves in a constant state of fear which then produces extremes like violence, trepidation or withdrawal. Changing the thought patterns that lead to this route, however, are possible. In fact, we can address the mind and stop it from fooling us at any point. Perhaps more easily than regulating our thoughts is allowing our practice of conscious breathing to do it for us. After all, conscious breathing regulates what is *triggering* those thoughts through purposeful redirection of cerebral-energy flow, which is more effective and permanent.

As our psycho-somatic connection employs messengers such as peptides and neurotransmitters through conscious breathing practices, the brain is more able to decipher the difference between real threats and fabricated threats. In sum, these messengers transmit information, oxygenate cells, and most importantly align our will with our mind. The effects are reassuring and calming thoughts. After energy is exchanged in these endocrine mechanisms, chemicals released into the blood and brain signify to the body that everything is okay. The more this happens, the more it becomes habitually ingrained (as is the case when the stressful triggers of trauma occupy the superhighway as well). The new patterns that are created re-align the neural networks in the brain and reform cellular connections that cause the body, the nervous system and brain to operate differently. Between the hypo-pituitary-adrenal axis and vagus nerve, the two info-energetic super-highways, the whole of our mind-body connection comes together. By consciously breathing, we create a balanced resonance and even energy flow up and down the vagus nerve and integrate the HPA cortex with that resonance so that our body can respond with neurotransmitters instead of reacting with adrenaline to challenging situations. Our vagus nerve is more likely to step around a problem if it is dancing than if it is just sitting still. The conclusion is this: *Conscious breathing not only repairs the body and changes unhealthy thought patterns, but mitigates the effects of anxiety by reconnecting the mind with the body so that they operate under the same singular intention of balance.*

The Barrier of Ego

I ask my students on many occasions: *Do we really have control over our own mind and if not, who or what does?* Psychoanalysts and others would say that it is the "ego" or the "fear-based" aspect of mind that directs our thoughts the majority of our waking hours. The term ego was coined first by Sigmund Freud as part of the realistic mind that mediates between the desires and the super-ego. A more esoteric concept of the ego has more to do with our mental life than our self-esteem. I would be willing to argue that it directs the large majority of our thoughts and actions. Our ego is deeply embedded into our DNA and it was born as a reaction to the separation from oneness—from God. The ego is a sort of massive defense mechanism. It's our way of dealing with separation from God, and so it interprets everything around it as separate. Including our body, mind and soul, which in essence, are one entity.

When the "voice" of the ego is not allowing space for oneness, feelings or internal release, what occurs is a psychosomatic disconnect. That is, the needs of our body are not correlating with the needs of our mind. The body wants to relax and rebuild, while the ego-based mind is on high alert, provoking a reaction. At worst, the ego is reacting to stimuli that are preparing us for fight or flight. The mind can be a mad scientist and the ego it's experiment.

Often, the ego is the only thing that stood in the way of getting many of my students to take a conscious breath. Too many of us who experience bouts with anxiety know that our egoistic mind robs us of enjoying life to its fullest and allowing us to see the eternal bliss of the present moment. It even incapacitates us from recognizing our immediate surroundings for what they really are. At this point, you may say, "Yes, but how can I experience total bliss if I'm worried about feeding my children or being on time for work?" Do not expect peace on your way to achieving it. Our challenges are to be honored and our work here and now is part of the process of growth. We must, however, prioritize our self-awareness and our wellness if we want to make gains. Nothing can go well around you when you are not well. When we choose to become conscious of our breath, we override the high alert, fight or flight and egoistic mind and allow the "higher self" to run the show. Conscious breathing can be done at *any* time—Beginning a short regular practice is enough to convince us that it works.

By not taking time to regulate our breath and regulate our mind amidst those challenges, we begin to do things unconsciously, allowing the ego to take control. A regular practice of breath control, whether through meditation or *Pranayama* can help your body-mind regulate itself so that you automatically become aware of the breath in the moments that it can benefit you. When we practice this and other forms of breath control, we not only regulate our breath and mind in the present moment, but set a precedent for those times when a false sense of urgency arises in our day. The ego, this "lower self," however, is not easily swayed. It doesn't simply crumble at the foot of the heightened awareness that we achieve—partly because we need it to survive and accomplish things in this world. It is reinforced through material wealth, status, acquisition and recognition—all of the things that our world is built upon. In this modern world especially, the ego can easily run amuck. It is important to recognize that the ego isn't just some greedy aspect of our mind, it is, as Eckardt Tool put it, "identification with form, primarily thought forms." It can remind us of any difficult past event, create any future scenario to worry about, make us desire or need something that doesn't serve us or attach distrust to anything or anyone around us if we let it. The breath is our best weapon. It is our connection to spirit, the teacher, the disciplinarian of our ego. I often say, to authenticate ourselves, we must move ourselves out of the way.

Conscious breathing is a rare opportunity to not only silence or occupy the ego, but reform it. The more we engage in conscious breathing, the more our ego is trained to remember what is important. The more we *respond* to life instead of react, we create added levels of awareness. Responding with conscious breathing creates the awareness that *I don't have to identify with the challenge I'm dealing with right now; I can deal with it without allowing it to suck my emotional energy.* One who carries sufficient awareness develops the ability to respond and, therefore, *responsibility.* You have a responsibility to care for yourself and we start gaining a sense of responding to the world around us. Often when some of my students were lashing out or acting inappropriately, I would simply ask them, "Are we reacting right now or are we responding?" Usually, they could immediately tell the difference. It's a simple question but one that reminds us that the ego wants to react—It is laying there in wait, ready to get pissed or blame somebody or something. It wants to create drama and pain so that others may notice. An unconscious waste of energy, indeed. Our ability to consciously connect to our breath is our gift of gifts. It is through the practice of controlling the breath that we begin to take back control of our minds, and therefore our lives. It introduces the ego to our *true self*, and, in time, can introduce us to the universe that lies within us.

✦ CHAPTER 2 ✦

EDUCATION AND TRAUMA

An Intro to the Culture of Trauma

Out of the empty, dark tunnel comes forth a wind bringing the smell of bitter coffee and the soft scent of Islamic perfumes mixed with a lingering stench of urine. The roaring headlights ahead illuminate specks of dust throughout the subway station as the dim-lit track escorts our arriving westbound L train in, clacking and screeching to a halt. The metal doors slide open and a swarm of humanity presses out of the packed car before a new mass of us load ourselves in. It is early February in Philadelphia and I feel a brief sense of satisfaction knowing that I remembered to wear two pairs of socks on this chilly Tuesday. Others boarding the train have their steamy caffeinated drinks, whether in a Wa-Wa cup or prestigious Starbucks holder. They have their briefcases or book bags, their children strapped to their back or hanging from their arms. For some, the fresh, cloudy, snow dusted morning means another day on campus, maneuvering the path of a career. Some are headed to the office or the conference room. Others, on the opposite track are returning in their scrubs from a long night in the emergency room. Working men with thick arms are sporting their battered construction gear, covered in dried plaster. Along the walls of the station, beings in tattered clothes are slumped over, disoriented or faintly engaged in their own chatter. They are broken and strung out—some beyond hope or repair. The mechanized silence of the subway car is a deceptive top layer of existence, as pairs of eyes stare off, their dreams cry out beneath earpods and Iphones, desperately trying to connect to a better world, one of meaning. The soul of an American city presses on in the daily grind of those that know how to keep pressing on. The fabric of Philadelphia shows a rich history of success and opportunity, but within that fabric is the grimey layer of survival. Those born into intergenerational poverty have known nothing but setbacks, shortcuts and bad breaks. Call it a karmic debt, *Bardo, Samsara,* call it a legacy of colonialism, racism, classism. Spirit science and social theory collide in the confines of my mind as we pull into the 48th St. station. Why are all of us packed onto one planet? Where are we going? The gray sky appears as I tighten my straps and emerge from the underworld on the zipping train past columns of brick row houses that reflect back a sense of nostalgia in the peering sunlight. It is a new day in the city of brotherly love and sisterly affection. The doors slide open and my thoughts divert to my students. Their empty sighs and stinging words...their sense of regret and guilt. Their patience and impulsiveness, their advantages and disadvantages, their spirit...All of it, like the smells of the subway station, blend to create a story of juvenile justice in urban dystopia.

Panda is with me. My *aunty.* A "south Philly" native and amazing teacher, Panda was a staunch humanitarian and animal rights activist. She is about 5'0 tall, fiery and feisty, dyslexic and working through ADD and ADHD. Panda and I are buddies, partners, family—in place where true friendships are hard to find. We look out for each other. We have a coded language and an intuitive understanding. It helps that we're both *Paisans* (Italian-American) but even more importantly, we both believe in what we are doing. We both acknowledged that although the idea of the juvenile justice system is an atrocity, it's much worse if the kids inside don't have good people to turn to. Panda could easily average over 20 conversations in the morning before we even get to the building, the whole time claiming to be exhausted.. I'd seen her free-style rap, buy a homeless man breakfast and curse out an irresponsible driver all in one morning. As we enter the newly built DHS (Dept of Human Services) complex and swipe our badges, we pass through detectors and beeping portals, winding our way into the school area. The white walls become suddenly alive—adorned with artwork from the students. Colorful portraits, signs and symbols of street life rage, hope and despair speckle the hallway. The Juvenile Justice program is within the district of Philadelphia but our building is housed by DHS—a complicated relationship that is still being negoti-ated to this very day. All within the same building is a residents' judge, (sometimes) their lawyer, their teacher, their social worker, their principal, their special education teacher, their counselor, their Psychiatrist. Collectively, we "service" juvenile delinquents.

An adult counselor props a door open down the hallway and calls out sternly, "hold that rap," to the emerging teenage inmates or *residents*, who filter out one by one, following suit in a straight line. The first face in a line of them stares forward lifelessly and the row walks silently out of the cafeteria toward the school area. They are attired in blue sweats and plastic flip flops with white socks and are in line from shortest to tallest. Panda and I stop, as is expected of us, to allow the unit to pass. I glance at the passing faces, recognizing a few—many of them appear both fierce as lions and as frightened as chickens in a hen house. The 12 are an array of skin tones and physiques—

representing the many mixes of racial and ethnic Philadelphia, but categorically, mostly Afro-American, with a sprinkling of Puerto Rican "creolo" and one or two "Caucasian" and even fewer Asiatic faces. When transitioning from classrooms or from their "unit," they are to remain silent. With the exception of some quick cackles, mumbles, or single coded words, their walk is a quiet one. A few nod their heads at me and smile at Panda. Most of them have been badly burned—on the inside and out. Scars and tattoos mark their fingers, forearms, necks and cheekbones. Many cannot lift their head or eyes to greet a passerby. Their pain runs deep. Their sense of loss, heavy. Anger often swells in the cold, frozen waters behind their eyelids. Although some are like proud ships sailing onward into the stormy night—strong enough to infuse hope in all of us, most are merely numbers in an institutional holding house. For them, there is no present moment. Tomorrow is everything.

Despite the circumstance, the youth bring their flair, their wits, their theatrics into the classroom, for within the spectrum of their personalities is an uncanny ability to unapologetically break social norms. Despite their imprisonment, they speak, act and think as they wish—sometimes to their detriment, of course. The irony is clear. In some cases, they are more "free" than those professionals working to liberate them. Many are eager to go to school, and, in class, they'll sound off through free-style rapping or regal stories from their "hood." Most are quiet, however, hesitant to engage anything or anybody too much. They are distant and laden with a sense of desperation. The rambunctious few that somehow made a bad decision and ended up "pickled (incarcerated)" are seemingly quick to leave. They stand out in the group like a deer in headlights—They listen to their elders, teachers and counselors without pushback or hostility. The counselors (2 to every unit) serve as in-house parents/

security guards that escort the residents wherever they go. These embattled and overworked caretakers sit in our classrooms, providing a layer of security. Other than that, they remain distant from the affairs of the school or the needs of the teachers—entrenched in the daily grind of managing resident life upstairs *on the unit*. They break up fights, resolve conflict, lock up "huts (prison cells)" and scorn unacceptable behavior whenever possible—even after a 16-hour shift with no sleep. They know the residents in and out from head to toe. Many are from the same neighborhoods and know the struggles of life in Philly. Only through my friendships with a few of them was I able to interact with the residents in a *one on one* context. Similar to many of the residents, those who spend too much time at "the youth" center seem to be swallowed into a numbness. Despite the schools' best efforts to fuse an academic culture into the setting, most residents don't value their education much and have already become disillusioned. Most have other plans. For some residents, it only takes a few days or weeks before the flush of boredom and or disillusionment sinks in. Their light fades and their voice disappears into the deep dark tunnels of the *school to prison pipeline* and the further "criminalization of America." Now, more than ever, there are more juvenile detention centers and more inmates to fill them—the penal-based justice system is finely disguised as restorative. It does not stop crime and by all accounts, does not reform, or heal, juvenile delinquents. It is my hope that this book provides a formula for change.

One March morning up in the faded four walls of the "girls unit," I and my co-teacher listened to a 15 year old student give a passionate monologue about her aspirations to be a writer. She touted her interest in certain modern classics like the "*House on Mango Street*" and "*The Color Purple*" etc.. She wanted to read as much as she could get her hands on so that she could enhance her writing. "You can bring books for me!" She exclaimed. That evening, I went home and scoured through my book collection, gathered some possible interests for her and made some photocopies of excerpts. The next day, I entered the unit(common area), excited to share with her what I'd found. The same girl sat slouched in the corner of the room and the look on her face was completely stoic. I showed her some of what I brought. She was oddly detached, eyes staring off into a seemingly different dimension. It was as if she forgot what she had told me the day before. I'm not sure what had happened in the period of 24 hours, but on this day, she just wanted to stay in her holding cell. She told me she was "done bein here." Then, without warning, sprung up and scoffed at the group, "Y'all don't know me... It don't even matter, I don't even care no more." Her inspiration to write would, perhaps, manifest another day, as trauma-related anxiety reared its ugly head.

Trauma-informed education is a catchy phrase these days, and at juvenile detention centers and holding houses, the effects of trauma are ever present in the daily experience. While difficult to statistically surmise, the majority of our students had experienced acute forms of trauma at some or several points of their lives. Many had been continuously exposed to an environment charged by traumatic events and some would argue that they grew up within a familial or cultural context in which their bonds to others were reinforced through trauma (known as "trauma bonding"). Two young ladies, for example, become best friends because they both lost their brothers to street violence. The many conditions and related disorders stemming from trauma-related anxiety were a major part of my dealings throughout this "study-story" and we will explore some of them as needed. Although my clinical degrees and academic credentials related to the field of trauma were few, my everyday experience teaching incarcerated youth served as a motivator to learn more, and find solutions. My students and the pursuit of coping mechanisms to help them, ultimately, informed my methods and discoveries. One discovery that became painfully obvious was that trauma-informed education could benefit from including an emotionally-spiritually conscious narrative and realistic informing an inexperienced teacher of the full parameters of how TRA debilitates the learning process.

Cultural and Racial Trauma

Lest we not forget that the forms of trauma take a distinctive shape when exploring or evaluating TRA in vulnerable populations. Being impoverished or a minority in America or anyplace where one encounters a daily struggle with their identity in the face of a majority culture that has traditionally imposed their value system is sometimes more than a Pyscho-social challenge, but a series of traumatic experiences. Tarana Burke and Brene Brown disclose the vulnerability of black America and the collective trauma embodied by white supremacy in their book "*You are the Best Thing.*" The expose reveals the many layers of shame and subjectivity experienced by black youth while growing up in America. One could argue that being black in America, alone, is a traumatizing experience. This vulnerability is found in all aspects of African American culture—revealed in language, gestures, values, beliefs and norms. Such works, along with the highly acclaimed "*My Grandmother's Hands,*" by Resma Menakem, reveals the degrees of impact of traumatic events on the mind, body and brain. In impoverished communities in America, especially those of color, trauma is literally found in the cell makeup of the body—from how one walks to how words are spoken. Many of the terms used by black Americans, for example, reveal a history of violence and oppression that is firmly embedded in thought patterns, mental schemas and or bodily movements. A slouching posture, a sexual innuendo, everything reflects something that was learned from being stripped of power, freedom and dignity at the onset of slavery. The word "swollen," for example, was always used in my upbringing by African-American friends when they referred to someone being bitter or resentful—a direct reference to being swollen after a beating. In Philadelphia, such references are numerous even down to the famous "scrapple," which is a "poor man's breakfast" consisting of wheat flour, pork skins, cow tongue or any other various leftover animal parts that could be fried and eaten. A word carries a meaning as well as a frequency. The frequency is purely energetic and has implications of the users intentions, self-worth, beliefs and behavior. Nobody wants to eat "scrap," which is a synonym of "garbage," but they do. Essentially, it is important to note that trauma is not just internalized from events in someone's life because something happened to them. It occurs through historical legacy and is carried down through DNA, then expressed through socialization and culture. The legacy of racial injustice in America is a very recognizable trauma that I witnessed all of my life as white male and more importantly, as a divinely inspired being. The work that needs to be done to clear this trauma, some refer to as karmic debt clearing, is a true undertaking. Then again, spiritual growth is an undertaking for us all.

The Hijacking that is Trauma-Related Anxiety

A traumatic event in our lives is like an earthquake on the ocean floor that is our emotional stability. It ruptures and rips the psychosomatic foundation, leaving our waters to cast title waves to the shoreline of thoughts that mold our mind and body. TRA is more than a negative emotional result of certain triggers, but an energetic and neuro-physiological hijacking that creates a slew of disrupted patterns found in our energy body down to the cellular structure of the brain and body. Its effects are encoded into the fabric of our being—manifesting through our daily cognitions and actions. Trauma is defined as a "totally unexpected experience which the subject is unable to assimilate" (*Critical Dictionary of Psychoanalysis*, Charles Rycroft, Penguin Books). That experience is so unacceptable to the conscious mind that the memory of the event is repressed. That is to say, it is censored from conscious memory while continuing to exist in the unconscious mind.

"I feel like everybody in here is low key stressin.. Even when we chillin, somebody dealin with something. I know for me, I always got low key stress, but it's worse in here." J.M, 2020

"It's when they lock my door, ...that's the shit I can't take." D.T., 2021

The simple statement above from a couple of my students epitomizes the daily burden of TRA. Those that experience a trauma-related anxiety disorder are often on constant alert, unable to take social cues, and many times viewing others there to help as sometimes threatening. They are many times distanced from the immediate conversation. On the surface, they could appear very quiet or calm and even attentive. The ego, or external social conscious personality, does its best to cover anxiety, but it soon emerges in one of its many potential forms. It is like a snake in the jungle. In recognizing its many forms, one must look for every sign of movement in the trees, and in the many coverings of the earth below. The snake can encroach with many tactics—appearing in a multitude of colors, postures and modes of movement. While the symptoms and the results of anxiety may be easily identifiable, the "middle" manifestations and emotions of those symptoms are not.

"Once incarcerated, children are at risk of physical and psychological abuse, sexual assault, suicide and other harms, including inadequate educational instruction. The use of solitary confinement further deprives them of social interaction, mental stimulation and key services during a critical time of adolescent brain development. Risks are heightened for children in the adult criminal justice system, which is focused on punishment rather than rehabilitation and treatment."

I have seen everything from over-elation to extreme anger as a result of generalized anxiety, which afflicted most of our population. One day on the unit when a group of 14-15 year old boys was locked down, a young resident desperately called me over to him. I could see his pupils were dilated and heard the tension in his voice. He was trying to desperately connect to something that could allow his mind to escape from the triggering of lockdown. He locked his eyes into mine and with a tranquil voice to cover his great urgency, he murmured, "How do you pray?"

While many (I would say most) experienced a state of generalized anxiety, a smaller, perhaps %10-%20, could be considered ADHD, ADD, PTSD and or RAD (reactive attachment disorder). Please note that attention-oriented (ADD, ADHD) and compulsive disorders (OCD) which result in hyperactivity are, again, results of anxiety.

Those who are traumatized are known to turn small things into big ones—external stimuli, whether a phone, a pen, a piece of candy, an image or spoken word or the presence of another human being with certain features can trigger a barrage of self-defeating and defensive thoughts. Those thoughts ignite a pattern of adrenaline-feeding emotions, alerting the nervous and endocrine system of the body to produce a repeated, heightened physiological response. This is especially true with young people who have not yet developed coping mechanisms for their traumatic triggers and find themselves in a world of "fight or flight." Anger, as well, is an emotion stemming from this pattern, as aggression is merely a manifestation of fear. The unfortunate reality is that trauma becomes physically ingrained or hardwired into the developing neural-endocrine systems of our youth at a young age—and the younger the age, the usually more unchanging the pattern becomes, unless there is intervention. A lot can happen in a single moment for traumatized youth. In the center, RAD was a common condition of those who had committed violent crimes, but also for those who did not. This condition's symptoms include a lack of emotion or abnormal response to normal emotional triggers—whether it is responding adversely to something universally pleasant (such as a bunny) or someone who was there to help (such as a counselor). It also included a generalized state of anxiety, which is illustrated in J.M's narrative. Many of the young juveniles had experienced ASD (Acute Stress disorder) as children, which occurs within the first month of a trauma-related event. In some cases, of course, they had come into the unit immediately after a traumatic event and were completely unadjusted. Untreated ASD usually evolves into PTSD. Needless to say, these children and teenagers were extremely vulnerable—and many of them, if not, all of them, were subconsciously well aware of it. Whether it is through a phobia or trauma, I assert that there are no such instances as "irrational fears." The stimuli that trigger both trauma-related anxiety (TRA) and associated phobic disorders present a real and present threat to the resident and result in the same energetic and hormonal response. For all of these conditions, the resident experiences a patterned response, beginning with the associative thought that the trigger. It ends with an emotional experience and an embedding into areas of our physical body. Emotions are simply feedback devices that tell us where the energetic imbalance is in the body. What is key to understand is that the afflicted responds to their *perturbations*, not their thoughts. Perturbations are the generating power behind the energetic, nervous, hormonal, chemical and cognitive activity associated with negative emotions.

Let's begin with an initial thought—*I see a fire, it reminds me of the fire in my house when I was a kid*. After the sight of the fire and the initial thought, there is the energetic response or disturbance in the biofield. This would appear in the biofield as a fracture in the astral or pranic energy flow coming into the body through the chakras. Following this, there is the perturbation. The host of perturbations that accompany the negative emotion stem from the negative thought. Removal of the perturbations, therefore, has a circumventing effect— restoring energetic activities to normal with the subsequent host of the negative emotions. This is why the ability of someone suffering from TRA to observe their own thoughts is paramount. Observation steps in the way between perturbations and emotions. Meditation and conscious breathing exercises, some immediate and some used in the long term, specifically allow us to observe the mind and the trigger, before it causes the chained pattern reaction. The chain reaction of trauma-related anxiety to a trigger is as follows:

EXTERNAL(trigger) ↓
↳ negative thought / association → energetic disturbance
→ perturbance → negative emotion

When the brain is enabling the excessive secretion of cortisol and there is hormonal imbalance, attention is diverted into a hyperactive "fight or flight" mode. At this point, a perturbed response is almost impossible to avoid. This mode results in the common "limbic hijacking" that occurs when chemicals called Catecholamines including adrenaline are released during a stress response. Dopamine is included in this category of responses and this is why I later advocate for non-dopamine rewards for residents, which only adds to their hormonal imbalances. When our cerebral activity prepares the body for the threatening scenario in our environment, there is a substantial deficit in our mental focus. Of course, this activity can happen gradually on a level of slow release or even as a general state of being. This is trauma related anxiety. J.M's description above illustrates that even those with "low key stress" are in a constant state of low level hijacking of the emotional part of the brain. This is the catalyst for hyperactivity—excessive or hyper sensual intake creating unnecessary preparation for action. It could lead to underlying or extreme nervousness and with those who are incarcerated, often anger. At worst and on rare occasions, it could manifest into violence toward self or someone else. I have witnessed this total limbic hijacking in the prison and classroom where an individual becomes extremely hostile under normal, harmonious conditions. It is as if they are taken over by a force beyond the immediate environment or a switch of one-directional electro-radiation is turned on within them. Their eyes fixate, their facial muscles clinch and they spew rapid words of hostility that usually come out as threats or degradations. During such an episode, of course, the higher cognitive parts of the brain, those used for critical thinking, analysis, emotional intelligence, language etc... are not activated due to peptides and neurotransmitters pouring into the limbic system—the reptilian or old part of the brain we depend on for survival needs. A young man in the prison once rammed his head against his window, shattered a glass platelet of 1 inch glass after being triggered by a certain type of music associated with past trauma.

Physiologically, these disorders produce harmful levels of adrenal-cortisol that causes energetic and hormonal imbalance and can eventually lead to a host of chronic health issues. I witnessed students internalize the pain or reaction to triggers and begin hurting themselves. Some would rub the eraser from their pencil deeply into their skin until it bled. In a drastic case, a student drove a pencil tip deeply into his hand through the other side. Such behavior is so symbolic of the inflammation occurring in the body as well. At its worst, young people with chronic TRA can become suicidal. The task of dealing with mounting threats and potential problems or uncertainties of life becomes overwhelming. It is well known that the brain isn't fully developed until about the age of 25 and Cathay Caruth, a trauma theorist, reminds us that trauma "creates irrevocable damage to the psyche." She goes on to say that it "fragments consciousness and prevents direct linguistic representation." I would add that trauma can be reinforced from thought patterns and emotions, but also directly into the cellular structure of muscles and nerve fibers that have been continuously fortified by a conditioned response to various triggers. In Sanskrit, thought patterns that integrate themselves into our physical bodies are called *Samskaras* (not coincidentally, similar to the word *scar*). The breaking of these patterns is the reason why I advocate for conscious movement and the simple, yet, miraculous therapy that rewires the brain's response to trauma-related stimuli, conscious breathing. As you will discover in these pages, conscious breathing proves that a re-routing of nervous impulses can commence and real healing in the psyche and physical body. It can rebuild the damaged patterns that exist in our fields and body. First, let's engage trauma where it lives and dies—the spirit.

◆

A Spiritual Narrative for a Conscious Experience

Without using the "s" word too much, let us just define the abstract concept of *spirituality* as *the awareness of and engagement with consciousness*—that is, the consciousness existing within us and beyond us. Many associate the concept of *spirit* with that of the unseen or *ethereal*, but the workings of spirit can be understood through engaging consciousness in both the ethereal and physical realm. Consciousness is the source of all things, physical and non-physical. What is perceived by 5 the senses, the thoughts of the mind, the emotions, good and bad, are all spiritual engagements.. All of these, including the five senses, help us learn about aspects of Consciousness. So, spirituality can be as much a physical part of life as an ethereal one. Consciousness flows through the energy body—that which inextricably links the physical body with astral and celestial levels (as discussed earlier). We can observe our own movements, thoughts and emotions from consciousness, although we may have a difficult time observing them while we enact them. Simply put, we cannot observe Consciousness, but Consciousness allows us a space from which to observe ourselves. In Sanskrit, this concept is called *Brahmacharya*. Gurudev reminds us that Brahmacharya means "moving through the infinite" and where we learn to "see ourselves as consciousness." This 1st takes the skill of self-observation. Some of the most powerful activities and lessons are when we allow our students to observe themselves and critique or just reflect on their own actions or thoughts. I would sometimes begin the class by saying a word like "harmony" or "strategy," and ask them what images and emotions are conjured in their minds. Sometimes I would directly ask them, "Is it possible to observe ourselves?" In one class, I had them role play a bird that followed them around all their lives but they never knew the bird existed. This spiritually oriented therapy is just a tool, but an accessible one that I could adapt to the prison setting.

Ultimately, what our traumatized youth need is therapy through *abreaction*. An *abreaction* is kind of a "shake-up" or "coming back to God" event. This doesn't have to be physically painful, but it jarrs the system enough to reroute old thinking patterns and trigger hormonal changes. Any birth or rebirth involves a culminating breakthrough moment. An abreaction may also be small enough to be almost unnoticeable or it may be of such proportions that for the duration of the process, the subject will undergo an extreme emotional experience matching the intensity of the original traumatizing event. A therapy with Psychoanalytic roots, the effect is to release the repressed memory (the valve in the diagram opens) so that it floods the subject's consciousness and he or she re-experiences the emotions of the traumatizing event. This is a moment of catharsis; once the event is released the subject is free of the repression and of all the neuroses caused by the repression. It is a moment of liberation.

Let's recognize that aversion is a form of bondage. We are tied to what we hate or fear and this is why the same problem, the same danger or difficulty will present itself over and over again in different forms and aspects of our lives. An abreaction is a breakthrough from this cycle—from this "attracting" our own aversion towards us. It is when we come so close to the actual thing that we fear or hate, that we have to deal with it in a different way—we have to face it head on. The abreaction can only be as unpleasant as the emotions caused by the original traumatizing event. The level of the client's distress usually has an effect on the therapy modality (or combinations thereof) used. The traditional clinical and institutional settings in which the residents are housed and treated uses no such therapy, but a great day will be when young persons with trauma are able to avail themselves of such therapy. Why? No repression = no perturbations = no trauma-related anxiety. One of my students walked into class everyday and brought his chair to the wall to face everyone. He wasn't the only one who positioned himself like Wyatt Earp, but he reacted to me one day when I was behind him watching his computer. We'll call him GT, and I learned that he had a fear of men (maybe white men or authority figures) standing behind him because he was thrown into a choke hold when he was younger. His reaction was not irrational when a teacher or counselor would stand behind him. In this sense, he was bonded to his aversion and it caused him great oppression. I know not how he further coped with his TRA, but an abreaction would look like this: Someone would stand behind him and GT would be instructed to tap several acupressure points from the top of his head to his ribcage as he experienced the fear or anger. He could say an affirmation out loud that could help him accept himself and move on from the triggering scenario such as *"Although I have fear when there is someone standing behind me, I deeply love and accept myself."* He may experience overwhelming fear and have to stop, but the procedure keeps happening until the reaction subsides. This method is called EFT tapping and it could be one of a few that sparks an abreaction. I personally would use a conscious breathing technique as well. Unfortunately, as one could imagine, I could not use this approach in the institutional setting.

We can not only observe the effects of our reaction to things, but observe ourselves consciously breathing through thoughts and behavior. Just as we can close our eyes and observe how we feel, we can guide ourselves into "deeper" modes of meditation to experience the energy body. We can experience consciousness by *becoming* Consciousness. Our cultural paradigm is founded upon the idea that consciousness does not exist beyond the waking and non-waking experiences of human beings. Even as I type the word "conscious," spellcheck reminds me that it cannot be used after the word "becoming." Despite its shortcomings, exoteric scientific methods do provide us with useful tools to understand the physiological side of spirit and we must remain within these academic realms to describe events understood by its associated fields—anatomy, psychology, physiology etc.. We can, however, learn about our "spirit"—by observing that we are more than just our thoughts, actions and emotions. We can experience more than just the 5 senses and have access to an awareness far more profound and dynamic. **The fact that we can observe all of this proves that there has to be a source state of our observation. That source state is our spirit.** The continuous correlative and interconnected existence of the energy body shows us that nothing exists on its own. Through the vantage point of the energy body, we can study and explore the consciousness that permeates all of life—including our own. The implication of meditative breathing activities that allow us to discover consciousness for those who have trauma-related anxiety are incredible. First and foremost, it can allow those with anxiety to observe their emotions and thoughts from a different vantage point. Second, they can come to realize very easily that engaging consciousness can allow them to identify their own triggers, emotions and thoughts that result in their undesirable behavior. Finally, it can allow those with anxiety to observe that *what* they are experiencing is not *who* they are.

Scientific-based educational theory does not take into account celestial/astral or energetic forces at play in our behavior and objectifies thoughts and emotions as if they are isolated events of the mind...Although physiological and psychological terminology is used throughout this study, I have found that the exploration and explanation of trauma remaining solely within those realms is limiting. While the platform of trauma-informed education speaks to symptoms and causes of trauma, it does not include referencing the spiritual domain and related conscious experiences (*concepts such as consciousness, breath awareness, meditation, prayer, higher self, responsibility, time, ESP, ceremony, collective consciousness, etc...*). Mindfulness is interjected as part of the platform, but it is referenced with 2-3 activities that to me, are temporary ways to decompress from distress, not address TRA. One of these for instance is "single tasking," or doing one thing with total attention. This classic example of mindful behavior does provide a platform for gaining greater awareness and certainly, if done on a regular basis, could train the mind to focus while performing a task. For those with trauma, however, the ability to concentrate distances the mind from even approaching an activity like this. They cannot just "focus" or "slow down." The state of anxiety that exists with most juveniles with TRA must be engaged in real time. My students would simply not participate in such activities because such activities had no *meaning* for them. Maybe a group of teenagers who studied mindfulness and its influence on the brain would appreciate or enjoy the exercise, but it would not be accessible to the repression and pain that a traumatized young person carried with them. TRA needs to be addressed on a spiritual level—a real level with meaning. "Spiritus contra spiritum" (Spiritual crisis requires spirit cure). These concepts that I mentioned above are just as much scientific as spiritual and objective as subjective; "Believing" in them takes the same quality of mind as believing in any religious or educational doctrine.

Picking Fruit

I have found that the approach to some of these conscious experience-oriented topics at first brings confusion or resistance, but after a proper familiarization, they provide clarity for students from angles of perception that were otherwise closed. I would often introduce the idea of spirit to the students through an exercise called "picking fruit," that was shared with me by a former mentor. It is endowed with archetypal symbolism and allows the student to see themselves in a new light. They create their own version of a picture entitled "picking fruit." Their drawing may take many forms depicting many scenes and perceptions of what it means to "pick fruit." Among many of the symbolic features they may include on their drawing is a reference to the sky, sun, or some feature on the horizon. This represents their awareness of something "greater than them" or a presiding force that is ever-present or omnipotent. Taken from the archetypal theory of Carl Jung, picking fruit reveals someone's fears, hopes, regrets, failures and supposed spiritual awareness. When my students would self-reflect on their drawing, we would engage in a conversation about spirit, which was usually a great way to establish the existence of spirit as fact and use it in the classroom as a tool to gain self-awareness. It didn't matter if someone believed in it—it was there on the drawing to be recognized as symbolic. My own authentic self does not adhere to "believing" in something—I either know it or I don't. When I was asked if I believed in the symbols of "picking fruit," I merely returned the question and asked if the student felt their drawing was an accurate representation of themselves. The proof was in the product.

The concept of spiritual awareness was also epitomized by the singing bowl. The sound of the bowl, for example, was real to them. I rang it before every 1-minute moment, so it provided them with meaning. It created behavioral and energetic change, drawing them closer to consciousness. A simple establishing of this small ritual inspired one student to write the following:

"When we start class with the bowl, everything changes. It's like a switch goes on and I wake up...At first I didn't like it, but now its ok.. I think it wakes everybody up and we look around at where we're at." J.L. 2019

Concurrently, I found that many incarcerated youth experience trauma-related anxiety paralleled a desperate need for spiritual engagement through inner exploration or personal practice (rather than an external search for God or religious doctrine). One reason that conscious breathing generated so many positive results is that it served as a successful spiritual medium that represented no one religion or belief system. It was accessible and spoke directly to not only our collective experience, but to the wounded spirit—and the youth took to it like a hand instinctively reaching to cover a wound. Conscious breathing at its rudimentary level, requires a subtle quality of self-efficacy. Being able to regulate our breath takes calculated effort, or "will intention" and observe the positive results from the discipline that is applied. That said, for our purposes in teaching those with trauma, we must engage the "physical" side of consciousness or spirituality when re-routing them. If they never experience a different side of themselves, how are they to realize that their own transformation is even possible? Healing involves, among other things, a continuous reflective experience and dialogue between the emotional, astral and physical. This happens through meditation or forms of conscious breathing and bodily awareness and is reinforced through self-observation.

If we are educating those with trauma, how can we not seek simultaneous healing for them as well? Are they not learning through healing? I realize that I cannot *prove* the healing quantitatively in these writings or the influence of spirituality in my teachings, but my work undeniably relied upon it, despite it being relegated by behavioral and cognitive theorists for decades. Trauma can be found on the physical, mental, emotional, astral and celestial planes. It is a fissure in our connection to consciousness, but it can be observed and repaired. A broken bone can cause physical suffering as a broken part of the spirit can cause mental or spiritual suffering. We can heal the bone by engaging the physical— with attention and practice. As such, we can heal the spirit by engaging the ethereal—with attention and practice. *I propose that conscious breathing and meditation before class mitigate the effects of trauma because it allows for an individual and collective interaction with consciousness through ritual. It fosters self-efficacy, spiritual responsibility and "innerstanding" and provides a platform in which one can retrain their response to trauma triggers and release their deep-seated repression.*

Spirituality as Responsibility

We've all heard the number 1 new age credo "I'm not really a religious person, but I consider myself to be spiritual." I'm guilty of using it a few times as a quick "go to" response when asked about my religious beliefs when teaching at the center. After a while though, people wanted to know what it meant, at least for me, to be "spiritual." I elaborate more on this in the 2nd part of this book in the "Spirituality and religion" chapter. To keep the concept of "spirit" secular, I emphasized that a belief in a *God* was not necessarily the focal point of spirituality. To me, the focal point of spirituality is our *responsibility*. It is our ability to respond to the world that makes us spiritual. The most spiritually aware or "conscious" people that I have known, ground their work in responding to life's demands, not reacting. Spiritual people respond to lies with truth, respond to aggression with harmonization (not necessarily peace) and respond to need with compassion. One who reacts is not observing or addressing their own negative actions or emotions, which are lacking consciousness. If someone steals something from me and I get upset, I am reacting based on fulfilling the egoistic mind, which personalizes my experience. Our experiences are not about us(the ego), they are about how the self (higher consciousness) responds to them. This spiritual being does not judge things or people as good or bad, right or wrong. The spiritual minded person is able to respond, not react to the world—hence their wisdom is not found in what they believe, but found in their *responsibility*.

The form of discipline that I could instill best at the center and found best to work for myself was one of responsibility—the ability to respond to the world based on context and circumstance, with self-awareness and mindfulness. *Responding* often involves, again, first observing emotions before acting upon them. Those who were responsible began to trust themselves and in turn, could be trusted. They could reason. They could discern. Additionally, someone who engages their spirit through ritual or disciplinary practice becomes more responsible through their dedication and devotion. Young people eventually come to understand that being dedicated or devoted to something, anything, brings not only focus, but identity and purpose. I will tie in the importance of identity as it is integrated into a curriculum of spiritual responsibility as this work progresses. One student that you will read about, "W" demonstrated that his small role as ringing the bowl and facilitating meditation was important and brought purpose to his day. It reframed his identity. As he became conscious of this role, he became more purpose-driven, more responsible. The 1 minute moment defied duality and intensified responsibility—for one brief moment, there wasn't us and them, good or bad, black or white, just the breath, the self, the inhale and exhale, which were all equally vital. Undoubtedly, spirituality was rarely discussed as a concept, but it permeated the nature of my relationship with my students.

The 1-minute moment that I eventually incorporated gave credence to all spiritual beliefs systems and it was introduced as a "moment to meditate, pray or reflect but mainly to focus on the rhythm and existence of the breath." This awareness of the existence of the breath allowed for the window of consciousness to slide open. Some may have explored being conscious of their own body and mind while others found it to be a time when they reflected on their own beliefs. One young man wrote that it "gave (me) a time to think about God." As the spiritual moment that I instituted with them provided them with more emotional management, I allowed them to develop their own responsibility through various allotments of exploratory time. The opportunity to discipline the self came through the 1-minute moment, but the opportunity to find truth in the rest of the time together was earned. True liberation was never given, but found within each resident who allowed the 1 minute moment to work for them. I was responsible for instituting the moment and allowing them the time to explore its fruits throughout the lesson. Some never closed their eyes or found it necessary to participate. **Some took that responsible step toward self-awareness and placed a soft foot on a path that could transform their entire life.** The void in our education system is in its need to convey the importance of self-awareness and responsibility through practice, and allow the personal journey of spirituality to unfold uniquely in the life of each child.

Meditation and Mindfulness: What is the Difference?

Mindfulness could be dubbed one of the top buzzwords of the 21st century, undeniably. To me, it is both an ironic reference and one that represents a broad spectrum of mental activities.

It has been accepted and used by the scientific community as an umbrella term to encompass contemplative activities having to do with creating a *quality of mind* that is reflective and aware. Coined by scientist Jon Kabat-Zin, an American professor who uses his teachings for what he calls MBSR (mindfulness-based stress reduction), mindfulness has taken education systems across the country by storm. Perhaps more than ever, teachers are seeing the value of awareness-based activities for themselves and their students. Mindfulness certainly has bridged the gap between the scientific community and eastern religions or mysticism where contemplative techniques and activities have been used for centuries for purposes of spiritual growth, not reducing stress. In schools, mindfulness is used to combat stress, create positive classroom relations and even improve test scores, which are all scientifically backed results. Here is the major difference between meditation and the trending buzzword.

Mindfulness works to create a quality of being that cultivates inner peace and uses various techniques that could include forms of meditation or not. For example, a mindful practice may be the "do nothing" exercise that has participants observe their every thought and feeling while doing or saying nothing. Another requires students to make only one movement at a time in a game format. Certainly, these are ways that could enhance the ability to slow down, observe and or gain a reflective awareness. Such techniques of disengagement were not well received in the group setting at the center for a number of reasons, but I hope they benefit others in schools where children could "do nothing" without the triggering of inner turmoil.

Meditation is as much a practice as a state of being. The act of meditating involves a total focus on the inner world. There is no meditation "activity" or meditative "thought," there is the act and the state of meditation. While meditating, one may reach *Samadhi*, or a state of bliss that creates an expanded awareness, detaching the mind from the world of the senses. It was never used as it is now—to combat stress and anxiety. In fact, meditation is not the best immediate remedy for anxiety because usually the meditator will not be ready to enter a state of release from the mind. This is done best through mindful exercise first— such as Yoga or Capoeira Angola. Meditation is used in the vedic tradition, to gain knowledge of the higher self, and, ultimately, superconsciousness, and it is one of the more subtle and refined activities of any *Yogi* or *Satsangi* (seeker of truth).

The detention center classroom setting dynamic proved time and again that both hyper-anxiety and social pressures were ever present amongst the students and more "meditative" activities often uncovered trauma and produced reactionary emotions. The adjustments that I had to make along the way, as you will see in the next chapter, were critical. In the classroom, I employed what some would call Dialectical Behavior Therapy, which is used when there are limitations with time and circumstance. Technically, I used the mindful practice of conscious breathing which could be labeled as a dialectical therapy since it was in the group setting and produced discussion and reflection. I used a few quasi-mindful activities in addition to conscious breathing, but meditation proved only effective in the one on one setting. I found that a combination of mindful, consciousness and dialectical-based exercises worked best in the group setting when supplemented with a curriculum rooted in spiritual responsibility and identity.

The irony of the term *mindfulness* is that it emphasizes the word "mind." Those who have incorporated meditation as a lifestyle and have thorough understanding of its internal mechanisms know one thing—that meditation, nor the self can be "full of mind" in achieving anything. The mind as an independent variable can both inform and disrupt our ability to meditate, but it must be kept at a distance. For most, the mind is a hodgepodge of desires and egoic interpretations of past and future, pulling us in different directions, triggering various emotions. It is the mind that leads us astray from our true self. The mind needs meditation and fine-tuning for it to work to our benefit. When we direct the mind so that it can "distance itself," then we have reached a state where we can immerse ourselves in consciousness. To me, meditation is more about consciousness than it is about mind. Therefore the term mindfulness can just as well be called *mindlessness* when being paired with meditation. So we ask ourselves, what works? Meditation, mindfulness or both? This narrative is not a comparative study of meditation or mindfulness per say, but one that tells the story of a real process where using techniques to help traumatized youth and prevent others from invoking trauma had varying results. It included mindful meditation at times and consciousness-based activities, some used for prevention and others, such as the one on one session, used for treatment or therapy. The conclusive results of the study are explained in the qualitative section near the end of the book.

When Mindful Meditation and Trauma Don't Mix

Life would be great if we could just all sit and meditate lifes' problems away. Not surprisingly, it doesn't work that way. Especially with trauma. I agree with the premise put forth with many researchers that meditation ignites the symptoms of TRA and is not easily performed by those with trauma-related conditions. While mindfulness intervenes with a far more broader array of activities that could produce desirable results, there is still always the variability of trauma-related anxiety and the challenge for those traumatized to partake in any contemplative activity in any setting. The bottom line is that sometimes it's best not to pour water on fire. The following was written by David Teleaven:

"For people who've experienced trauma, mindfulness meditation can actually end up exacerbating symptoms of traumatic stress. When asked to pay focused, sustained attention to their internal experience, trauma survivors can find themselves overwhelmed by flashbacks and heightened emotional arousal."

He goes on to say that "...mindfulness doesn't cause trauma, but it may uncover it." He cites an impressive study at Brown University, "The Varieties of Contemplative Experience" by clinical neuroscientist Willoughby Britton. Britton has done extensive research and talks seeking to bridge the gap between neuroscience and traditional contemplative studies that create a better quality of mind, such as attention practices like meditation. In my experience with the youth at the center, they best responded to contemplative activities when the social factor was eliminated as much as possible. My findings show that mindfulness could be used in the classroom to create a more positive and peaceful space for learning to take place, but there is no evidence that it could help those suffering from trauma related anxiety to heal themselves. Guided or unguided meditation proved to be more effective when it was used in the one on one setting and I witnessed the direct healing effects that it had on numerous occasions. **I call for a trauma-informed approach that is beyond mindfulness because mindfulness falls short of restorative healing.** Both mindfulness and meditation must be done with an added spiritual dimension that includes self-efficacy, gratitude, empathy, discipline and responsibility which I found were greatly needed in the setting. Mindfulness may change the temporary state of being, but experience with consciousness is what begins the healing process.

It must be stated that some of those who are traumatized respond well to meditative activities or mindfulness, and others do not. Each case is different. Additionally, it is crucial to note what type of exercises are being used that represent "meditation and "mindfulness." Finally, we must remember that to be trauma-sensitive, one must be in-tune with the context of where they are working and who they are working with.

Real Solutions for Real Problems

Call it self-awareness or spiritual intelligence, our traumatized (and non-traumatized) students benefit exponentially from developing it. Something as simple as having a daily ritual that recognizes the higher or "better" self doesn't need to be "spiritually," much less religiously affiliated. This work puts forth the notion that the current model steeped in penalizing and victimizing does not serve incarcerated young people with viable coping skills or tools for adaptation. It conditions them to feel helpless and dependent. It does not provide them with a platform for self-efficacy or recovery. Most of all, it doesn't expose them to a form of therapeutic, inner exploration that can be experienced through daily meditative practice and used as a tool for overcoming the effects of trauma. Inner exploration teaches them to not point their finger at others or compensate through overindulgence, but to honor the inner gifts that they discover...Through the belief that they can be successful, the awareness of their own unique potentials and their ability to maintain self-discipline.

Yes, they committed crimes and made mistakes. I've concluded that most of my students "knew better" in their doings, but the role of history and socio-economics obviously brings a variable of desperation into the framework of their morals and ethics. Knowing better, however, shows a disconnection between mind and self. It shows a lack of responsibility and or awareness of consciousness. I use the term consciousness here because consciousness does have a lot to do with conscience. In fact, within our Latin languages, there is no distinction between the two words. In the regular attempts to interact with their own consciousness through my class, residents explored that aspect of themselves that "knew better" and allowed it to take root. Consciousness fed their conscience. In this, they come to better learn why that voice wasn't directing their behavior. Taking time to engage consciousness showed them that their outer world is a reflection of their inner world.

As found by Gerritsen and Band, "contemplative activities... related to self-awareness... directly reduce symptoms of anxiety and stress disorders." It is conscious breathing that I have found to be the most effective tool and or form of therapy when combating stressor-related disorders or any other form of anxiety. I acknowledge that we live in a world of sensual perception and we must make observations from that vantage point but make no mistake that the fullness of (1) what can be observed with the senses and (2) what can be observed as a result of expanding consciousness... are two different things. I once did an activity where the students plugged their ears for 3 minutes and they were only allowed to move their mouth when they spoke to each other without making a sound. We wrote about the experience. So many of them both acknowledged how the sounds around them greatly influenced their behavior and the gift of hearing alone, was a tremendous blessing. Gratitude could be called the bedrock of spiritual responsibility. Becoming appreciative of what you do have in a place that has stripped you of everything creates a feeling of gratitude—a great place to start the healing process and sure up a slice of spiritual responsibility through an experience of conscious observation. I left them with the quote, "Best to be in a prison with friends than a garden with strangers."

Hyper Trauma and the System

The "low key stress" that the above student, J.M referred to, to me, is the underlying result of a continuous presence of perceived danger or uncertainty that remained a constant with most kids in the center, even if they were otherwise stable before they came in. This state may or may not be in addition to the stress of those with PTSD or acute anxiety, but it certainly was an underlying condition that wore on everybody's ability to communicate with clarity, to focus and function. It is no mystery that damage to the brain thwarts the ability to learn. As the traumatized mind finds ways to adapt to every environment and deal with the potential of triggers, it cannot be expected to attain much information for leisure or intellectual gain. By the same token, it is not the inability to learn that confronts those with TRA, but the lack of focused awareness that is required to learn. The brain is an amazingly adaptive organ and it will strive to cognize and make meaning of information, but it cannot be preoccupied with survival or safety needs while doing so. Maslow's basic pyramid of needs reminds us that before intellectual or "esteem" needs are fulfilled, a sense of safety must be intact. So why do we expect children who are traumatized to learn at the same level as others? If we see *special education* as the solution to educating all learners, then why does special education not address the debilitating level of emotional unrest? Modifications of instruction and adaptations in lesson delivery do not account for the neurological damage done by emotional trauma. The traumatized may benefit from accommodations that increase their test scores, but such accommodation often builds more walls around them. They don't need more modifications to the delivery of instruction, they need modifications to the delivery of meaning. They need purpose, they need safe space, they need healing. They will not heal from confinement or modifications, they need a whole new curriculum—one that results in self-awareness and emotional management. I call it *beingness*. *My claim is that without regular techniques that promote a sense of spiritual responsibility and self-awareness education only adds to trauma.*

The truth is that we have all experienced trauma to one degree or another: The most common being the very first episode being our own relatively harsh entry into the world from the birth canal. Most of us, however, after that event, soon adapted ourselves to a relatively stable situation that provided us with a degree of love and nurturing. Others began a life (at some point in infancy) that lacked provisions of safety or security, disabling them to develop a normally functioning brain and or gaining a sense of trust in the world around them. Some lives are traumatized continuously from the onset, beginning with a lack of safety in their immediate environments or abuse and violence at a young age. That suffering is internalized and programs itself directly into the pathways of the nervous system, affecting every interaction of that individual for, in many cases, an entire lifetime.

The school in the detention center, of course, was not your everyday school with "homecoming," "decorate your locker day" and "school spirit." It's norms, rules and values reflected a subculture of hyper-trauma-related anxiety. This was part of what J.M refers to as "low-key stress" and it includes the trauma incurred from the legal and criminal justice system. This degree of TRA results from the anxiety of traversing the proceedings and legalities of the court system as well as being held in a detention center where they are subject to being confined. It also includes the process of getting "booked" or "placed" into a new and challenging circumstance. As D.H. reported, many times, the youth are behind locked doors for the better part of the day. This is psychologically debilitating. Indeed, it is potentially traumatizing to even the most well-adapted persons. Those already dealing with a host of issues can easily become overwhelmed. I observed that many do not complain due to extreme cultural pressure rooted in hyper-masculinity (discussed in part 2). Some, however, "crack." Residents who are locked in their room don't have the option to be claustrophobic. This is a part of the hyper-trauma that may "mold" the young person, but also scar him or her as well.

Punishment may stop some behaviors, as Pavlov has proven, but punishment doesn't stop anxiety and certainly doesn't heal. Being that a large percentage of residents regretted their decisive action that brought them in, many of them overstayed their punishments. Some of you may assert, *It doesn't matter, they should be punished for their crime.* Well, yes, but all behavior is contextual. Those working with the delinquent population are constantly negotiating the dialogue between trying to honor the punishment, but at the same time provide the youth with hope and a restored sense of trust in themselves and other people. Our punitive system seems to forget that these young people go back to communities, not just their bedroom.

Victimizing

There were those with more sympathetic approaches who coddled the residents, which was certainly understandable. I felt that this was more of a "victim" approach and treating these young adults like helpless infants who were victims of the system wasn't improving their capability for self-efficacy.

Despite its loving intentions, the "victim" approach does little to build discipline, character or responsibility. Though I delved into this approach and concurred with the idea that we as teachers are in place of the parent, I soon realized that the teacher **cannot be** the acting mother or father or grandmother. It was best to me to never assume which aspect of familial love a student was lacking in and work on giving them the tools first to love themselves. Coming from a background of martial arts and having a Marine as a father, at times, I did wonder whether some kids needed the "old fashioned" discipline that "teaches a lesson" through discomfort or some kind of deeper deprivation. The truth is that the youth were already in pain and already deprived. They suffered the pain of trauma, neglect, abandonment and or everyday abuse or violence. Most abhorrent, they suffered the deprivation of human relationships rooted in trust, comfort and reciprocity. Maybe some of that "man to man" physical punishment that they experienced outside of school produced a degree of discipline, but it didn't take me long to realize that most of my students had suffered enough beatings already—by the path that brought them there. Sometimes short term physical punishment is, undoubtedly, more effective than long term psychological punishment. Neither is restorative, and neither heals or provides hope. Psychological punishment, deprivation, is, of course, the philosophical basis of the justice system. *Lock them away and make them pay through loneliness, fear, captivity, madness, lack of sunlight, etc...* The current model is applied to juveniles and adults under the same umbrella of punitive justice. Granted, sentencing is usually not as long term and most of these youth are placed in a home before a year's time. While some services are offered to juveniles in the way of restorative justice, I will soon point out the reality of such a platform. Our current system leaves the incarcerated youth with few opportunities to truly reform themselves through a change in self or a shift in perspective toward life.

In reality, the system has only diverted the youth to deal with traumatic pain through seeking a dopamine rush (video's, social media or junk food, usually high in sugar) which aligns with the "victim" approach. These are all used as rewards for good behavior or good merit in the juvenile justice systems across the country. What is most likely more beneficial and rewarding for these students would be a dopamine detox and courses on emotional intelligence or mindful practice. While certificates of merit or candy bars provide temporary satisfaction or social recognition, what really remains with the resident after they leave the system? A need for more sugar and a certificate that has no value in the real world of work or entrepreneurship. How has their physiological response to triggers changed? What discipline or inner trust have they established that allows them to better respect themselves or equip them to deal with the outside world?

The hyper-trauma related anxiety incurred from prison certainly only added to the pushback I received from those students who resisted responsibility-based discipline. Most teachers seemed to conclude that we had to deal with trauma as a part of the education process. Many teachers across the country are now required to complete a rudimentary 2 hour-long certification exposing the signs and characteristics of trauma. This condensed glimpse into recognizing the influence of trauma-related anxiety provides few or no management techniques, nor methods of adaptation that one could implement with an individual or student or group—much less a healing-oriented curriculum. For my circumstance, a classroom of traumatized black and brown teenagers, it was worthless. From my observation, those working directly with the young people on a daily basis take several years to understand (if ever) the dynamics of trauma-related behavior and many who eventually did, were only able to do so because of their own upbringing or experience. The "energy" of trauma-based anxiety, especially in a group setting, can be overwhelming for any facilitator/teacher who may be sensitive, emotionally fragile or untrained to deal with its many manifestations. The slightest or most subtle error, when teaching a class or facilitating trauma-informed therapy, can, unfortunately, be detrimental to the educational or healing intentions. It can also wreak havoc on the lesson and the experience of those in the room wanting and able to participate. **Not knowing the physiological or mental effects of trauma, of course, when teaching traumatized youth can lead to an insurmountable level of confusion on the part of the teacher or counselor, which often leads a professional to respond with impatience, frustration, misjudgment and miscommunication.**

It was fascinating to see how in some instances, it was the students who knew a great deal about handling trauma in the classroom. I remember observing a young teacher flustered during a discussion with a few students that turned volatile and some of the other students reminded her to keep teaching and just ignore them. Easier said than done when trying to conduct a lesson, but it becomes an artform. Students would often warn me if one of their own was volatile or having a bad day. On occasion, one would flat out say, "bro we traumatized, we can't be thinkin of this other stuff." Until I learned more about the needs of these students, I struggled with adopting the best ways for me to express myself with them and still command a friendly respect as a trusted teacher. At some point after I implemented the breathing techniques that I will discuss, I had to be the person *that I truly am* when with them; A person that they viewed as genuine and able to provide the voice of discipline, caution and care that they needed to learn. Despite any psychological conditions or any other "dysfunctional" aspect of their behavior, they were very intuitively aware of the authenticity and ability of the adult in the room. They were afraid and fearful on a certain level, but expressive and unafraid to take chances on another. They constantly demonstrated in their writings (I would say more so than many of my suburban students from the past) that they had feelings and needs and they were aware that they needed help.

What is Missing from Trauma-Informed Education

A teacher is constantly adapting to a trauma prone scenario until they achieve an energetic "homeostasis" with the students—which could take years. In the classroom, disruption hangs in the balance as a constant variable and anger or violence is always only a few words away from the present conversation. Not all teachers use the same tools and not all are aware of the degree to which trauma became a factor in learning. Most of them will probably not know their students' ACE score and, understandably, do not have time to explore the psycho-social background of each student. I would get to know a student only after they showed respect and we developed a safe rapport where they felt that I respected their trauma and I felt they respected my intentions. It was not a requirement to adapt a teaching style toward trauma sensitivity, but many teachers in at-risk environments learn to integrate intervention methods within their delivery from the onset. In my case, implementing a disciplined-based, mindful approach, by utilizing meditation and breathwork allowed me to gain a better understanding of how anxiety and trauma played a role in relationships, and particularly, learning. Unfortunately, as you will read, many of the relationships that I developed were fruitful, but were short-lived. Instead of gaining a chance to become a consistent influence in someone's life, the "placement" or relocation of these young people ushered them out of my own sphere of influence as swiftly as an early winter wind along the Delaware river. Too often, residents who were eager to learn more about meditation, breathwork or consciousness, were deployed back into the streets.

Trauma—informed education is a wonderful idea, but it must be implemented with more authenticity, depth and breadth—and not just in underserved communities, but across the board. Though trauma takes a different shape in affluent or suburban school districts in a general sense, it is still present and crippling to those children trying to fit the socio-educational mold in place. Trauma-informed education must also leave space for a child to explore their own *inner world* or consciousness through consciousness-based activities and engagement of mind/body/spirit, which I will discuss shortly. Additionally, the goal of this trauma-informed approach should not only be to create a more employable student, but a more self-aware student. Indirect trauma intervention often takes the form of "anger management" or "life skill" lessons that reinforce job training and career skills only. This, unfortunately, in my observation, had the effect of narrowing the scope of restoring our residents. It did provide glimpses of responsible behavior and professionalism for them to emulate. Unfortunately, many were unable to build on such emulations because they were encapsulated in a world of fight or flight existence. Tenets of emotional intelligence and self-awareness must not only be associated with "getting a good job." It diminishes value of such essential traits in the eyes of the youth. These are humanistic and conscious forms of intelligence are critical to lifelong success and the ability to adapt to a changing world. As I will demonstrate, mindful practice such as conscious breathing as well as meditative intervention promotes responsibility, awareness and emotional intelligence. In my experience, completing worksheets with readings and vocabulary associated with emotional intelligence does not.

I would say emphatically, that properly informed and presented, trauma-based lessons that address anger or anxiety could be extended to illuminate a young persons' horizons far beyond what job they could attain. A job would only be part of what they could achieve as responsible and self-aware human beings. In the average educational institution and certainly in juvenile justice centers, mindfulness is a start, but it must be supported with a non-linear, consciousness-based curriculum in a separate class altogether. The current model, defined by written, step-by step sequence-based models that include phrases like "active listening," "controlling emotions," do not provide space so that emotional intelligence comes to life. So, students were being asked to "manage emotions," but not given any techniques that would inform this and actually produce desired results. They were told to listen actively, but rarely get the emotional support that can help them manage their tendencies not to.

Many of the basic tenets of trauma-informed education, such as not punishing inappropriate behavior, are unknown by most educators. While many who are trauma informed attempt to "fix" a child, what is actually needed is an attempt to "heal" the child. Ultimately, I feel that the academic sciences that inform public education need to begin researching, promoting and legitimizing breathing and meditation techniques as a major form of trauma-based intervention and create a curriculum around emotional intelligence and consciousness-based healing. This goes across the board and I can tell you that it is needed just as badly in suburban or affluent schools, as I have spent enough time in them as well.

Unequivocally, I found that guided breathwork is something that our population greatly benefits from and immediately sparks an empowering and responsible mindset.

True empowerment is the authenticity gained from discipline and practice. The individual whose consciousness has ripened into an authentic identity of acceptance can manage their emotional triggers, motivate themselves and take responsibility for their actions. The whole of Vedic science and an extended scientific research is available for us to create change. On occasion, I had my students chant *So Ham*, which is that mantra that invokes authenticity. Its literal translation is "I am that I am." *So Ham* is not a religious chant, it is an energetic chant. It is not a religious chant, but an energetic one-rooted in self-awareness.

An interventive mindset focused on healing just as much as learning is what is needed by teachers with students with TRA. Without individualizing the issue, we must openly admit that traumatic episodes have created friction and chaos in our lives. We must openly acknowledge it in the classroom without making it a crutch or an excuse. It cannot be swept under the rug anymore and allotted to a few students who have been diagnosed with PTSD. It is widespread and it is detrimental to learning. 1 in 4 children by the age of 4 in the U.S will have witnessed a traumatic event—this doesn't include trauma incurred from neglect or poverty. Mindful and meditative practice in settings where trauma-related anxiety is ever present contributes to growth and paves the way for learning through a newfound awareness. It's time to stop thinking that we can address trauma by teaching kids to change their thinking on their own. We must be willing to dig deeper and take the chance of "offending" the few who are resistant to spirit science. Our young people, more than ever, must learn to self-authenticate and become aware of their true identity—*beingness*. A meaningful part of the shared human collective consciousness. That said, being honest about how trauma affects the mind and body and establishing a real practice with real techniques is a way to maximize that change. Mindfulness helps, *beingness* heals.

I would venture to say that nearly every child in America experiences unnecessary anxiety to a degree and more and more they are experiencing forms of trauma. From school shootings to social media sabotage, trauma can now take many forms. What is our education system doing to keep up with it? Not much. The problem is that we have yet to understand it as a crisis. Technically speaking, trauma-informed education includes "examining the influence and impact on students in our schools of factors such as racism (explicit, implicit, and systematic; and microaggressions) as well as poverty, peer victimization, community violence, and bullying." This is where trauma becomes sociological as well. As with many categories of psychological conditions, lines separating one disorder and the next become sometimes blurred as layers of symptoms appear and change. What becomes essential to realize is that trauma interferes with learning—in a big way. Even at the lowest level of Bloom's taxonomy which is designated as "remembering," can be a daunting task when the brain cannot give attention to processing new information because it is preparing for a situation of distress. I noticed TRA as a constant distractor (even when remembering or understanding was achieved) when executing academic skills that reflect these learning modes. High level brain activity such as applying, analyzing, evaluating or creating is improbable. Realizing this, however, when teaching traumatized children, can invite every interaction to be an intervention. Sometimes, by just walking into a room and giving an authentic smile or cracking a dumb joke to the residents, I could see it lightened their load. Working with such populations requires a huge amount of patience. Unfortunately, the state and its demands for performance do not leave room for much patience in schools. Administration and teachers are continuously bombarded with needs for more data collection to meet performance criteria, more educational platforms to payout more universities and tech companies creating those platforms and more technology to fuel the ever-growing information matrix. Where are we going with all of this?

◆ CHAPTER 3 ◆

ENTER THE CLASSROOM:
THE 12 TIPS OF LEARNING THE ROPES

The city of brotherly love and sisterly affection was gearing up to rally behind their dubious super bowl team, the Philadelphia Eagles, when I moved into my aunty Panda's apartment in *South Philly* in January of 2016. The blustery cold took its toll on my energy while squeezing furniture up the stairwell, but I showed up for work at the center the next day with a sore throat and wrinkled shirt, ready for a fresh start. I was excited to engage the residents and determined to impress my principal, who had built the center program from scratch. My style of teaching had always been explorative with an emphasis on presenting content in a manner that inspired emotion. I held tightly to the idea that igniting the spirit of my students was the catalyst to inspiring them to learn. In the past, I would introduce the Italian Renaissance, for example, by beginning with a photo of *La Pieta'*, and without delving into the religious or cultural significance of the statue, I would have the students write about how this piece of marble invoked the emotions of a mother losing her son. When teaching the civil rights movement, I had students take the role of walking arm in arm with Martin Luther King across the

Pettus bridge in Birmingham. **I wanted my students to connect internally, to feel compelled, to dive deeper into the personal meaning behind the content. Essentially, I always chose inspiration over information and my critical views toward the education system were already in place when I joined PJJSC.** Coming into this new, highly secured facility, I felt that staying adaptable would be my greatest strength. I guessed that these young students, the residents, would need structure as well as inspiration. Soon, it became clear that the school provided them with a small dose of both, there was a huge space for improvement. My own teaching style and methods would prove to need quite a bit of tweaking as well. Little did I know, I needed the structure that I would later advocate for. As I wanted to create a foundation and scaffolding for the students, I needed to implement it into my delivery from bell to bell. I came into the center believing in freeing the spirit of my students so that they could learn, and I left the center acknowledging the power of responsibility and discipline that actually made it happen.

From the onset, I wanted to make it my mission to build a pedagogical base that could anchor them in a sound daily practice that would reveal to them their own potential. I wanted to provide them with scaffolding to understand important concepts and push themselves beyond their current levels of reading and writing. I wanted to provide inspiration enough for them to recognize something more than the mundane. By the same token, I wanted them to feel the universe inside of them. I did not know what it would look like, I just knew that I was not to inform, but to transform. Nearly 5 years later, there were transformations abound. Undoubtedly, it was I who was transformed.

◆

The Trials of a Beginner

My first day, I was immediately assigned to travel upstairs, where the residents resided, for my classes. It was termed going up "on the unit." Each unit (or grouping of 12 residents) existed within a set of 3 "pods" who shared a neutral common area that was used if the group was unable to report down to the school area. There were no desks, no chalkboards or smartboards. Some pods had a ping pong table, but the area was mostly barren until residents brought out plastic chairs to partake in the class. I elected to take some books to share, soon finding out that whatever I brought didn't spark interest, and whatever I left behind, they preferred.

The plans to integrate meditation into my classroom were part of a personal legacy I brought with me in the last several years of my teaching-prior to that in a D.C. charter school. Though my approach was organic and maybe unorthodox, I was certain that the residents could benefit from the influence of mindfulness—even if I had to come up with my own brand of it. After all, meditation had literally saved my life. I was certified in Vipassana and had been studying different traditions for well over 2 decades. I was a quiet advocate while learning as I practiced, focusing on the ability to manipulate energy, which included training in Capoeira Angola as well. By the 2010's, Jon Kabat-Zinn's "mindfulness-based stress reduction" was a topic that many had heard of. Certain programs in Baltimore and New York that utilized Yoga and meditation in schools had been well underway. At PJJSC, I quickly found that I would have to start from the beginning. Capoeira would have been perfect for the population in the center, but it was or course, out of the question. I had to be strategic and creative. The high security operation had regulations on nearly anything that involved kids doing more than sitting in chairs and reading, drawing or writing—or in the case of their music class, recording beats and rhymes. So, meditation it would have to be.

It took a few weeks to learn the ropes of teaching on the unit and "vibing" with the setting— maybe even a few months. Under my staff badge and buttoned polo shirt, I was a pure seeker, an exploratory soul with tribal tattoos and callused hands who had returned from living off the grid over the summer and tangling with street Capoeira in Brazil. In the detention center, however, I had to keep a tight and low profile—a return to professionalism. Every action invoked a rule referring to something about that action. Learning to close the heavy unit doors quietly behind me, or not to say first names and or not asking too many questions, were just a few items that helped us avoid triggering anyone or breaking any rules. There was a tremendous energetic adaptation that had to be made to spend hours upon hours in a place that held such pain within its walls. When it became overbearing, I would think of the residents who had to stay for months without ever leaving the building; And the counselors who sometimes did 14-hour shifts. It was not a place for one who thrived in nature or open spaces. I witnessed many residents who suffered from anxiety deal with the added challenge of claustrophobic interference. I got my own dose of it one Friday afternoon when most had left the building and I found myself stuck in an elevator with no cell phone and an emergency button that was not functioning. Even while teaching, our learning experience never ceases.

I remember my very first class period vividly because my lesson was a complete wreck. The students cared nothing about what I wanted to teach and desired instead to talk candidly the whole time. They were masters at cutting through the structure or protocol of things and deformalizing anything. They wanted to get to the point. One particular student that had such a resilient and positive attitude, wanted to know my whole life story, what "hood" I was from and why I wore a copper bracelet. They were feeling me out. A decent rapport started to develop between myself and my 2nd period 16-17 year old group of young men. There were some "tough customers" who sat in the front and critiqued everything that I brought forth, but they were all amicable. They seemed to enjoy some stories of Brazil and constantly encouraged controversial discussions, and I later understood this as a way to convey to me that there was more under the surface of their rambunctious energy. The honeymoon would soon be over.

In most of my classes, by the end of the first week, my students still seemed a mystery to me. They were quiet and tactful, with some boisterous and mildly disruptive. One day, I decided to take a chance introducing them to a silent guided meditation at the beginning of class. I introduced the idea of meditation and explained a little bit about how giving the brain a rest was good for mental growth, strength, calm and focus. As my 1st period commenced, I demonstrated good chair posture and some of them unabashedly began to mimic me—others somewhat straightened up in their seats, amused. Of course, the majority of them just stared at me—especially those in the back. Some were tuning in out of curiosity. They all seemed surprised that I was even trying such an endeavor. Some became automatically distrustful and shook their heads, "naw man...I ain't doin that." I commenced with a silent 30 seconds. I closed my eyes and reminded them to just focus on their breath and visualize it moving down to their belly and back up. I told them to try for 30 seconds, and guided them through a process in what was the longest thirty seconds I have yet to experience as a teacher. I know that there was little participation because when I opened my eyes, they were still all staring at me. Not one had closed their eyes. Maybe one kid in the corner held his hands open and did the breathing. They were, on a positive note, respectfully quiet! The 2 counselors that sat in the class void of any response whatsoever. I think they were in a state of disbelief. The exercise was basically ineffective.

In other classes, I tried it and I received mixed reviews—mockery included. Some kids hummed aloud, others chanted the "Om" sound super loud and a few would purposefully interrupt with jokes or freestyle raps. I realized that if I couldn't make this moment a special (or at least respectable) one for them, then it wasn't going to work. They had to see the sanctity in it and be willingly silent or it couldn't be practiced. It wasn't something that could be done nonchalantly or in passing. Some kind of meditative moment before class and I was certain some would like it once they could get used to it (or even tried it). So, I went back to the drawing board. The next trail brought even worse results. I figured I'd try a silent meditation and not guide it so much as to let them explore their own breath and the feeling of stillness. This would be part of a more relaxed approach which included telling them about the connection between the mind and the breath, posture and the mind briefly beforehand etc...They were uninterested—some were mildly annoyed. I commenced again, **and about 20 seconds into the meditation, a resident, the only Caucasian student in the room, flipped a table up into the air and stood up screaming in anger. He stared at me with a murderous glare as I asked him kindly to sit back down.** The counselors came over and apprehended him while the rest of the unit broke out in laughter. "White boy crazy as @#$%." I calmly asked if anyone else had any objections to the meditation. One kid said "That shit don't work." Another said "I'll slap that shit." One did speak out fondly "It's cool old head, go ahead." Little did I know that the mixed reviews from this one class was just a sample taste of the variety of reactions to come. And I would have to suffer through one trial after another of failed attempts. *Rule #1, Create intrinsic value for them before attempting the meditation exercise.*

Mistakes and Mishaps

Though my lessons were often well-received, my first year was riddled with "meditation miscalculations." So many variables interjected themselves into the setting—most of which I had no control over. The greatest hindrances being a general unfamiliarity with mindfulness activity, classroom etiquette and lack of group cohesiveness at the center.

I attempted to befriend the guys in a way that they could see that meditating and doing well in school was cool and I could be someone they could relate to. Not a good idea. To do this, I took a sympathetic tone and listened to their problems and issues, trying to placate any of their demands so that they saw the power of just being peaceful and friendly. This approach would prove to fall short of my responsibility as a teacher and I would soon pay the price for it. It did create a few positive relationships and most of the residents were indifferent, but the "peaceful prophet" style would not provide them with what they needed. They didn't need a friend, they needed a teacher. I made the mistake of bringing in oatmeal cream pies for some of the classes that participated in meditation and did their work. It soon became a dopamine/glycemic distraction and it created a need that I could not routinely promise to fulfill. I had fallen into the "victimizing" mode and the boys soon played on my sympathy. They began to expect the sweet treats and complain when there were none. I gave one and they wanted two. They hid the one I gave them and said they didn't get one, they bullied others in the class to cop an extra one. The "reward" approach was not working. I even had a good group in my afternoon class and looked forward to seeing them until one day I was walking past their line in the hallway and a few gave me their usual fist bump until one of them asked "Where are our cream pies at?" I said, "Not 'til Friday, you gotta get the job done this week." He responded, "@#$% you then," and the entire unit laughed. The feeling of betrayal and hurt sunk into my chest. Maybe they didn't like me as much as I thought. It was a wake up call to readjust my demeanor. I took the comment personally and thought to myself, some are hungry enough to bite the hand that feeds, so the oatmeal cream pies would be no more. I realized that I was kowtowing to them to pacify them; And when our friendship was not honored with sweet treats, it was no longer valid. They less respected me as a teacher. My relationships became inauthentic and worse, conditional upon rewards. It's easy to like someone who feeds us—and take advantage of someone who fears us. *Rule #2 Do not try to make friends.*

The year presented more challenges, as I incorporated meditation into more classes. My own readings in Taoism reminded me that there had to be an opportunity in this challenge. I certainly was waiting for it. There were some moments of success, of course—and these moments fed my desire to improve and continue. Days and nights were spent trying to figure out the best way to manage a group and get them to participate or at least remain quiet. Each time, unintended variables would interject themselves in different sessions. Disruptions, setbacks, changes in scheduling created a nightmare for my flow and ongoing routine in the classroom. If one session went well on one day, I would come in and do the same routine with them the next day and they would lean back in their chairs and ignore me. Of course, there were always new residents being admitted and they were either silent or "filling their oats" in a posturing fashion. One unit, who had enjoyed the meditative moment for a couple of days did well until a new admittee showed up and right in the middle of the breathing instructions blurted out—"What the @#$% is this?" or "Who is this dude, Buddha??" It flustered me. It was humiliating because I allowed it to be. Not only was I pissed at the student, but pissed that the meditation was just not working. The next day, I conversed with a student who enjoyed the meditation and asked him what we could do to make it more interesting. He said, "Nothing...Just don't get pissed when they don't do it." The response struck me in a variety of ways. It reminded me of my high expectations. It also reflected back my own hypocrisy. I was asking them to do something that I myself could not fully embody—remain mindful under pressure. **How could I expect them to be patient and breath when many of them were on the brink of breakdown? How could I allow them to see the value in stillness and silence when their world was about action and assertiveness. How could I expect them to put their ego aside, when I could not?** By taking things personally, I was not understanding their predicament. In hindsight, it wasn't something that I could immediately notice, much less change, so more sessions were interrupted as I figured out how to keep implementing the routine without being too attached to it. Tricky. The good news is that the meditations hadn't yet become a complete flop. *Rule #3 Do not take things personally.*

Then, one weekend I had an idea. I was doing my own Sunday morning Sadhana and I rang my singing bowl and it suddenly dawned on me—it was time to bring the bowl into the center. The vibrations would clear the environment and surely bring attention toward the ritual. I could better influence the vibe of the room and create an energetically pleasing space—*this would surely get them to want to participate.* That Monday morning, I unzipped my tote bag and brought out the bowl. All eyes were drawn to it immediately. I began to speak about the bowl and the power of vibration or frequency. They asked questions. Each class seemed intrigued. They asked how much it cost, where I got it, what was it made of, etc...They wanted to ring it and when I told them I cannot allow them to handle it, they felt slighted. Although the novel idea of the bowl brought some mild interest into meditating, it caused just as much distraction. Students would talk about the sound while we meditated. They wanted to look up and hear different size bowls. After the novelty of the bowl was over, however, they fell back into a mode of mild disinterest. Though ringing the bowl brought some meaning and sanctity to the situation, it did not have a disciplined routine to accompany it. I didn't yet attain their participation. I wasn't speaking to their spirit. How could I think that a material object alone would solve my problem of creating sanctity and silence for a meditative moment?

During this time, frustration became my bedfellow. In typical Taurine fashion, I bulled forward and struggled to implement the meditation into the beginning of every class no matter what—even if I had to endure the worst criticism or ridicule. Hardly meditative. I would assume the chair posture after ringing the bowl and a student in the front row would start "raggin" on my shoes while another would make semi-comedic threats of hitting me with the bowl. **During the borage of distractions, I would attempt to remain calm to "show" the others that it didn't bother me. After some reflection, I concluded that my response wasn't showing them anything except that I had an ego and they could get away with bullying me.** I was forgetting rule #3. Some would participate, but get restless within the moment. Others would partake for a few days and then opt out. If at one moment, I seemed out of sorts or with ulterior motives, they would verbally destroy the meditation, lesson or anything else on my agenda as they saw fit. By asking them to do something completely out of the ordinary, many reacted with negativity. A big "aha" moment came when one quiet student told me to ring the bowl but not to do meditation. It was that I realized that I had a piece of the puzzle in hand.

Those with TRA needed constant stimulation—the bowl appeased them, but the silent moment that followed was ominous and even triggering. It dawned on me that I needed to guide them through it. The silent moment left too much room for error. But what could I do that could provide stimulation or guidance but allow them to tap into their inner world. Guided meditation was too intimate and had a repulsive effect. On many days, I found myself tied up in knots with a new issue and very few options of solving it. I began to react to interference and criticism by justifying what I was doing. One day, I began explaining the concept of the 3rd eye in what I thought was a very grounded and relevant explanation and a student in the back of the room called out— What the #$%^ you talkin' bout old head?" I challenged him and criticized his outburst. We nearly faced off. He was wrong about his interjection, but in one way, he was exactly right. What WAS I talking about? How was it significant to him or others in the room? I'll never forget this comment because it seared into me the rule of "relatability..." *Rule #4 Meet the students where they are.*

Although they were labeled as criminals, many of these young men and women had a general sense of respect, humility, honor, calmness, balance—all the things that meditation embodied and enhanced. So why couldn't they connect with it? I took a harder look at my actions, my procedure, my energy. It became clear, all of it needed an adjustment. My 1st year had ended and that summer I led some workshops at a recreation center in west Philly. The next September began with a bang. One morning, some of the guys were "freestylin" and refused to start class. Before reacting, I observed my emotions, acknowledging how I would normally respond. Although I would typically be at ease and ask them to please focus on class, I would get tense and be pissed on the inside, showing anxiety toward their disregard for protocol. This one time, I observed how I would normally act before I responded. Then, it became clear—I had just as much anxiety as they did. I wasn't responding, I was reacting. Whether it was the pressure to produce quality lessons or the fact that I really didn't have everyone's attention, I was uneasy. I had a passive aggressive approach and it sent mixed messages. It showed that I was uncertain of myself. Self-observation helped me to realize the importance of finding the solutions to problems in real time. Their freestyling continued; **And then I noticed something. Freestylin' was a form of meditation—a form of being present.** In fact, freestylin requires total immersion in the present moment in that a good freestyler creates rhymes based on what is in his immediate consciousness. Some of these guys were excellent at becoming present. Meditation is a type of freestyle, so I began to freestyle with them. I made a rhyme about stillness, "So hold on to ya seat and just try to chill, you don't know who ya' are until you stay still..." etc. They laughed. My "corniness" points soared that day, but as teachers in the youth, we took any points we could get. Now, if *I could only get them to observe their breath as if it were the subject of their rhymes.* Just as problems presented issues to ponder, I began to observe and let them solve themselves. When I was able to become present, the solutions to problems began to appear. More importantly, I was forming a template of lessons that allowed them to explore consciousness—life in the moment. I was also seeing how their form of meditation was a form of therapy. This began a turning point where I refused to give in to anger or anxiety.

One day, I saw some guys writing graffiti on the table and

I walked over to them and sat down. They looked up and one of them kept writing as if I wasn't there. I subtly interjected, "Gentleman I see we have some talented artwork but that needs to be erased." One responded, "Da' $%^& outa' here man, go teach." I thought for a second as they chuckled, defacing the desk with hashtags and street names with the last of the counted pencils that I had sharpened for the day. I took a slow deep breath and waited for my response to come... "Guys I don't have to clean it up, the maintenance man has to do it... I'm just speaking for him because I know he doesn't make a whole lot of money and probably wants to go home and feed his children after a long day of scrubbing toilets and desks... It takes a lot of time to scrub down these tables. But if he doesn't get to it, I will. It's cool.. So handle it however you want and I'll leave you guys alone now and get back to the lesson." I don't know where my words came from but I knew once I responded with a conscious breath, they would reflect an inner peace. I got up and walked away. Toward the end of class, one of the guys walked up to me and handed me 3 pencils with nubbed erasers. He simply said— "We erased it" and he got in line quietly with the group as they "sized-up" from shortest in the front to tallest in the back, ready to head upstairs back to their unit in silence. Static from the counselors walkie-talkie invaded the silence and the command to move was given. **I looked at their stone-cold faces. They stared ahead, some slouching, some straight up with hands clasped behind their back. One made eye contact with me and seemed to silently say, *Why are you really here?*** A sense of accomplishment came over me. At that moment, I witnessed that the "worst" of these "bandits" just wanted to do the right thing. I didn't totally believe what the young man told me until I walked back and examined the desks. They were indeed clean. I finally learned to not take things personally. And I also realized that progress takes time.

I had to learn more about them. They wanted to respect me, to learn from me. But it was I who had to lead the way. It was I who had to figure out how meditation could fit into their paradigm—not mine. The method would come and I had to remain patient. *Rule #5 Be patient by using strength instead of force.*

As my paradigm adapted and observations grew keen, it occurred to me that it was time to better understand the complexity of trauma-related anxiety, which I found was more internalized than the type of anxiety that I experienced. I knew that I couldn't make assumptions about their needs or how they manage their emotions. Nonetheless, they revealed to me the depth of their anxiety and it sparked a re-examination of my approach and method. It became apparent that I needed to first study trauma and learn of their own methods of adaptation in a world that was basically foreign to me. I needed to be willing to learn as much as I could teach. I needed to accept them more for who they were. "We cannot change what we cannot first accept (Carl Jung)."

The Revelation Comes

From the first weeks of teaching, I was aware that most of the residents suffered a great degree of abuse and degradation. I knew they were hurt, but I was only beginning to scratch the surface by my 2nd year of how many ways the ugliness of trauma could be manifested. It had much to do with their ability to stay focused, complete a task, attain new information, enjoy simple things, and feel safe amongst a group of their peers. A general distrust of the world is very much a part of the malaise. Some residents were just uncomfortable with silence. Most would not close their eyes and almost all of them had the initial impression that meditation was a waste of time.

At this point, I was teaching both English and Social studies and seeking to engage them in something novel but *powerful*—literally. They loved *power* to an obsession. To them, *power* ruled the world—it was something that they sought, maybe just to be in control of their own lives or maybe to have power over others, but nonetheless, they were intrigued with the idea of dominance. How could I capture their attention with something powerful, yet innately peaceful, zenlike or intellectual?

A student had me click into my personal YouTube list one day and came across some martial arts training videos. He begged me to show some of them. One highlighted Bruce playing ping pong with nun chucks. The guys were fascinated as I briefly, but passionately, explained his life and philosophy. They were glued to the screen "...Ohhh...eew...$%^&, he thurl! The poignancy, the precision, struck a deep chord in them. The group consciousness seemed to collectively admire the show of power—but in addition, they saw the result of mindful discipline. They saw "responsibility." Of course! The answer was right under my nose the whole time. I had to stop thinking like a public school teacher and start thinking like a martial artist. My life experience held the answers, it held the method. Martial arts brought power and peace through discipline. Maybe I couldn't teach Capoeira or find the perfect meditation, but I had to bring form to those things in the classroom. Even better was the interview with Bruce Lee who discussed the power of authenticity, the importance of "expressing your true self." I had to remember how I learned martial arts. I had to understand the training regimen and traditional moves, but at a certain point I and all others have to adopt their own style. It was time to tie our belts..

They each received a diagram with a house. They wrote basic observations of the house for the 1st half of class. The 2nd half I had them add features that they wanted. We reflected on how each house was connected in its frame and structure but how each became a unique expression. The first part of the house represented the disciplined foundation of building the house, the 2nd part represented the freedom gained from that discipline. This was the path of learning.

So, I began to teach them martial arts—academically. I began to get tougher with them. No more sympathy. They began to see my passion. I was realizing that I had to risk losing my job to gain their respect—and they had to see that I was willing. I had to assert my alphahood without publicly claiming it. No more goody goody school teacher. These guys were at war and they needed a general. We began to research martial art styles and origins, analyzed the philosophy of the Shaolin monks, the Nubian wrestlers, the Samurai, and took notes on their training methods. We delved into the Afro-Brazilian fight dance of Capoeira Angola, a martial art in disguise. They began to see that consciousness was like martial arts—all inclusive. Martial arts wasn't just something one did, but something one became. We wrote, discussed, and reflected. It captured their interest for a few weeks and they began to think about power very differently. On showing the respect and interest gained from the philosophy of balance and self-defense, the students wrote the following samples:

"...I was thinking that some martial arts are better than guns because a bullet can only go in one direction...I seen the monks fly around and nothing could catch them."

Another wrote:

".. It's like you know you gonna be straight because you can handle the situation...If I knew martial arts I would be like a warrior... I wouldn't think about carrying a gun because I wouldn't be scared."

A third wrote:

"They up early in the am doing they training and that's' thorough because you know they are serious....I would take

their class and learn them kicks and spins. I already do some of that $%^& for real...I like the drip (clothes) they on too..."

Of course, at times, delving into martial arts within a classroom setting, placed me in a controversial position with those who didn't make the philosophical connections. Some associated martial arts with fighting instead of a study of awareness. When I was approached about the kids learning martial arts, a counselor who had witnessed the lessons stepped in for me and reported that it wasn't making the boys violent, it was giving them something interesting to think about, to emanate. *Rule #8 Teach only what you're passionate about.*

At this point, I only facilitated the meditation if I was in the mood. As the meditative moment began to fade into the background and I began to start class with flare and fire, the energy picked up, but the academic progress stayed stagnant. The guys liked class and learning was fun, but they were not making the connection to academics. One day, someone asked why we didn't do meditation anymore.. Ironically, the singing bowl had now invoked a symbol of punishment for me, so the stimulus had gradually diminished my behavior. I fell victim to my own conditioning! I saw meditation as slowing us down. Besides, in the school, some found it pointless, some looked down upon it, some counselors and most fellow teachers seemed mildly amused or indifferent. The results weren't yet convincing, so I didn't proceed with the same zeal as I had developed in teaching the martial art themes. Of course there were exceptions—especially with the counselors on the DHS side. Those counselors who saw the benefits in it often inquired for more. At one point, I was transparent with the students about my own disappointment with the meditation and told them it just wasn't worth it. There was too much distraction and there was no way to get everyone to be still and silent at the beginning of class. Some students appreciated the vulnerability and began to encourage me to start doing the meditations again. When the youth believed in something, nothing would stop them from speaking up. As the martial arts lessons grew thin, I turned back toward the meditation, this time with a new vibe. I was forgetting that with a group of incarcerated teens, my passion was best demonstrated as an inner flame than a raging cauldron. Although the fire helped the day pass, it wasn't who I was and it didn't help the youth learn to control their own. *Rule #9 Stay the course.*

Upon observing what I disdained about the public education system in general, I concluded that there were a few things that I could do in response to that disdain—instead of being bitter. I re-examined my blueprint. I discovered that the conventional seating arrangement was less than ideal for cultivating beingness or responsible learning. Most of my guys would never sit in front or behind one another and as soon as class would start on the unit, they would grab a chair and place it against the wall. In the classroom, the rows of seats created a distancing effect for those in the back. Why force students into a world of squares when I was teaching them from a place of circles? One day, I placed on the chairs in the shape of a "U," so that they could see me, the lesson and at the same time be on an equal playing field (spatially) with each other. It was like adding a touch of magic.

This single event inspired me to re-incorporate meditation as a regular practice. It added a much needed element of structure. That's when I realized that I was not bringing enough structure—plenty of inspiration, but no structure. I learned that above all, whether it was seating arrangements or meditation instructions, I would "suggest" a certain way to get best results, but never force or implement a practice as a rule. By the same token, I began to develop a higher expectation over time, without becoming too rigid. I stopped trying to build the fence higher, but stronger. I still was beginning each meditation session with my usual spiel and awoke one day to cut that out as well, based on the response of a student— "Old head, you don't gotta explain why we doin, it, just do it." Yes. Some were now guiding me as to what they needed. The cohesion between routine, discipline and energy was taking shape.

To be honest, it was rare up to that point for me to get it *exactly* right. At every turn there was, still, a new challenge. When I was demanding, they retracted, when I was lenient, they digressed. As expected, a few classes wanted something in exchange for their participation. Otherwise, it didn't have a purpose. They were in survival mode. The idea of silence, peace and focusing on their breath had no immediate visible results. Peace was something that happened somewhere else. Silence was "Joe" (for suckers) and breathing was nothing to even think about unless it stopped happening. Some days I would be at wits end trying to explain things, so I would write a quote on the board and let them dive into it. One day, I wrote, "Tranquility is courage in repose." I did a lesson in *metaphor*. The youth delved into the collective consciousness. What else is associated with courage? I asked..."What else is tranquility?" We discussed why people act with such violence when everyone just desires peace. As I sat on the L train going home that day, I realized that it was I who needed to embody the quote. I, myself, was the final piece of the puzzle. Until I was the master of my domain, they would not believe in my technique. I had to show them that I was a warrior—not one who listened to directions, but who acted with courage and lived by my own code. I had to be impeccable with my words and actions. That, they respected.

One even brighter moment in the darkness came after a bad weekend on the unit and the kids were locked down (in their "huts") because of fighting. A group that complained incessantly about meditation and had power conflicts within their ranks got into a huge brawl. It was no surprise. More on power conflicts and gender later on. That Monday morning, they looked ragged and slowly circled up their chairs, sitting in silence in front of me. Some had casts on their arms and black eyes. Their counselors were tight jawed and fed up and it appeared as if quite a battle had been fought amongst all of them. The alpha looked at me with wide opened eyes and calmly said—"We need some meditation, O.G." I was quietly elated. I could not have foreseen that this class, this moment would be a turning point. For some reason, I picked up the bowl and looked at them all first with clear eye contact and did not say a word until they looked back in silence. Then, I began to count down 5-4-3-2-1, and struck the stick to the bowl creating the ever-familiar echoing ring. Their eyes closed and I instructed, "Inhale 5 and exhale 5 beginning *now*. I counted down again, this time as a cadence for their inhale. **Some closed their eyes while I counted. It was miraculous. I counted 5 again for the exhale and they followed the count to a "T." Some even made a mudra or hand formation with their fingers. There was not a peep, not a distraction.** I rang the bell after a minute. Afterward, they proceeded right into their warm up exercise and I began the lesson. I can only say that an energetic force enveloped the unit that day. A spiritual force or source of inspiration different from anything else that we had experienced. Even the worst of critics participated and integrated themselves into the presence of the room, seemingly entranced by something that was undeniable. We had found the method. We had found the "1-minute moment."

The 1 minute moment provided the anchor that I needed to embark into the abyss. I could now inspire them as well as ground them in a disciplined practice that could quell anxiety. It became clear that the same discipline that the youth rejected was the discipline that they craved. How could I think otherwise? It made total sense. The 1—minute moment would lay the groundwork for spiritual responsibility. It laid the foundation of our new house. By establishing this ritual, I began everyday by greeting them the same way and deferring to something that was more important than I was—Consciousness. I built my new approach to teaching after the 1-minute moment commenced and could observe a whole new side of my students and their trauma-related anxiety. Before, I had only encountered what didn't work. Now, I was cultivating what worked. I could only begin deducing why. So I began to take notes. Now that I had them somewhat focused, I wanted to address their trauma and create opportunities to learn.

The Magic of Animal Archetypes

Part of the anxiety that trauma creates is the need for constant engagement or stimulation. The youth were always hungry for something—anything. Sometimes martial arts and even the 1-minute moment didn't cut it, unless there was a helicopter shooting flying dragons out of the sky at the same time. They had their "full moon" days and I had to adapt. I had stopped giving out sweet treats because of the effects of hypoglycemia on the brain and behavior, and my new disciplined approach wasn't very reward-based, so they begged for any video that displayed something of value or entertainment—usually a thematic display of yes—power, status or conflict. This was exhausting for me. Most of those requests were for *trap* music with some of their favorite rappers. I entertained the reward if they did their work and gave them a video or two at the end of class. With so much gun violence in the city, my only rule was that the video could not display guns. I would negotiate and reach a compromise with a highlight video from "Animal

Planet," tying it in with a written response. One day they requested Animal Planet instead. I asked them what it must be like to live in the "the wild.". They connected immediately—and had questions. I told them of my encounters with stingrays, alligators and wolves. They had stories of their own—about raccoons, rats and even horses. A unique equestrian culture still thrives in West Philadelphia to this day. In a way, they lived *in the wild* as well. **Tying lessons to animals was leading me into the world and symbolism of archetypes, which are the woven patterns of human collective consciousness..**

Animals are one example of archetypal symbols that innately connect with our consciousness through our DNA. Our collective human experience holds a common language of symbols that are universal in their meaning—to nearly all of us. Animals, planets, themes of nature, emotions, geometric shapes etc... I started realizing the power of archetypes when I saw the unifying effect that animals had on us as a group. The boys were able to tap into their emotions through not only the beauty or grace of animals, but the strength, ferocity or agility of them. The young ladies of course, leaned toward the *cuteness* factor, but they also valued the masculine traits. The animal kingdom became our 1st archetypal theme. I showed them my own fascination with animals and it inspired us to respect their innate knowledge. **Through the creatures of the earth far and wide, we discussed the emotions related to fear and its ability to both motivate and stifle. It was a perfect trauma-relief therapy.** We highlighted behaviors of resilience or adaptation. We spent a day on the chameleon, a day on the squid, a day on the black panther. It inspired us to look at our own animal brains. Many of the students opened up about how they react to things and why. In one lesson, we read about the 1st nations tribes and their concept of the spirit animal. They looked at where their animal-spirits were on the medicine wheel and made connections with the theme of that quadrant (see medicine wheel image). Many identified their "spirit animal" and wrote about the common traits of their personalities or demeanor. Some were foxes, others were birds or sharks. While Panda followed through with a lesson on veganism, they wrote the following poetic verses about their connections with our winged and four legged friends:

"The hawk is my spirit guide because he's always on the hunt. He's sharp and thorough. Don't make the mistake of thinking that he'll crash because he flies straight as an arrow."
R.N 2019

"The owl is my spirit guide because she's always lookin out. She's hidden and wise. Don't make the mistake of thinking she won't see you because her head can turn in any direction."
F.W 2019

After a while of course, the boys would want to see the conflicts—the epic encounters between hyenas and lions, hippos and crocodiles. All of these archetypal battles of the mind spoke to their collective inner civil war. We all were battling the lower self to become our own master. Animal consciousness was ingrained in all of us to a certain degree. I told them the 1st nations story of the red wolf and the blue wolf, always dueling inside of us, representing the lower and higher self. We pondered the winner of this battle. I asserted to them it was the one we "choose to feed." They wrote about which wolf they fed and how. We read about the scorpion and the frog and how despite the frog providing a free ride across the river, the scorpion still bit the frog. The story led to a lesson on nature and nurture. They enjoyed the simple lessons drawn from these tails because the lessons were neutral and meaningful. They weren't graded harshly or judged while interpreting the stories—and it led to nearly total partici-pation. The lessons were neutral because I wasn't forcing them to take a stance on something and they were meaningful because we could all relate on a deep subconscious level to a beautiful aspect of consciousness. The archetypal symbolism of each animal became a new part of their identity—almost like a totem. They related to embodying the hunting skills of a hawk, the courage of a lion and the watchfulness of an owl. The connections were directly relatable, as well, to the world they experienced everyday and without having to give details of their lives, they could emulate their struggle with the tact and grace of all the wondrous creatures of planet earth.

The all-time favorite video of the youth was the footage of three elder men of the Masai tribe in Kenya who, in sandals, calmly walked up to a pack of 15 lions and took their fresh kill to bring it back to the village. We were able to role play and they empathized with the men through the scene and every carefully planted step that inched the men closer to the lions. Their ability to put themselves "in the sandals" of these tribal hunters was so complete that many of them actually couldn't help but to stand up and emulate movements of the men. In this footage, the boys not only saw the power of composure, but the strength of identity. The men knew who they were. They were hunters, they had responsibility to their community and they understood the power of their own confidence to the point where they could risk being torn to shreds by a pride of protective predators; The universe did not bring harm to these men because they self-identified their role in the great collective consciousness. The boys experienced that with this type of spiritual assurance, we have the ability to create our own reality out of a host of situations, even the most desperate. They saw spiritual responsibility in action. In the lesson, which I'll share in the next chapter, we would link *consciousness* with *courage, cooperation, culture* and follow through with almost any form of exploratory writing. One wrote in his journal when asked about the connection between courage and beingness—

"They (the men) showed that being conscious brings you courage ...and you have to be focused in your heart to be focused in your mind..." B.D, 2018

Amazingly insightful words that I could never take credit for. This was a typical case of a student finding deeper meaning in such teachings. I asked them to use the words consciousness and identity in their response. Some were a bit more literal:

"They were sturdy (strong) the whole time and even when they back was to the lions..They had a lot of courage hadda move fast, luckily they had consciousness." A.F 2018

"The lions were afraid of the men because they felt the men were together and the men had no doubt what they was doing." B.F.

Archetypes as Identities

Archetypal themes became a cornerstone of my lessons. They brought leverage for me and camaraderie into the classroom. I eventually saw that archetypal tribal roles activated a memorial identity in my students as well. The builder, the artisan, the doctor or the shepherd. They all seemed to connect immediately with a role that supported a healthy and balanced community. The girls got into a debate about whether females should be expected to fight in wars or why there should or shouldn't be rites of passage. At one point I assigned them roles to play in a dialogue facing a certain tribal challenge such as a food shortage or a pending storm. More time to develop these scenario based lessons would have been optimal and certainly a more long term student circumstance could have produced incredible results. When young people identified with responsible roles in their community, they felt needed. They saw less need to compete and more need to work collectively to figure out solutions. I remember asking at the end of discussion, what does it feel like when someone tells you they "need you?" They all answered with astounding positive affirmation.

So the archetypal lessons continued and I used a medicine wheel (see diagram) where students could pick the 1 of the 4 or 8 archetypal roles in which they identified and they could begin assembling the parts of their new identity. This identity linked them not with likes or dislikes on Twitter or some music star that they don't know or a social construct that separated them from others—**In this identity, they could see what was buried inside of them. They could feel the energy of life through archetypal memory. They could justify their existence and by identifying with the aspects of their ancestry, their planet or an element or a season or animals, they could link themselves with all of creation.** This link was more meaningful than perhaps any other activity that I could facilitate.

Storytime

What they really loved most about English class, arguably, was stories. I say *arguably* for a reason—some of them could tell a story and create an argument at the same time. To most, a well-told story, whether true or not, sparked a magical connection with the collective consciousness. I remember after watching the whole film of Life of Pi, which they enjoyed, and nobody ever asked if it was based on a true story. It didn't matter. To them, it was true, and they, perhaps, didn't want to know otherwise. The world of adventure, fantasy or imagination gave them a place of retreat—maybe it reminded them of their youth; Maybe it rekindled the escape "place" they went to in times of trouble. That place seemed so far away by the time they got into their teens, but with a good story, their inner universe would come alive once again...This is the power of collective consciousness. There is no need for fact checking or evidence, a story transcends such pettiness. It allows us to become the characters, to become the protagonist or anti-hero. We automatically are attracted to the archetypes that match our experiences, or the experience of our soul journey.

The residents themselves were storytellers. They used imagery and rhetoric in recalling their own personal legends. Indeed, stories are the veins that carry the blood of experience. Animated, descriptive and comical, they articulated their run-ins and experiences when the spirit moved them. In one class, we researched the role of the griots in West Africa. They identified with this ancient teacher-like entertainer that was a central cultural figure to most tribes. The griot performance paralleled elements of jazz, hip-hop and break-dancing, so the residents connected with the figure in dynamic ways. The griot, of course, never had to persuade his or her students to write. This was my job and it was not a 1-2-3 process by any means. "You all have great stories, you just have to recall them and use your speaking skills to build them or your writing skills to validate them..." I conveyed to them in my best persuasion that today especially, the pen was mightier than the sword. Admittedly, getting them to follow the steps of the writing process was insurmountable for the most part. Many were able to write a great intro to their story and then the will to articulate through the written word faded. This was due to their lack of vocabulary and organizing their ideas into a draft. **Again, they produced writing when recognizing something relevant in their lives needed to be expressed on paper—even if it was a story about a pit bull sleeping on their porch or how their parole officer dressed in purple suits.** With so many different levels of writing and speaking in just one class, I had to keep the assignments approachable and build scaffolding for as many as I could, meeting them where they were. The desire to bring the inner story to the written word, to claim their sovereignty for a brief moment within the walls of the prison was a rare, but wonderful moment. Whether they finished their story or stopped in the middle of it for whatever reason, there was often camaraderie, laughter and nostalgia in the room when it was time to write or tell stories. The ingredients for empathy. The world of storytelling opened a different dimension of communication— one that required them to know their audience, to use non-verbal cues and persuasion. Their stories kept their spirits alive. At times I would intercede and slightly coach them and sometimes I would fade into the background and allow them to fly—through an open sky of expansion and self-recognition. Whether from their peers, teacher or counselors, interpersonal praises were a needed form of support. To know, someone related, to know someone cheered for them or at least listened, made the difference. It was the *beingness* gained from authentic emotions, empathy, and ritual. These were the new components of the classroom that fused together to make things work. When there was laughter in the room and it was not at the expense of another, I knew things were ok.

My own spirit lifted by year 3. In the 1-minute moment, they heard certainty in my voice, clarity in my tone. School began to be an uplifting experience for those residents in my class, even if they were in a miserable mood. Some days, of course, nothing worked. Some days it was just good to be with them and for them to know I was there. The key was that I was always myself and after the 1-minute moment, I didn't block them from being themselves. I encouraged authenticity and didn't replace teaching them with assessing them, We never excluded humanity or spirit from the lesson. Fear and anger were frowned upon for the most part and we didn't allow prison walls to silence the stories that were yet to be.

Some call it emotional or social learning, but it's more than that. It was organic and authentic. The new method and culminating archetypal themes birthed many moments of collective awakening that illuminated a new dimension of the bright minds before me. The crucial component was to let it emerge whenever it happened. Instead of forcing a lesson objective everyday, I stated the objective and we worked our way through it until I felt they did their best with it. This allowed the space for them to eventually show me how they could understand what I wanted them to understand. By creating experiences in consciousness and self-awareness built on a foundation of identity, a degree of trust was created in the room.

Real educational experiences reflect real learning. The effects are lasting and the hormonal shifts that occur in such moments create a lasting imprint in the neural networks of the brain. The limbic system, the seat of emotions in our brain, can open or close access to learn. When we involve the whole brain in our lessons, learning occurs at all levels. Building a true culture of learning, even on the worst days, allows young person to experience emotional intelligence and collective consciousness. Lessons of such become woven into the fabric of their personality and demeanor. The few days where I tried to force them to learn something (which is a violent trait of our educational philosophy), were days where I lost them almost permanently. This is where a teacher's intuition has to guide them. I was fair about how much pushback I would tolerate from the lesson. Their resistance to emotional intelligence on some days was understandable. Their disinterest in poetry or imagery or symbolism on another day was expected. It was my responsibility to present it as relevant, but most importantly I had to gauge how they were feeling that day. What had happened on the unit the night before? Who was not present? Our *1-minute moment* helped this "check-in" and allowed me to test the waters and feel out the temperature of the group before objectifying the whole setting for the day. It always amazes me how teachers are expected to mandate a conversation, mandate an objective and mandate an outcome for every class on every day that they teach. It's like demanding that everyday on earth be sunny. *Rule #10 Listen to Bruce Lee and "Be water, my friend.."*

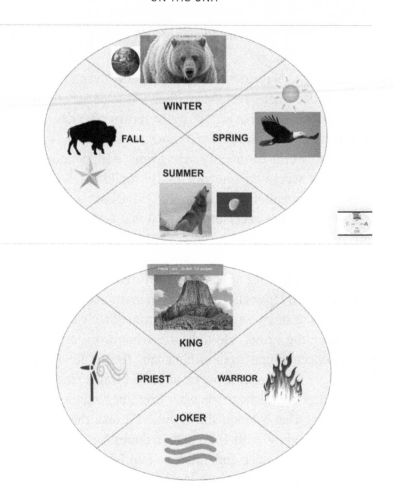

Examples of archetypal "medicine wheels"— These wheels follow the Lakota tradition and there are others with different symbolic representations in the 4 quadrants. The 4 quadrants always represent (counterclockwise from south)— birth, life, death, rebirth and then all the other associated concepts, animals, elements, personality traits, celestial bodies align with that quadrant. Have the students choose an animal, celestial body, season etc.. through different wheels and allow them to discover the traits of that archetype, finally connecting those traits to their own.

The Story of "W"

An unforgettable resident we will name "W," was a classic case of the unfortunate recidivism that we experienced in the center on a regular basis. "W" was a return offender and had eventually been in the center 3 times for 3 different offenses. Residents were commonly appearing within months or sometimes weeks in and out of the building. Some, who detested my meditation pitch at first, came back a second time and showed more acceptance. "W" was a perfect example of this. He was an alpha type—unmoved by authority/regulations or even social norms. He had a strong physique, a chiseled face with a beaming white smile which he rarely displayed. He was about 16 when I first encountered him in my social studies/life skills class upstairs and I could tell immediately that he held sway over the group. He did little schoolwork and did not meditate, remaining stoic in his chair. He left for 6 months before I got to know him, but came back. I walked into his unit and his first comment to me was "Don't be ringing that bowl and putting that Voodoo shit on us." I'll take that bowl and bust the window with it." I didn't doubt him. "W " could single-handedly start and finish a multi-person brawl and swear up and down that he had nothing to do with it. I asked him why he thought it was "Voodoo." He blurted, "cause they be doin that shit and cursin' people." I asked him if he thought that I was a bad person. His retort, "*maybe.*" I consented. The next day, I began class without meditation or the bowl. We began a project of making posters and "W" took advantage of his dominance of the class (and the teacher) and made a caricature of me and my exaggerated boney head, meditating, with closed and crooked eyes. It was actually a pretty good sketch and I let his group present it—I shared a laugh with them and gave them an "A" for the illustration, but a "C" for not finishing the academic portion. They were mildly surprised that I didn't get offended. "W" surely couldn't accept my passive response. Accordingly, he tore up the whole poster and threw it on the ground—He smiled unwittingly at me as if to challenge my peace and I nodded my head up and down softly. I'd never been physically attacked by a resident, but the possibility was always there. Our principal was punched in the face later that year. Still, I felt "W" didn't hate me as badly as he postured. The next day, I had pasted all of the posters on the wall, including the torn one which was taped together as finely as possible. We began class and "W" asked why I hung his groups' poster up—I said "Because I thought it was good and I'm not throwing it away...Plus nobody ever drew a picture of me and I'm proud of my new portrait..." Something odd then happened. A small smile appeared from the crease of "W"s mouth and his eyes brightened with humor. His classmates sat silently and seemed to wonder what would happen next. He turned his head sideways with his eyes big and chin up asking, "How come you don't ring that bowl anymore?" I told him that I didn't want to offend anyone and I didn't think the group liked meditating. There were a few instances like this when I said the right words—in many other instances, I did not! He seemed to be scanning me and testing me further to see if I was actually someone who he could trust—or at least someone that he actually liked. Another resident said "Naw, we like it." W interjected, "Lemme ring the bowl." I relented and decided to make an exception by having class begin from that day forth with "W" ringing the Tibetan bowl. Some exceptions were for the better of all. "W" still didn't meditate, but he instructed the others to do so and made sure they were quiet. I showed him how to count aloud for a 5-5 breath. The class followed his lead. Aside from a mildly aggressive approach, he was an awesome facilitator. "W" began to do well in his other classes and showed a love for art—He soon learned that his art teacher was my friend and "aunty"—Panda. Panda and I would laugh and talk about him for the few weeks that he was one the unit. One day, a devious resident poured some paint into Panda's coffee mug while she was presenting a concept and she nearly drank it before a counselor intervened. When "W" saw it, he leaped across the room and unleashed a slew of punches on his mischievous classmate—landing himself in solitary confinement, "the rubber room." I ventured up to his unit immediately to touch base with him. I was denied entry, but sent a message of support for him. Despite his violent response to the incident, "W" showed character—he showed that he truly was a warrior and had love for the teachers that cared for him. On my way out, the counselor was happy to share with me that he saw "W" meditating in the rubber room to pass the time. I never suspected it. I guess he just didn't want to partake in front of his peers. Panda came into my room the next day and asked me if I was able to speak with him. I told her that he was in the rubber room—and meditating. We both paused and smiled. She walked over and embraced me. Most hugs and or contact was discouraged even amongst staff because of PREA laws. We hugged until my eyes teared. "W" was our pride. He defended Panda and showed me that what I was doing had real value. He was willing to pay the price to defend what was right—yet he was a criminal. Why? Had anyone ever shown him a different way? To me, it revealed once again that young people make mistakes. When they are traumatized, in need and at-risk, those mistakes can have ugly consequences. So many times, however, residents like this are more loyal, more compassionate and more heroic than some of the very public figures and authorities that keep this system profitable. The next week I had everyone circle up their chairs as usual, but "W" didn't emerge from the room. I asked where he was. "Released." The rest of the unit looked at me with quiet inquisition. I felt sentimental for one moment and then someone blurted a question—"Could I ring the bowl now?" I shook my head no. "That was only for "W" to do.. now the bowl comes back to me. Let's straighten our posture and prepare to observe the breath..." "W" was back out in *the trenches*. Another soul released into the hard Philadelphia streets to search for their mojo, their big break or moment of truth. I only hoped his character would bring him the good things in life, and his angels would protect him as he protected Panda.

"W," and, of course, most of the residents, were dealing with trauma-related conditions on a day to day basis—whether it be the sometimes traumatic experience of just living in the youth center or the past events embedded into the consciousness that they brought in with them. Many end up heavily medicated and some suffer withdrawal symptoms from what they have been cut off from in the streets (or their place of refuge). Education was made meaningful for "W" after he made real connections to his teachers. It didn't matter what his skill level was, but when he bonded with someone, he produced effort beyond expectation. Nobody knows what he dealt with beyond the walls of the center. I sensed he along with many had seen horrific things. For some, the youth center is the safest place they could be. I was shocked to learn early on just how many of my students were homeless. For some, the center was their home. School was at least entertaining, at times. Three meals a day and a bed to sleep in with no immediate threat of violence was a refuge. For others, the center became a nightmare and school, meaningless.

The Story of Jo

Along these lines, there was Jo. Jo was quite tall, unorthodox and lanky with big lips and carried his soft demeanor with a loose strut. He was an oddly happy young man. He arrived into a unit that consisted of a group of pretty rough customers, who had a very distinct pecking order. They were not adverse to even threatening me from time to time and some days, they firmly conveyed to me that they were not doing any school work. Jo was an exception. He asked questions about the material and enjoyed finishing his assignments. Completing his schoolwork seemed to bring a normalcy to his life there at the center. He was ambitious and had a positive outlook for the future and seemed to transcend the environment with an airy demeanor. Extroverted and interested in speaking to crowds, he wanted to be a sports broadcaster. Then, he changed sportscaster to Youtuber, then back to radio host. He was somewhat eccentric, well, quite a bit eccentric. After I was able to establish some fluidity in the class and start with a short mindful minute of breathing, Jo realized that he found something else he was interested in—meditation. The three fellows in the room who participated in the meditative session seemed to want to try anything to establish some kind of uniformity in a unit that ran amuck with defiance and power struggles. I began a guided breathing exercise one morning and saw that all 3 of them were clinching their foreheads during their meditation, as if trying to experience or see something out of the ordinary. It was symbolic of their moment to moment experience. I rarely observed my students intently while they were breathing, but this revealed the level of strain that they carried with them all day, day in and day out. Being stuck with a bad unit could be torturous for some residents who weren't accustomed to living with thieves, drug dealers, much less, killers. After Jo's whole unit was locked down for a fight amongst themselves, Jo was the only one who asked to come out of his cell to do some schoolwork. In the solitary confines of the lockdown, Jo and I discussed his writing and worked on a personal narrative. He was certain that he would be released soon and inspired to get out and move on with his life. His face gleamed with delight and he spoke about doing meditations on his podcasts. He seemed unbothered by the hostility of his classmates. The class came out from lockdown for two days and then, one morning later in the week I reported up to the pod and they were on lock down, but Jo was not there. The counselor told me that the unit turned on him and he was badly beaten. He was in the hospital. An emptiness came over me and I left the pod with no desire to teach. It had happened before, but this time, it felt like a friend, a younger brother that was hurt—a young brother with a spark of life and hopefulness in him that, sadly, created a target for those without that spark. *Rule 11: Don't underestimate the mob mentality*

By the time Jo was released from the hospital, I had a different class that period. I went to visit him after school one day to see if he was alright. The counselor told me that he was in his "hut" but it might not be best to go near him. He had been wrapping his bedsheets around his body and head like a monk and "saying crazy things." He also was on lockdown for threatening a counselor. This was not the Jo that I knew. He was damaged—dealing with his trauma by adopting a reclusive character. Maybe that's what he needed to do, but it didn't look good to the establishment. I knocked on the door— Jo? "Who's dat?" he sharply replied. "Mr. Biseca." There was a long pause..."I just wanted to say hi and see if you were doing ok." He snapped—"Get outa here old head, you can't do nothin for me. You're just a teacher..." You don't know jack." I told him not to forget what he learned—to stay focused on his vision... "Don't let it stop you Jo, this is only temporary, stay strong..." I walked away and nodded to the counselor who seemed to be relieved that I was leaving. From behind their doors, some of the others started cursing at me "Yea we tipped on your boy and we'll tip on you next." Some began asking for treats or snacks. I opened the door to exit and heard Jo screaming and pounding on his door behind me. My blood ran cold as I felt the tension, passing through the sterile unit area. I can still hear his voice echo, bouncing off of the concrete walls. Like a house of mirrors, it exuded an eternal emptiness.

Maybe he was right—I was just a teacher and I couldn't do anything to really help him. I shouldn't have been so naive, I should have warned him about keeping good relations with the unit and focusing on "being in the present moment," dealing with the present circumstance. I should have known things were going to happen when I saw the boys tightening their foreheads during meditation. If he was more aware of his environment, Jo could have seen it coming. Trauma is contagious and violence is its main symptom. They both spread like wildfire. Dammit, I could have prevented it. Jo, if you are out there, I know that you made it through. Let's get that podcast going. Tell your story Jo. *Rule #12: Don't become attached to anything or anybody.*

The Triumph of HH

Not all stories have endings and certainly, not all are so bleak. The universe certainly gave me reason to hope at every turn, with every new group. Although there was a time after Jo's incident where I ceased meditating in class, I was quickly blessed with a "soon to be" source of inspiration. I had my own room by year 3 and it was at that time when I acquired "HH," a group that left a lasting mark on my experience at the center.

I grew accustomed to a variety of circumstances and commentary in the moments during meditation and had instituted a few chosen responses to that commentary. While my eyes half closed during the 1st session with HH, a kid about 6 feet to my right quietly murmured, "What if I cracked you in the jaw right now, what would you do?" It was a group of 18–20-year-olds who were seasoned juvenile veterans of the system and the streets. The real risk of the moment laid in not so much the threat, but my response to it. Which gradually became more along the lines of "...That's not a nice thing to say.. and you don't have to participate if you don't like." I eventually came to realize that such threats were not as imminently dangerous as they seemed. The student in the front row that made the comment was moved to placement one week later. Eventually, I realized that when some of the rougher residents like something about you, they test you. HH, as most other units, poignantly assessed the thickness of my skin, my confidence and the conviction behind my method. They tested my morals, questioned my beliefs...some days I felt as though I was making my case to *Saint Peter* or *Djehuti*. They were cunning and ruthless, unceasingly trying to negotiate for videos and free-time. Some days I just did not want to be there. Their tests of me expressed a very streetwise technique culturally embedded in the way of life *on the bricks*. They knew if they scared me enough, I would give into their demands. Plenty of situations arose where I was challenged because of who I was or how I looked. I worked with other teachers who never dealt with one physical threat or behavior issue. That was a result of who they were. Maybe I was a gluten for punishment. The young men applied their tests with great effectiveness on most authority figures in some way. Of course, it is something one realizes only after going through the trials of failure. I later realized it was also a way they helped us understand them and the world they came from. I stumbled a few times prior, but managed to weather the storm without flinching in the HH unit. For that, most of them began to respect me.

One day, while addressing the usual assumption that I smoked marijuana, I was in the middle of my explanation (that I had found something more lasting and meaningful through meditation) when I noticed how interested they were in the supernatural and various mental states. I spent considerable time showing them evidence that meditating and different forms of breathwork was a form of getting high from your own hormones—only the high was internally induced and it had tremendous health benefits. Some of them missed getting high from weed so much that they were willing to try meditation. At one point, a few of them had a revelation about the power of the present moment. One concluded, "There really ain't no future and ain't no past—it's all in your head," after a brief discussion. "Exactly!" I said. "Time is all in our heads and it's time that creates anxiety." They were not only catching on, but becoming quite existential. We read about the Iroquois rite of passage and vision quest. One day, we had a "hold the breath" contest." After I showed them a Navy seals challenge video and we read about how holding the breath actually makes your body stronger and blood flow to your brain. When that went well and inspired them to get to their daily assignment, we then tried a meditation contest. It came back to the old adage—"Inspire them first, then you can teach them." The game was simple—whoever could maintain their posture and silence with complete breath control would receive a prize. They nearly fought over who actually won and there was plenty of cheating, but I gathered that they got the point. Irony at its best. My own fault, of course, so I tailored it back a bit. A certain spiritually—oriented quality took hold of the classroom culture. They began to open to a perspective of universal consciousness.

It was HH who named the exercise "The 1-minute moment" based on our conversation about the power of the present moment. They became the 1st group that identified with and sincerely practiced "1 minute moment," a truly organic technique that emerged from a collective conscious experience. I could have never forecasted the camaraderie, however, that evolved over the next couple of weeks. At the time, we were studying the American Civil War and I, accordingly, tied in the theme of "discipline" as they investigated life as a black soldier during the war. I decided to show them the film "Glory," the historical drama about the famous black regimen, the 54th Massachusetts. It was a hit. Their meditations became impeccable. It was then when I became inspired to compile my notes and write this book. All 12 of them sat up straight and followed the breath count, sitting in complete silence even after the meditation was finished. The group started to develop a type of rare togetherness that we all found surprisingly enjoyable after a rough start. To see the boys asking questions and doing their own research about soldiers in the 54th was awe-striking. We held discussions about race and the legacy of slavery. The boys expressed their personal understanding and offered rich perspectives. We laughed and shared emotions that the film brought us to encounter. They identified with Denzel Washington's character, *Private Trip*, and responded in their journals to the scene where he stole shoes. They were able to metaphorically put themselves in his shoes— A mark of empathy. Ironically, Denzel's character was whipped for stealing shoes in the film. The boys responded:

"...He was tryna stay out of trouble but needed shoes to be a good soldier. I woudda still copt em (stole them) and risked the punishment... #$%^#@ got beat for nothin back then but now we get put in jail..." G.N. 2018

"The old man called him a #$%^ but he was just bein' real...Old head was tryna look out but he didn't have no right tellin private Trip what to do." H.M. 2018

A culminating moment in the film came when the soldiers were preparing for their final battle, which would ultimately lead to their own demise—The night before the battle, Morgan Freeman and Denzel Washington and others gave epic performances singing gospel and depicting the negro spiritual "call and response" tradition, including clapping, percussion and lyricism. The boys were enthralled with it and after making me play it again 3 times, they actually started a live recreation of the scene—and song, in the room. I stepped back and observed them producing their own version, snapping the pencils for clicking sounds, thumping the desks like conga drums and taking turns rhyming as if they themselves were going into battle. It was also clear that they were in that same mentality as the soldiers. It was a moment of realization that stands out in my 15 years of teaching. The final scene of the film, when the men storm the confederate fortress only to meet their glorious demise, our room full of young men and two counselors, myself included, held back the tears—maybe not so much for the soldiers of the 54th, but for the memory of them that has been lost or abandoned in a country that they've never been able to claim as their own, no matter what they endured. Despite all of my experience in the black community, it was a moment when I fully grasped the tragic plight of the black man in America. It was the only class that went beyond meditation to true fellowship. On that day, I reflected as I watched the boys unpack the purpose of the film and it dawned on me that after all that lesson planning, the calculation, the instruction theory and copy paper, the real lesson came when they felt empathy for those that came before them, for each other and even for me. They internalized the strength of their ancestors as seen in the film and applied it to their own struggle. They were thankful that, oddly, a white teacher shared the story. They found a precious gift— the gift of interconnectedness. They also found a piece of themselves that would always stay with them—a new identity of authenticity took shape. On that day, that single class became more than informative, it became transformative. My time with HH allowed me to witness what could be if schools or prisons focused on cooperative engagement and conscious experience in forming a common bond while learning. Trauma needs emotional release and avenues that release it. If we could inspire our students to approach knowledge through their own emotions, empathy and conscious experience instead of challenging them with the next "repeat what I do" task, then maybe they could develop a greater love for learning—and a greater awareness of who they are...not just through their grades and test scores. That moment in HH brought a crescendo of hope to my room and a bright star in the long night of my juvenile justice experience. My spirit was lifted. Things were changing. The day that music arose from the hollow desks and wooden pencils, their scope of identity and selfhood brightened our room like the fresh rising spring sun over 48th St. For that one moment, we had, together, overcome.

Moving Forward with 1-Minute Moment

Whether it was the need to conserve energy or the natural progression of things, I began to validate meditation through my explanations far less before beginning the "1 minute moment." I simply ignored any resistance or groans or side conversation and proceeded with the routine. The ringing of the bowl and scripted instruction seemed to quell most conversation automatically. One day someone said, "Don't explain the shit man, you too *thurl* (thorough)...just ring the bell." Normally, I had spent time trying to hush the talk and brief the group about why conscious breathing was good for everyone before we partook (It also was done for the new additions to the class who might not have known what was happening), but as time went on, I rattled off 2-3 quick reminders, then presented a brief opportunity for questions after it was through. I had to keep things moving. One reason for this was that although I knew that explaining aspects of the benefits helped some kids take to it more readily, I began to see that it had the effect of a sales pitch. **In a society where young people are constantly fed persuasive rhetoric (from the media, political and education institutions), skepticism runs high especially with black and brown juveniles. For each new resident, some white man sitting in front of them, ringing a bowl and telling them about how to manage their emotions must have been nerve-racking to some extent.** I was well aware of this, so I only diverged when prompted. The 1-minute moment soon became a class ritual that the students and I owned. New admittees almost "had" to buy in due to social cohesion and normalized effect that the ritual brought. I can honestly say that after suring up the 1-minute moment, there was never a conflict in my room afterward. African author, Malidoma Some, said "A community without ritual is no community at all." He was right. Ritual creates collective awareness, commonality and demands participation.

By year 3, I was also strengthening my own personal practice and "Sadhana" every morning as I further developed the 1-minute moment in all of my classes. I began to incorporate different breath sets for different classes, depending on what I felt they needed. I deepened my study of the respiratory system—and the effects of various breath control exercises on hormonal secretion and brain function. Some classes needed a *Buteyko breath* (4-inhale, 7-hold, 8-exhale) to redirect hyper-anxiety, and some needed a 7-11 breath to wake up. The standard "go to" was the 5-5-5 for balance, focus and clarity.

Like clockwork, everyday, I held the bowl out in front of me. I didn't say anything. My eyes would only move toward those still talking. At that point, those who noticed would begin hushing the others and soon the class would fall quiet. I began with a quick phrase of inspiration and reminder to keep the spine straight with no muscle tension, breath down to the navel and *become* the breath, "nothing else." I then would ring the bell and begin.. " *aaand inhale, 5-4-3-2-1, exhale 5-4-3-2-1, hold,* so on and so forth. Structuring the meditation as a regimented routine that was an essential part of beginning class with a specifically allocated minute created uniform participation even in the most challenging of groups. For some it was 1 minute, for others, I could tell that 30 seconds was enough. It usually ended with me saying "Any questions?" or "good job" or "How many were able to slow down the breath and follow?" Afterward I would interject a proverbial phrase or a routine reminder such as... "We take a moment to breathe because a person who is in control of his breath is in control of his mind"...or, "A man in control of his mind is in control of his life." All of these elements—the reference to mental control, the disciplinary tone, the ritual presentation and sound of the bowl, contributed to a successful method—and I defined that success by what happened in the next hour. Each one of the youth found meaning in at least one of the elements of the structured ritual and the format allowed them to participate freely without being judged or lost at what to do. They could sit quietly or jump in at any time. Were there days where it flopped? Yes. Were there days where the group brought in energy that was too hostile for the whole routine? Absolutely. I became undeniably certain, however, that the work was ushering them toward an inner awareness that provided sparked self-efficacy and hope. As far as the imple-mentation, as soon as the bowl came out of my bag, the boys knew I was committed. My purpose was sealed. Nothing could deter me.

I started to see the results of the classes that participated the most and began surveying them to see if the effects that I witnessed were statistically observable. I kept my delivery authentic and transparent—most were aware that I was trying to see if meditation was helping them. I identified the *1-minute moment* as a way to begin an actual meditation since actual meditation was not effective in the group. Many reported that they did some meditation in their room in the evening or when they got up in the morning after doing some exercise. Gradually, groups of classes began to be more respectful, listen intently and complete their assignments. Even in "beef" they had among themselves, those contenders tried not to interrupt the flow of the room. Questions about meditation began to brew. Some asked if it helped cancer or drug addiction for members of their family. I saw a new side of them—a sense of responsibility way beyond what one would assume. Our team began to use PBIS (Positive Behavior Intervention Support) and it supplemented the incentive for them. There were marked changes in their behavior and motivations to participate in class after a good meditation. Kids were starting to ask me, "What we doin today *teach*?" Some of them even referred to me as "unc." The "1-minute moment" was far less elusive than the prior attempts and quite honestly, I never thought it would be as effective as it proved. The specifics of timed inhales and exhales brought a rhythm, a cadence to the ritual. It was an unspoken recognition of a spiritual presence, of a need for sanity and strength. It was bringing us from our different neighborhoods, ages and skin tones and intelligence types—all into the same singularity of sound, breath and consciousness. It was rewiring young minds and opening new channels of awareness. Most importantly, it was untangling the mess of trauma. As divine intervention would have it, I was soon given an opportunity to sit with individual students, which gave new meaning to meditating and trauma informed teaching.

◆ CHAPTER 4 ◆

ONE ON ONE INTERVENTION

With handcuff marks on their wrists, scrapes on their faces or even bullet holes in their arms or legs, residents entering the "in-take" units were usually recovering with an immediate traumatic or semi-traumatic event. **Some were on crutches or freshly bruised from street altercations or altercations with the police, and a great deal of them appeared bewildered upon entry to the facility.** For a few months in the early winter of 2020, the "DHS side" of the complex was out of compliance due to shortages of staff and taking residents to the school area was off limits. So, teachers had to travel to the units to teach, like I had done my 1st year. I was assigned two in-take units. This was my opportunity to try some 1 on 1 meditations since they were spending most of their days in their cell. After proper arrangements, I set up 15 minute sessions with 4 students per class . I had convinced my principal that meditation helps set a calm precedent for the *intakes* and allowed them to decompress from the stress of street life. It was time to do some therapeutic work with meditation as the modality. My sociology degree and meditation certificate would have to cover my credentials. Though it only lasted only for a couple of months, this calm period before the storm exposed deeper layers of institutional trauma, and medical, social-emotional and psychological issues that I would have not seen as a regular classroom teacher.

In the months before the Covid-19 pandemic (from January to March), on my way to the intake wing each morning before my 1 hour of sessions, I would glance at the Rachel Remen quote tucked away on the wall behind the art room—"Our humanity is far more powerful than our expertise..." It was a reminder that although I was supposed to be focusing on reading and writing for the one hour, it was secondary to helping them cope with trauma. By all accounts, including Maslow's "hierarchy of needs," emotional stability had to be prioritized before intellectual achievement. I decided to mix in a little of both and fuse in some spiritual responsibility. It was the one on one sessions that brought me to the realization that mindfulness or *Dialectical Behavior Therapy* that I was using in the classroom—which was serving to be more of a preventative measure, but meditation was showing to be undeniably therapeutic for those survivors of trauma. My proof was not recorded by statistical or quantitative data, so I began documenting the changes in a journal.

Medicine on the Unit

I didn't truly learn about the degree of prescribed medications that the residents were given until I sat on the unit in the morning before school started. I would guess that roughly %15 of them were on mild doses of heavy meds (Adderall and Ritalin were the most popular amphetamines and a wide variety of antidepressants were given for both anxiety and depression, which I found to be very disturbing). Although no sleeping pills were distributed, these other drugs, of course, had addictive potential at almost any dosage. Some of the youth could claim a pharmaceutical certificate with all of the knowledge of both street and prescription drugs. Some would offer me "medication services" for when they got out and they were unafraid to tell me what they could get for me. Drug possession and distribution ranked as some of our top offenses and many were awaiting to serve their time to literally start back on the block again when they got out. School and the justice system was just a game to them and some were able to play the system fairly well. **Some of them were booked with 10's of thousands of dollars on them from distributing kilos of cocaine. They had gone from riding around in their Escalade and eating cheesesteaks everyday to sitting in blue sweatpants asking for an extra lunch tray, without a dollar to their name.** Drug culture was certainly its own beast and many parts of Philadelphia were notorious for it. *Kensington*, for example, was one of the city's blighted drug infested neighborhoods where within a square mile, over 1200 people died in 2021 alone of unintentional drug overdose. One of the guys who came to like me suggested, "I know you be down Kensington, Biseca—What you need and I'll hook you up when I get out?" I told him to see if he could get me some Turmeric.

Incidents involving the effects of prescription meds were not mine to trace or document, of course, but I saw them as being an undeniable factor in behavior. One young fellow, that first week of one on one sessions, (whom I eventually developed a relationship with over a few trips in and out of the youth) made a conscious choice to get off his meds as a spiritual sacrifice during the month of Ramadan. Two days later he punched another young man (with whom he was friends with) in the face due to the anxiety of withdrawal. The other did not retaliate because he, himself, was Muslim. Others were experiencing withdrawal from street drugs/pills (hallucinogens, opioids and benzodiazepines), and being switched over to in-house drugs brought episodes of hormonal imbalance and emotional turbulence while in the center...Adverse drug events and reactions were uncommon or undocumented, but upon such an occurrence, residents had to spend time with the pharmacist/doctor. Medical information was not shared with teachers unless it was significant or related to others in the room, but one on one sessions opened my eyes to the massive amounts of pharmaceuticals dumped into the bellies of these incarcerated teens. Of course, street drugs were a plaguing issue before and after their stay. There is a whole study to be done on this phenomenon if it could ever be explored and or exposed.

The Case of "T"

My first one on one session was with a young man of Puerto Rican heritage who we'll call "T." He was addicted to Percocets and now on antidepressants at a low dosage. He wore a rosary and clung to it as he told me that all he could do now was pray. He had been evicted a few years prior and watched his grandmother get dragged down the steps of his apartment by housing agents. Surely, a traumatic event. I asked him if he prayed the rosary. He didn't know exactly what I meant so I showed him how Catholics prayed at each bead of the necklace. Like all forms of spiritual discipline, it tied in with conscious breathing. I didn't exactly encourage the act, but he seemed interested and voiced that he wanted to try it. I made the suggestion that he would benefit exponentially if he learned to breathe consciously with each bead, since he was adamant about praying. He wanted to learn prayers and I didn't know any except the *Our Father* and *Hail Mary*. He wanted some different creeds so we made some up. He told me that he believed in angels and he liked boxing. The word "warrior" resonated with him right away. He told me how his uncle rode horses in Puerto Rico and his posture and demeanor immediately became proud, masculine and stoic. He clearly embodied the warrior archetype—I encouraged the peaceful warrior in him and reminded him that being a warrior was not about being at war, it was about being able to prevent it. I reminded him that I was no priest, but I thought that it was good that he kept his spiritual life alive. He agreed to try the meditation with me and folded his hands in prayer when we began. I showed him a more relaxed hand position as he took deep breaths into his chest. I asked him to see if he could expand his belly not his chest when taking the breath and keep it quiet—"This is a real deep breath," I affirmed. He nodded his head and from there he must have gone into a deep state of consciousness in a few minutes because he did not open his eyes when I asked him too. A big smile came to his face after an extra minute. "One more time?" he asked. He seemed to rediscover something that he thought was not part of his everyday life—peace. He was astounded that simply breathing consciously was healthy and spiritually gratifying. He had found a new place to focus—inward. By going there, he had realized that it was alright to just *be*. "T" became the first of dozens who sat with me and found the activity of breathing to the diaphragm, rhythmically and consciously, to be mysteriously soothing. In his time on the inside, it became his preferred "medication."

The Story of "Y"

I decided to use some form of accountability and record keeping of these one on one sessions so I gave the students a short survey about how the meditation made them feel and if they thought it was useful. These "exit tickets" soon began to show me that I needed to take note and record of the sessions as they were happening. I chose to include here the story of "Y" to illustrate the climate of the streets. He was locked up for a typical gun possession charge on two occasions. We immediately had a candid conversation and I asked him why he felt the need to carry a gun. He told me the recent story of him playing basketball with a friend and they decided to make a $5 wager on the last game. When "Y" won the game, his friend left and returned with a "gliz" and shot him in the ribs. Since then, he has had acute anxiety, having already lost his brother to gun violence a few months earlier. **The bullet was still lodged in the back of his ribcage and though there was no pain, he was reluctant to take deep breaths. He told me that he smoked as well and that his lungs were weak.** He was almost certain that he would lose his life within a short time. I coached him through a slow diaphragmatic breathing exercise and he soon found the confidence and comfort gained from breathing deeply. This was an occasion where in addition to meditative exercises, spiritual and emotional counseling was badly needed. As "Y" gradually slowed his breathing down and released some surface anxiety, I spoke to him from the heart, and reminded him that the key to making the best of each moment was to learn to be in control of the breath. *One who is conscious of their breath is conscious of their surroundings. They can create their own reality from within.* I reminded him that only he could control his own destiny, and that he had much to live for. The new technique became a new best friend. "Y" quickly became a fan of conscious breathing and the last session we partook, he had told me that he meditated every night before bed. He also believed that his lungs would get strong again and planned on quitting smoking. I don't know his whereabouts, but I have a feeling that he is enduring and thriving. He wrote on his exit ticket, "I'll be meditating for sure and I think I'm gonna show my mom."

The Life Saver Breath

In extreme cases like Jeel's, it was a matter of emphasizing a single pause and immediate shifting of energy flow. Those cases where residents were quick to react to everything around them, I would focus on the power of a single pausing breath that I referred to as a "check" breath before thinking or acting on their emotions could save their life. This involved immediately closing the mouth and bringing the inhale down to the belly, then holding the breath for 5 seconds. Each second stood for one of the 5 elements. Holding the breath brings immediate oxygen to the brain. This check breath could also grant them the crucial second of divine intervention that may keep them from doing something to land them back into the center. The 1-minute moment was the time where we reinforced that ability to pause.

The Case of "Jeel"

This narrative would not be complete without the story of Jeel. Jeel was an incredibly traumatized resident who was placed in solitary confinement on numerous occasions for erratic behavior. It was later found that he was "cheekin" his meds, or not swallowing them when they were given. When I first encountered him, his energy was unnerving and his eyes shot from one direction to the other. He couldn't fixate his vision on one thing for more than 3 seconds. Instead of schoolwork, he was often given a computer to take his *Iready* assessment (online learning and assessment platform most likely soon to replace teachers), where he would switch screens to play video games. I noticed the compulsion and offered to take him for a few one on one sessions. **Gaming, I do declare, is the complete opposite of mindfulness—*video games and trauma*** *do not mix*, **despite the illusory engagement with the mind they provide. Maybe that will be the title of my next book, so let's leave it at that.** It certainly wasn't helping Jeel, as I witnessed his anxiety worsening along with his subsequent tantrums after the games. At first, Jeel did not want to sit down at the table with me, and, although we kept the door open, he refused to go into the room. I asked if there was anyone that he trusted to sit in the room with us while we do some relaxation exercises. He told me that he wanted to talk with his social worker, not with me. It was understandable. He was not ready and needed some more intervention. I was a complete stranger with a strange idea. This was an instance where along with gaming, meditation and trauma did not mix.

An added component of great importance is that those with acute trauma could benefit from breathing exercise but must first feel comfortable with the person facilitating it. This report could be immediate or need weeks to develop. Certain breaths are better for those dealing with more extreme states of anxiety. As a rule, the more intense the condition, the less regulated and more forceful the breath. **A long breath count would be suffocating for those already at high levels of an adrenaline release. It would be like throwing water on a blazing forest fire—it may dampen some areas but most likely would spread the fire in others.** Although I wanted to help Jeel and would have ideally implemented some conscious movement exercises for him, I decided to let the whole case go and hope for the best for him. Not surprisingly, another opportunity soon arrived. About a week after our first attempt, I was with another teacher in his pod, waiting to lead our afternoon class when soon a counselor appeared. He told Jeel's teacher that there would be no class and that everyone had to head back into their "huts." Since we had good relations, I asked him if everything was ok. **At that point, I heard yelling within the bathroom walls and saw water**

rushing out onto the floor. The counselor ran back into the unit and we both soon followed to find that Jeel had locked himself in the bathroom and clogged the toilet with his flip flop, while flushing it continuously. I hung around to help out the distressed counselors as we hastily rushed residents to their hut while they threatened to run out or "tip" on (beat someone up) somebody if the place flooded. We got them all into their huts and the counselors forced our way into the bathroom to find Jeel sitting on the floor in 3 inches of water yelling that he wanted out and couldn't take it anymore; He was hunched over and seated, with his arm hanging on the lever, exhausted from flushing it. The counselors went to grab him and drag him out. Something told me to intervene. I knew they would throw him in "the rubber room"—and it might be even more torturous for him. I stepped forward, "Wait...Let me sit with him... I can try something." The counselor looked at me and then looked at Jeel. "You wanna go with Biseca or go to the hut?" He couldn't immediately answer. His arm reached up and one finger extended toward me. We slowly walked to the small conference room and my thoughts circled around recalling which method to use. I went with intuition and stayed calm so that he would stay calm. "Do you want to change clothes first?" He looked up and a sense of semi-awareness came over him. "Yea." He knew it was a better option than being locked in his room for 24 hours. When he returned, I looked at him from across the round table and saw a tired, terror-stricken young man who was losing his capacity to maintain any kind of mental balance while in the youth center.

I began with, "Can I ask you something?" He shook his head no. Immediately, he requested, "I want outta here." I leaned forward, "I'm going to do my best to get you outta here but I need you to tell me something..." He looked into my eyes for the first time. "Do you care about yourself," I asked. He was silent. I probed further, "What I mean is do you want yourself to be ok?" "Yea," he said quietly. "Then can I show you one way to make sure that you're ok, no matter where you are?" He closed his eyes in silence but his face softened, which was a step in the right direction—any such attention was unattainable up to that point. I honed in, **"What I'm about to show you is for you only...and it can be used anytime you feel like you're losing control. I want you to use this to take care of yourself...and when you're feeling like you're gonna pop or like you can't take anymore, this is what you can do—are you ready to try?"** I told him that this technique is going to require *being a conscious warrior*—a master of your own mind. "...And it begins with sitting up straight and realizing that there is nothing to fear. I remembered his birthday was in late August—A Leo. I decided to throw some fire towards him so in a growling fighter man voice I commanded. "You have to be a lion!" His eyes opened. For the first time, our energy fell in sync. I demonstrated the technique. He watched. My voice became impassioned and direct. I continued, "If you discipline yourself and practice, it will allow you to lose the fear and doubt in your mind...but it takes time and practice...And the single best part of this technique is that the body can be completely relaxed." I used my hand gestures to show him how to close the mouth and take a deep slow breath down to the abdomen. I guided him through the exhale. "Look at the wall or close your eyes, whichever you're comfortable with...Now breathe in through your nose softly and when you breathe out, stick out your tongue like this." He made a face of disgust, but mild amusement. "Don't worry about what it looks like," I became stern. 3 breaths later, he was exhaling with his tongue out for each one while making a "Haaaa" sound from the gut. I told him that if he ever feels like he's going to snap again, do those 3 breaths and then take a slow inhale down to the belly. I challenged him to try a 5-5 breath for 30 seconds while I counted. He kept his eyes glued on the wall. At the end of the thirty seconds, he blinked slowly as if to realize that there was a part of him that liked it. It was a moment of self-regulation. I will not say that he was ecstatic, but he linked in and listened. His eyes lost the look of terror and angst. For the first time that I could see, he was in control of his thoughts. His throat Chakra had been completely blocked due to trauma. TRA grips certain energy centers of the Chakric system depending on the individual and the event. It causes blockages of the energy flow and depletion of cellular growth and repair. Jeel could not express himself through his own voice. After speaking with his social worker, I was not surprised to learn that Jeel had been in a house fire as a boy and lost his two siblings. His mom was a drug addict. He was just trying to process it all. He was speechless. For just a brief moment in time in the center, he found a way to take a break from processing it and cultivate a part of him that could help him understand who he was because of it.

One on One with PTSD

PTSD is simply a diagnosis of trauma-related anxiety that has been tied to a specific event. In the center, it was assumed that someone who was diagnosed with PTSD had experienced or witnessed a serious traumatic event. Many however, were not reported. TRA, PTSD and depression have a long list of similar symptoms. Fatigue, difficulty concentrating, irritability, substance abuse, hallucinations, paranoia, negative thoughts, feelings of guilt, a loss of interest in life. Hard to imagine someone dealing with any combinations of these doing their school work. These symptoms regularly appeared in my one on one sessions, but I never realized the significance of PTSD and depression in my classroom with the students. When I would return to my classroom to teach, it changed my whole perspective of the young people sitting in front of me. Those with PTSD had issues with proximity, for example, they couldn't bear an authority figure standing behind them. **One boy broke his pencil at the mention of the word "father." Some had seen their little sister get shot by stray bullets just outside of their own house. Some had witnessed atrocious crimes—and committed them as well.** There were plenty of those who were in for "catching a body" (murder). Philadelphia saw a spike in homicides yearly and by 2022, the rate was up nearly %30 from the previous year. The murderers were traumatized too. And the proverbial wall that they built around themselves was impenetrable. They didn't speak much, but, often, they were the most profuse writers. Some could fill up a single journal in a week with fascinating reflections and narratives. Out of respect for their privacy, I cannot share the details. In one case, I had an angry young man who admitted that he was waiting to get revenge or "get back in blood" when he got out for what someone did to his friend. I spoke with him about where we get the word "responsibility." We discussed the difference between reacting with the mind and responding with the heart. He privately opened up. After a few days of counseling and conscious breathing, he began to realize that It took courage to respond, not react. Though he didn't vocalize his intentions any further, I am certain that he changed his mind—Let's hope so.

After every one on one session, I walked the young men out of the room and often wondered if they would apply what they had experienced in our brief encounter at any time in the future. We could only hope. I strongly feel, however, that a single meditative session with someone who is well-trained and responsible can lay the foundation for a regular practice that will eventually create a permanent shift. I only wish I could trace or track such shifts with more scientific certainty. **I used science to study the breath, to understand the anatomical effects of conscious, rhythmic breathing. My own path, however, led me to a fork in the road, often splitting my method between science and spirit, and when I had to choose, it was spirit that always prevailed.** The one on one sessions were proving to be incredibly eye opening and I began thinking about preparing a proposal for the administration and DHS to implement a program. I needed a little more data and time to show that those who participated were less likely to return to the center. That was about the time that I walked into the teachers room one day and heard the news that an unprecedented virus was sweeping across China and was surely on its way to the U.S. There was talk of a worldwide pandemic. The energy of the center, the students, my colleagues, shifted into a quasi-frantic mode of preparation. Within days, I would see the end of my one on one sessions and life would never be the same.

The dozens of young men who partook in the one on one session intervention went unknown and certainly unrecognized, but it struck me as a powerful stepping stone toward meaningful and therapeutic interaction. The brief display of effectiveness that the one on one sessions demonstrated inspired me to track some of the progress and have the students write some short reflections at the end of each session. Some of them were able to fill out a short questionnaire. Most who were reluctant to write during class time, poured out thoughts and feelings gained from their meditation session. Reading some of their words from time to time reminds me to push for *beingness-based* intervention in education and juvenile incarceration. When I think of the subtle moments that I shared with these individuals who climbed out of the dark deep pit of anxiety to take a look at the garden that grew atop the surface, it reinforces my conviction that healing begins with a disciplined method and intention. It blossoms into a realization of individual consciousness. Each young man and woman in the center had a story, and it was, undoubtedly, difficult to choose a few for this book. I'll leave you with the story of "V."

The Case of "V," and Hopeful Victory

I was early to the unit one day and found the whole group in typical fashion watching *Fresh Prince* reruns and playing cards. One fellow, however, was sitting outside on the landing with an inquisitive look about him. He mosied into the room when I started class and I could immediately see that he was a loner. Energetically present and noticeable, "V" soon showed himself to be quietly ambitious and impressively articulate. He was unlike most in that he was willing to separate himself from the crowd. He didn't seek the approval of others, which so often led to anxiety for so many of these young people. "V" would sit on the veranda between classes, listening to the birds and enjoying the fresh air. An *old soul* indeed, I thought. He had his own way and certainly his own story to tell. By consequence, his unit soon became a one on one group and I would have my first session with him. He seemed curious about what I would share and after we exchanged pleasantries, he opened up about his situation. He told me that he was a "runaway" and that his father was in the state prison. His mother was alone and his older brother and sister had left the house. His mother, he said, was badly depressed and they had no money. He didn't want to do anything bad in his life, but he couldn't remain with his mother because no matter how hard he tried, he couldn't help her through her depression. He would feel the depression creeping into himself. He verbalized with great conviction that running away was his only option.

He was tired of being in and out of the juvenile system. He was tired of maneuvering the streets, working at the car wash to pay bills and sleeping abandoned buildings of *north Philly*, where police lights and sirens ruled the night. I asked him about his work papers and we began to work to locate his birth certificate.

"V" wasn't so much frustrated with the difficulty of his life, but what bothered him was not fulfilling some sort of purpose. I could relate. He wasn't afraid to go as far as possible to "become himself" and maybe return one day to buy his mother a house. I sympathized with him and his story resonated with me. There was a Shamanic quality to him and it emerged deeply when he spoke about his mother. I knew he had seen much and overcome great odds—perhaps even in other lifetimes. When I sat with him for our only one on one session, he told me all of this and I began to talk to him about what type of breathing and meditation may be helpful for him. He replied "I do all this meditation stuff already." I was skeptical, but we commenced. He was able to immediately slow his breathing and remain still. While others usually moved or chose to disengage after 1-2 minutes, "V" stayed calm, focused and completely unmoved. If I would have let him, I believe that he would have sat there for hours...I opened my eyes to begin to guide his consciousness back into the room and noticed he had a single tear rolling down his cheek... He didn't wipe it and I watched it roll down to his chin and even drip onto the floor. I stayed quiet. I felt it. The emotions began to swirl within me as well, but I decided to not speak. We both sat still and silent. He wiped two fingers across his face to dry it and placed his hands over his eyes. We didn't speak for what seemed like 5 minutes. "Did you like the breathing?" I asked. I removed his hands and affirmed. "Yea."

We didn't need to say much to each other at all for the next few weeks when I had him in class—it was almost a telepathic connection that just required a daily nod. There was an unspoken understanding between us that transcended the need to speak much. At one point, I had a moment with him and brought up the possibility of him getting into a job training program and finishing his degree. I told him that he could make a good life as a doctor, a teacher, but he had to start somewhere. He was surely bound for impactful work. He was fascinated with the prospect of being someone who people relied on. We linked with the school career liaison and discussed some job corp programs since he just turned 17...

A few months later, I received news that there was a ruckus in his unit. Amidst the mini-riot, a bigger guy pummeled "V" and my young apprentice found himself on lockdown for a couple of days. I spoke with him through the door window and all he could tell me was, "This ain't me, this ain't me...They throwin shade on me!" I slipped him my email address under the door because I knew he could leave for a placement at any time. He snagged it. Although there were resources at the school that could link him with the job program, I felt suited to help him as a mentor. Maybe I was just being "extra" as they say, but it was a rare case where I was willing to avail myself. Soon after, he ended up getting placed on a heavy dose of antidepressants until his court date. He came to class and sat there, somewhat lifeless. I made a typical joke that he would normally laugh at, but he was expressionless. He only shrugged his shoulders. I internalized it and kept passing out papers, moving forward with the lesson. It hurt to see him losing his will, his vitality. **But there was no time for expressing hurt in the center, for students and adults alike, hurt was a silent film being shown from within the heart vessel of each one of us that nobody spoke of**. Anything spoken in the center reflected the mandated norm of "keep it moving." I repeated with sarcasm to myself— *Keep passing out papers, collecting them, assessing them...*

keep carrying out the data production machine and hope that another youngster finds his way. Keep taking attendance. When "V" was finally released on his court date, he left without a trace and I could not catch up with him before his placement. He became another statistic, another captive soul, reprogrammed and packaged for the prison system. About 2 months later, I received a message at school that someone, a former resident, was trying to get in touch with me. "V" had called the school from an unknown location and asked for me, providing his first name. Nobody seemed to know where he called from and there was no number to call him back. I inquired, somewhat frantically, how I could find him. I found the placement center where he was assigned. I rang them and spoke to the receptionist. She reported that he had left "undocumented" several weeks earlier. I could only speculate as to where he would go. I hung up the phone, slowly walked to my room and sat in my chair, hoping he would call back. I looked around the silent room. I glanced at all of the papers stacked on my desk, the pencils neatly counted in a stack of twelve, next to the stacks of folders with hundreds of worksheets and assignment papers from all the residents. I thought of the trees that were killed. I thought of the hundreds of youth that kept coming into the center, year after year. I thought of wasted life and the drudgery of living in this world. A sense of great tragedy came over me. I thought of all of their stories—the ones known and unknown. The day passed. The week passed. The self-proclaimed "runaway" and his dream became a memory. But I know he is ok. I feel it. Sometimes I think of how when growing up we were always taught never to run away. Running away only makes things worse. But "V" knew, I swear, he knew where he was running to.

✦ CHAPTER 5 ✦

THE PANDEMIC HITS

The images of creeping plasmic colored graphics across maps noting the growth and path of a virus from China would be seared into my memory. During those first days in March when news stations in every room of the center blared the imminent spread of Covid-19, I ruminated over how to address it with the residents. The angst and uncertainty of the time no doubt added to an already tense prison environment. As the rising numbers of infections and deaths were preoccupying everyone, other teachers and students around the country evacuated their schools, beginning an era of virtual-based homeschooling. We, on the other hand, had to leave our students inside the prison walls. They and their counselors could not go home and were left in the center waiting while the virus crept its way through the city of Philadelphia like wildfire. It was a matter of time before someone brought it into the institution. That last day before evacuation leave, I spoke candidly with each of my classes. I told them what I knew and what I didn't know about this new strain of SARS. They had many questions. Some were indifferent. Some were more quiet than usual. The girls wanted to finish reading their poems about springtime.

Although the spread of the virus was looming and, in my mind, very serious, I consented and kept things light and breezy. When they finished their poems, I felt the need to leave them with something important, so we focused on the breath. I gave them instructions for the *1-minute breath* and a sample of the *breath of fire* to strengthen their immune system. We made masks out of paper towels and rubber bands and then the counselors lined them up to go back to their units. I looked at them one final time and thought about them having to stay in the center and endure what was to come. I was blessed to be able to leave, to go home and attempt to protect myself. We were all about to face a type of "inner journey," and semi-dramatic shift in our way of life. They would have to stick it out behind these walls. Before they left I looked them in the eyes and a message bubbled up from my core— "They'll see to it that you all have everything you need in here," and I pointed to the DHS quadrant. "Just make sure you have everything you need in *here*," and I placed my fist on my heart. They understood.

With the exception of about a dozen volunteer trips to print out materials and care packets for the students, **I didn't enter the school as a full-time teacher again until the following spring, one year later. Virtual schooling was a valiant attempt, but a virtual mess.** We did manage to work one on one with some students and there were instances of good days in the classroom. Were kids learning anything? Maybe a little. The 1-minute moment was sparse and it was virtually impossible to create the effect of the singing bowl through the meet-up channels of our online meeting. Quality group meditation relies upon the presence of a live facilitator, the sound and tone of their voice, the presence of their emotional content, their energy that connects with the partici-pants through subtle vibrations. Screens are distractions. Lessons, however, were still tailored toward spiritual responsibility and *beingness*. A few instances proved to me that covid was creating a slight deal of appreciation for others and life in general for those in the center.

When we returned in September of 2021, the pandemic was still raging, this time with new variants and the added vaccine dilemma. I had not taken it. My natural immunity had been tested a number of times and having studied the immuno-respiratory system for years, I decided that the vaccine was not for me. I did encourage others who were at risk to take it. Unfortunately, the powers that ruled weren't concerned with ones' antibody count or natural immunity even though two Israeli studies had verified that natural immunity was indeed more resistant to the virus than any of the vaccines. We had lost a dear member of the team from Covid and it was more than difficult to speak about natural immunity when people were lining up for the vaccine. Out of an obligation to authenticity, I had to be *about* what I said I was *about,* so I quietly faded into the background and observed the pandemic and vaccine hysteria from a place of non-reaction. Being the "meditation guy," however, wasn't a good enough safety measure and pressure mounted to get the shot. By that time, the sickness had taken a few rounds throughout the center, infecting dozens, maybe hundreds of students and counselors into the winter of 2022. Only 1 individual passed away, our staff member. Our schedule changed on a daily basis and there were often several isolated quarantine units unable to attend school. I kept my choice to myself for the most part and connected with the couple remaining staff who also defied the mandate and assumed responsibility for their own health and body. I discussed my position in one class and only because they insisted that I explain myself. I didn't sway anyone to stay away from the vax but only emphasized that there were natural ways of creating strong immunity. I did not identify with those protesting the mandate publicly, for they seemingly were not taking the responsibility of self-care to convincingly remain a non-threat. Freedom comes with responsibility.

The 2020-21 year was a serious time in the center and the residents seemed to tune in to class with a slight sense of urgency. We explored a variety of light controlled breathing exercises and I created more space to talk more about the effectiveness of conscious breathing in terms of the immune system, the health of organs and maintaining of energy. My co-teacher and some of the counselors seemed to be especially interested at this point. Something had definitely shifted from the beginning days of struggling to quiet the room so that I could ring the bowl. Whether it was due to the assault of the pandemic or a greater general sense of appreciation, the youth were interested and responsive. Wellness and self-care arose to the forefront of many minds. I, too, was more intentional and focused. Unlike most of the adults who were relying on the vaccine for immunity and the news for information, the young people and many of the counselors felt that something was not right and they were opting out for as long as they could. They instinctually sensed deception perhaps due to historical degradation and experimentation of the medical industry on African-Americans. I would estimate that nearly half did not agree with the vaccine mandate and there seemed to be a collective resistance from the whole DHS side of the center. My classes transformed into "literary" group therapy sessions. We studied rhetoric and persuasion the best we could—the students saw elements of it all in their music, politics as well as the media propaganda that seemed to be heightened more than ever. Students talked about how uneasy they felt about the future. One class was interested in the idea of people moving to Mars. After exploring the efforts and "philosophy" of Elon Musk and others, we decided it was best to wait it out here on earth. At all turns, I promoted the importance of being responsible, present and honoring the self. We talked about the wisdom of just observing all that was happening without getting emotionally wrapped up in it. Some days amidst the hopeless drudgery of it all, I would sit in front of them calmly, tell them what I was experiencing and allow the lesson to take shape as they responded to me. They wanted to be empowered in the truest sense, not indoctrinated. They responded to empathy with empathy. On the days when a few of them would express themselves through the written or spoken word, they showed a strong need to take care of others. They missed their families, they talked about how they just wanted to feel safe when they went home. Many started to sit up straight when I walked in the room—some of them even smiled. And despite the challenging chaotic circumstance of the whole pandemic presented on a daily basis and being socially outcast from the staff, for the first time throughout the day, I found myself smiling as well.

I would like to dedicate this paragraph to explain some of my final convictions and feelings with regards to the Covid-19 virus and vaccine mandate. With respect for the choices of all who read this book, I can say that each individual has a primary responsibility to honor their own intuition and inner voice. To take or not take the vaccine is a choice that goes beyond any social contract or societal responsibility. Until those in power, who mandated the vaccine, mandate equal housing, education, health care access for all, their deceptive mandating huge pharmaceutical and petro-chemical financial endeavors in the same vein of public health are remiss. Each has to investigate falsehood and truth. To date, no evidence can prove to me that Covid-19 could be passed from a non-host, asymptomatic individual to another person. This is never seen in nature and is not reflective of the innate immune system, which automatically elicits symptoms at the invasion of any viral contact. It was apparent to me that this was yet another divisive tool propagated by the world's most powerful industries to create future markets for themselves and ensure global dependency. The worldwide coercion utilized fear tactics and in the holy name of that which cannot be refuted— *medical science*. It was and is a highly developed plan that has been carried out quite well, forcing those individuals who were completely healthy and previously exposed to the virus, to take a synthetic mRNA-programmed injection— which itself is still cautioned by the creator of mRNA, Dr. Robert Malone, to be experimental in nature. Coinciding with the threats to the livelihood of those who retained their own sovereignty, this push for vaccines around the world has taken the form of totalitarian medical militarism. If there is one idea that arises of the many that have been missed, it is this. The virus, like all others, exists on a frequency, just as we do. As a glass breaks due to high pitched sounds, when a person's frequency is greater than the virus, the body will not house the virus. Because of the blessing of intense Pranayama and energetic practice, I assumed the responsibility of keeping myself in optimum health. I knew that if I were to deny the vaccine, I had to faithfully awaken before dawn every morning and do my 2 hour Sadhana (training). I not only live in accordance with the science of energy, I relied upon it to survive without a symptom thus far and not be careless around my fellow human beings. After 5 waves of the virus and still, no vaccine, I am satisfied to say that yes, I did. And after seeing those around me with the vaccine continue to get sick, I am baffled. I have become an advocate for natural immunity and strengthening the respiratory system through breathwork. Those that want to castigate me will not be the first and I can only say that I want us all to be well—black and white, left or right, vaxxed or not vax. Before we *see* truth, we must *be* truth.

Eventually the pathless path takes us onward and the

"writing on the wall" appeared for me by winter of 2022. It was time to resign and fulfill my role as a naturopath, assuming the warrior-shaman archetype. The ins and outs, ups and downs of the juvenile justice center forged my new identity with consciousness. Today, trauma related anxiety and associated disorders are my area of expertise. I don't know what people remember about me at the center nor do I care, frankly. There were many wonderful people there doing their own work on their own path. I do hope that the energy that channeled through me spread to the hearts of the incarcerated young people there. I'm now responding to my new identity within consciousness. As Victor Frankl said, **"It's not what we expect from life, but what life expects from us."**

◆ PART 2 ◆

THE SACRED SOCIOLOGY

INTRO

THE PERSPECTIVE OF SACRED SOCIOLOGY

This work has inspired me to develop and apply a perspective of "sacred sociology," which holds a view that humanity is a sacred entity, endowed with the collective consciousness that exists within each member of the human family, inextricably linking them with all others. Both individually and collectively, we are all ultimately striving for "the ABC's," that is, *Awareness, Balance* and *Compassion.* The constant striving toward these 3 exalted characteristics reflect our continuous need to mature into a stellar or godlike state of being. We are, in essence, no matter at what point we find ourselves on our soul's journey, seedlings to a new universe **Just as we watch our own children become "conscious" and grow into being,** *Consciousness* **watches collective humanity from the same perspective—evolving and involving toward oneness.**

Consciousness-based techniques, such as the use of conscious breathing and movement and guided meditation can act as catalysts for the progress of human consciousness on an individual and collective level—without the use of synthetic (*"without God"*) drugs nor religious doctrine. Sacred sociology holds that a balance between science and spirit is necessary. Thus, *awareness, balance and compassion* are sensible pillars of our collective sacred spirit. Evolving refers to what we learn when interacting with universal consciousness itself. Our *involving* refers to what we learn from interacting with others. In applying sacred sociology to education, trauma and juvenile justice, my view is that healing techniques integrated as educational practice would, at this juncture in time, benefit our young people and our society more than the traditionally aligned curriculum.

One aspect of this involving and evolving progression is rooted in the premise that breathing consciously with others and utilizing certain associated techniques creates a common experience that transcends any social identity— be it race, religion, gender or social status/class. The health benefits of specific breathing techniques are, of course, exponential, and its manifestations are universal. Sacred sociology reaches beyond positivist social science and extends into the wellness fields because the sacredness and social experience of humanity cannot be separated from the wellness of humanity—or its harmonious existence with the planet and all living things. Essentially, sacred sociology integrates spirit science into social theory and social research methods. The ideals of a common "synchro-destiny" of humanity and a collective movement toward a greater human consciousness are at the core of this perspective. I find that it is time to recognize the sacredness of humanity by recognizing its cosmic dream and unconscious tendency toward *awareness, balance* and *compassion*. This is the time, more than ever, that we need to fight with ferocity for the things that bind us together as human beings. There is certainly plenty that divides us. In this work, I can affirm 3 major findings or ideas that have presented themselves as very real and relevant, observable phenomena emerging from the research:

1. The legacy of corporate-capitalist, patriarchal/ monotheistic institutions, including criminal justice, health care and education, is directly contributing to the "school to prison pipeline" and the criminal- ization of the average American, particularly the impoverished, the African-American (i.e "black") and Hispanic (i.e "brown") underclass and most recently young women.

2. Beingness-based meditation, particularly, the "1- minute moment" and breath work can serve as a (secular) form of trauma-informed therapy in schools, programs and detention centers because it promotes emotional intelligence, self-efficacy and social harmony, and innately promotes a momentary transcendence of race, gender and religion, creating essential components for personal development and a cohesive school culture.

3. There is an emerging underlying consciousness among those of the urban poor that wants to move beyond poverty, violence and even race-conscious- ness toward a more spiritually aware, cooperative society with opportunities for all to work and exist in harmony.

The following is my own qualitative memoir that highlights the interactions of certain social dynamics as I experienced them in the center. They are not at the crux of the purpose in these writings, but provide an illuminating framework that exposes a more "involving" aspect of these findings as they relate to important sociological topics of the day. The variables of *race, gender* and *spirituality* are of great significance in all human societies, with Philadelphia being the epitome of pluralistic urban America. These social groupings, identity roles or "constructs," form the bedrock of consciousness for so many, and such identities have been reinforced through our socio-political and cultural history. For disenfranchised groups such as racial or religious minorities, women, LGBTQ, and impoverished people, such an identity presents an everyday hindrance toward economic progress and total integration into American society or privileges within that society. This work focuses on disenfranchised groups—particularly impoverished African American males, and recognizes the social reality of those at risk of existing within a circumstance of inequality. In a macro sense, we can recognize the sacredness of humanity as an essential principle of transcending social constructs as barriers while respecting culture as well as individualism.

The future of our species seems to very much depend on the recognition of our common human experiences that inextricably bind us together beyond race, nation, class, religion or gender. It was, however, these social categories that caused difficult or unavoidable dialogues and interactions with my students that led me to a greater understanding of myself, them, culture, history and most importantly, the need for change...It was our ability to become collectively conscious of our breath and observe the influence upon a daily ritual that bonded us despite the presence of social constructs. It was our ability, also, to recognize common archetypes and conscious human experiences that we could all relate to, despite our differences. **When issues of race or gender or any other political-social issue arose, I honored and discussed them thoroughly, but I *de-emphasized* their relevance compared to adopting a lens of consciousness that we can call "oneness."** I did emphasize what created commonality—such as the use of *empathy*, the expressions of human emotions and discussion of archetypal values (such as that of a *warrior, sage* or a *queen*) or even the response to art or music that had a universal sound or message. It was not my *maleness* or *whiteness* or *professionalism* or even my credentials that allowed me to connect and better teach or relate to my students. It was my humanity. I was received, accepted, and, in many cases, respected by these residents because I focused on the things that created commonality, most significantly, the sacred and subtle act of collectively controlling our breath.

On the Bricks

(a brief historical, socio-economic snapshot of Philadelphia)

Philadelphia's social and ethnic diversity flourishes, as any other international city. Within that diversity, however, is a highly stratified, polarized urban populace that is now experiencing the breadth of "neo-liberal" policy changes implemented by a new democratic party agenda as of 2022. This includes an allotment of more resources to the impoverished and disenfranchised communities, public services, as well as more contracts to unionized construction groups. The money and resource flow has changed dramatically since the Trump era and an emphasis on equity and inclusion has now taken shape in a city that desperately needed it. A city of continual mass immigration, like many has seen the "pour" morph into a trickle. Although Philadelphia attains roughly an %11 immigrant population, the incoming immigrant population has steadily declined since the late 1990's. The majority of these immigrants come today from west Africa, parts of Asia (Indonesia, Laos, China and Vietnam), central America (Honduras, Guatemala and Mexico), while a %13 of the city claims a 2nd generation Puerto Rican or Caribbean cultural heritage. %42 of the city is African American while %41 is white or white ethnic (Italian, Polish, Russian etc..)

In some ways, the challenges currently facing impoverished black Philadelphia are far worse than the problems outlined by W.E.B. Dubois in his famous 1899 work, *The Philadelphia Negro*. While, arguably, civil rights, educational access and technology (through the accessibility to information) has presented a broader framework of options for descendants of slaves, other tragic areas of difficulty have arisen. Gun violence, drug use, police brutality, the breakdown of the family unit and mass incarceration have emerged as debilitating issues in black neighborhoods, especially in the past 50 years. The famous MOVE Crisis that ended in 1985 with the killing of 11 sovereign community organizers (including 5 children) is seared into the memory of black Philadelphia. Hundreds were relocated after blocks of a west Philly neighborhood were burned from a fire bomb dropped by helicopter. The tragedy and horrific use of power paralleled the elimination of the black panther leaders of the early 1970's. This systematic brutality demonstrates how the black community was and is being purposefully destroyed and the black consciousness movement was institutionally neutralized during the late civil rights era. Recently, "gentrification" has fueled de facto segregation and the school to prison pipeline has become an unfortunate backlash of public education. While Philadelphia and its suburbs attain a substantial working and middle-class element, the majority is impoverished or working poor. One could argue that police violence has increased as well, but the lack of valid statistics from past era's (one without cell phone cameras) leaves that up for dispute. Nonetheless, a long history of police brutality exists within the city limits. Philadelphia is the 4th "most segregated big city" in the country, according to Phillymagazine.com in December of 2021.

Despite an increase in net-income and a rise in millionaires in the city, Philly is still classified as the "poorest big city in America." According to the census data of 2020, it carried a %25.7 poverty rate, which is the highest of the ten largest cities in America. While since 2010, substantial economic growth has surfaced in the city, poverty is still one of the core social issues. Black Philadelphia was at a %30 poverty rate, while white Philadelphia at %15. The Hispanic rate was at a striking %39. Perhaps surprisingly, Asian and Pacific Islander was at %32. An alarming %45 of impoverished females were unemployed. Philadelphia's growing population (average .45 growth rate since 2010) is unfortunately outpacing job growth. Of course, it does have the highest wage taxes in the country. Median household income was $45.9, but the city's impoverished neighborhoods struggle to yield half of that. Most of the income and wage increase by percentage are representative of those living in the downtown districts or the middle to affluent northwest quadrant of the city, with a high influx of New York transplants bringing an unprecedented amount of wealth to central gentrifying areas such as Northern Liberties, Fishtown and Port Richmond. South Philadelphia is also seeing a relatively large influx of wealth due to the New York exodus and building of continuous high end residencies. The poverty that crosses ethnic and racial lines, does not reflect those lines in Philadelphia's Juvenile Justice system.

Why, if poverty rates of Asians and Hispanics are even higher than African Americans, are an average of %90 of residents of Philadelphia's Juvenile Justice Center black? Is poverty not the issue? Why are black youth committing more crime? Is it by systemic design? Is it a lack of choices? A lack of family or community stability? Racism? These are not questions that can be answered by mere speculation. A thorough study of crime in Philadelphia might suffice. Perhaps it involves the study of police, socio-political topics and a countless number of variables that interact on a macro level.

This need for investigation is at the core of socio-economic issues in cities around the country. My work is not focusing on answering these questions. They are, however, very funda-mental and their implications are far-reaching—especially when delving into the issues of incarcerated young people in the city of Philadelphia.

✦ CHAPTER 6 ✦

RELIGION AND SPIRITUALITY

The many mornings when I would appear bright eyed and bushy-tailed on the unit or in our 1st period class, I was met with depressing, haunting looks of despair and fear. So many of the residents had witnessed death and tragedy in many forms, so many feared they were next. This "mortality anxiety" loomed over one after another and it surfaced in so many different ways. How could I expect them to write or become excited about learning? To think critically? Most were hurt and trying to come to terms with larger questions that could explain the fear of dying young, the loss of a loved one, the seeming hopelessness of life. It took me a while before I realized my method of addressing this type of anxiety was slightly off. A silent minute of meditation or mindfulness was not quite what was needed unless it included guided coping skills or simple instruction. The deep sense of grief for those who just lost their cousin, buried their sister or saw their father get shot was able to creep in during a moment of silence, which was too long of a moment. This is why the *1-minute moment* worked well. It could be tailored to 30 seconds or any other time frame. There was no religious or spiritual exploration needed, just practical application that brought a sense of stability and self-regulation. In addition, instilling a sense of spiritual responsibility proved tremendously valuable. This came from dozens of lessons (many of which are shared in later chapters) diving into the internal and external conflicts and perceptions of these students' sense of responsibility to themselves, their communities, their planet. In defining spirituality for this section, I will divulge all of that in which Emile Durkheim described as the "sacred" or what others deemed inextricably linked to a higher power beyond human control. We can now venture into that which the students and adults at the center viewed as sacred and adopt a lens of religious or spiritual aspects of their perspectives and experiences.

One day during the Covid epidemic, a case worker who was from the streets of South Philly volunteered to come in while I sat at my computer at home. She played a music video, "Ghetto Angel," for them and set up a writing prompt where they could express their own story of loss. It was superb. In my 3 years of teaching there, I never accumulated such levels of completed, written material. They wrote "bars" (rhymes) that would inspire even the worst critics of rap music. Their favorite line from Ghetto Angel, unanimously, was "I end up cryin' even on a good day(sic), why do I always question God, but I never pray?"

The Search for Something

It's common to see young people walking around Philadelphia wearing all black with black hoodie sweatshirts pulled over their heads or with shirts that say things like "trust nobody" or "only God can judge me." There is a fatalistic spiritual reference point in the lives of many who struggle economically or dwell in neighborhoods associated with violence. The psychology of *blackness* and its association with darkness or negativity is an interesting and perhaps, unfortunate parallel, but one to be explored. One observation that I could conclusively generalize was that no matter their predicament, most of the residents had an ever-present sense that there was an unseen higher power at work—even if they felt that higher power was working against them. **Very rarely did I encounter a feeling of disbelief in the spiritual domain or an abandonment from the awareness of a higher power. There was, however, an embedded distrust, and an overriding fear.** I would go so far as to say that most, including the religious (mainly Christian and Muslim) saw God as an omnipotent parent that was punishing them for their shortcomings. There was a lack of trust, in God—I would speculate due to the lack of trust in the world and ultimately, in self. Their lack of trust in the world perhaps created resentment, but that resentment seemed to simultaneously fuel a deep longing for someone or something *to* trust. One student wrote in his journal:

"I don't trust too many people because they do me wrong. Every time I trust someone, they do me dirty. Like someone snitched on me for something I didn't do to get in here. Some #$%^& on my block clutch and we ride together, but you never know...Plus sometimes I feel like if I trust God, he just gonna do me wrong too..." H.N, 2018

One thing was certain was that when the lights went out at night, the residents craved something to believe in. Their entangled outstretched inner child reached for any stable entity or idea that revealed a greater meaning. Yet, they masked their need for divine love with a slew of robust cultural folkways that demonstrated their love for others but kept it within strict parameters. An example of this was their sturdy handshake that ended with a quick mutual snap of the fingers, a real *Philly* thing. They searched both internally and externally for somewhere to hang their hopes, as seen in their writings, their raps, their tattoos, and heard in their words. Names of fallen relatives or friends were etched into their forearms, necks and any given nearby desk in all manner of fonts and sizes. They were in need of a code to live by. As noted by my co-teacher at one point, the number one book that the boys would gravitate to was "the Four Agreements" by Carlos Ruiz, a philosophical treatise on Indigenous spiritual wisdom of Central America that laid out a foundation for how to act with self-awareness. It was 4 simple agreements, but it provided them with an ethical compass from where to begin.

A fatalistic street bike culture dominates the cityscape where the youth often parade in groups through city streets on loud *supermoto* bikes with short mufflers and high RPMs, claiming their space in a city that has typically oppressed their voice. So many are injured on these bikes, yet along with other dangerous rites of passage, it is a way to connect with something greater. Riding gives an observable freedom and each time a young man from the neighborhood rides with a "click" (group), he believes in his click, his neighborhood. It becomes a type of religion. One wrote,

"When I'm riding its good when they see me. That's why I ride. Also, it gives me a chance to feel myself free and fast where I can just let go. I don't think it's dangerous it's what we do." H.N, 2022

The disregard for danger or safety reflected a fatalistic view, but the adoration of the rite of riding reflected a necessary cultural need to establish a rite of passage. I often shared the YouTube footage of the *Egbe* rite of passage, a West African tradition re-established in Baltimore, where young people pass into adulthood with prayer, blessings from the elders and a test of endurance. Riding bikes, to me, showed a longing for this type of structured and meaningful passage into adulthood that "proved" worth. As they wanted to be seen on the dangerous streets maneuvering their bikes, they wanted to be seen by their community, their elders and their God, overcoming fear and becoming an adult.

Religion Meets Meditation

Both the Christian and Muslim traditions are held in high regard in the black community and the black Muslim population has been firmly rooted in Philadelphia since the civil rights movements of the 1960's. A report in 2019 confirms that "We find that black Muslims experience greater residential disadvantages than non-Muslims in Philadelphia... Moreover, black Muslims face a double disadvantage due to both their race and their religion." Religious counselors, both Christian and Muslim would visit on the weekends and lead prayer sessions, which quite a few of the residents participated in. Some Muslim students questioned my meditation sessions and a few declined to participate. "We don't meditate, we pray." I would respond, "I understand, this is always optional...You are welcome to pray or take a moment of silence if you would like." At worst, there was an instance where I received a look of disdain from a Muslim counselor when doing the meditation, but, perhaps not surprisingly, most of them appreciated the moment. Although some initially took offense to the meditation and singing bowl, my Muslim students were often the most participatory of all. During Ramadan, many would be literally hanging their head, tired from fasting, but most would perk up for the meditative minute and attempt their conscious breathing. They surely showed an undeniable loyalty and sometimes devotion to something "greater than themselves." For whatever reason, there were far less *Kufi's* worn by 2022, then when I began in 2017.

Subsequently, the residents continuously wanted to talk about the nature of God and life. A need to recognize a higher force seemed to envelope both life in the streets and the confines of the youth center. Some would quote the *Qur'an* or Bible for me when an overlapping idea between beingness and religion emerged. Many of my philosophical tenets that arose in the room, whether that of spiritual responsibility or universal consciousness, were questioned through the lens of religion. One time I heard, "Muslims don't believe in spirituality, we believe in the teachings of the prophet." We effectively listed some of the core teaches of Islam and the prophet Muhammad and I had the students interpret them for me, culminating the lesson with a comparison between concepts. Most would shy away from religious debate and teachers certainly discouraged it. I saw spiritual responsibility as an inclusive approach. When students were able to understand the concept of spiritual responsibility by learning it from the ground up, they immediately felt able to relate and connect with the commonality of all of our paths. Instead of presenting the idea as a spiritual concept, I presented it in terms of everyday life, everyday values and important choices. We started with who we cared about and why they were important to us. We defined the difference between reacting and responding. Such questions as, what are the areas of our lives where we show personal responsibility and where can it be improved? Questions like these had a moral undertone, but never needed to be identified as religious. Discipline, character, emotional intelligence, self-efficacy and self-awareness are arenas where we all could apply a little self-reflection—this is a core idea of spiritual responsibility. The only thing spiritual about it is that it involves an awakening of the inner voice, a growth of our *beingness*.

Meditation and the 1-minute moment, innately sparked discussion about spiritual beliefs. I saw my role was to keep things neutral and allow them to discover their own inner voice. It was up to them if they wanted to label that voice. Successful students, in their classwork and spiritual responsibility, identified with consciousness, not with the social pressures of those around them. These students were the ones' who could observe themselves, manage their emotions and think independently. Meditation was a high order activity, not a therapeutic modification like the 1-minute moment. Those who could manage the stillness, the mental direction and the will to breathe consciously were inquisitive and avoided debate or minimizing of the activity. It was important to me to include all perspectives, not because it was politically correct, but because it was the only way to move forward and onward with the participation of the group in class. The residents knew what I was about. When I showed them that I would not leave them behind, despite how they felt about the philosophy, they moved forward with me. They bought in. More interested in learning about spirituality than practicing it, the experience of inner exploration *in school* showed them that they were connected to something greater, that they mattered.

I got a message one day from the digital sound teacher that there was a resident asking about me and wanted to learn about meditation. I was in my free period so I decided to walk over to her room. It was J.K, the same resident who flipped over his table during meditation near the start of my time at the school. His eyes lit up when he saw me and I'm not sure if he thought I would be mad at him, but I smiled and greeted him with a positive vibe. He had come back into the center a year or so later. Despite having some serious emotional issues, he was in deep pursuit of making meaning in his life. When he returned this 2nd time, he was no longer Jewish, but Muslim, and wore a Kufi. It wasn't uncommon for residents to change religions or to convert to Islam during their time in the youth.

J.K. had shown me early on that meditation wasn't for everyone and meditating in a group setting with young people was sure to trigger some imbalances and maybe even trigger episodes, or at least a social-political reverb. Ironically, he wanted to delve deeper into meditation during our second meeting. From what I could deduce, he was still experiencing trauma-related anxiety and he needed intense one on one intervention, which I was not able to provide. He was in the midst of spiritual warfare within himself. His studies did not concern him so much because profound questions lay in the forefront of his conscious experience. What happens when those questions cannot be addressed? Is he expected to dissociate his experience at school with the spiritual turmoil that fixated at the core of his being?

Despite my efforts to keep the 1-minute moment a secular practice, the spiritual implication and substance of it as a form of "meditation" was always begging for interjection. It wasn't long before I had prepared answers for so many common questions directed at me—such as, "What God do you believe in? Do you pray? I thought meditation was for Buddhists?" Perhaps the most memorable and common question I would get was, "Is meditation prayer? I stumbled around the response to this many a day and always tried to answer it the politically correct fashion, but finally found the best way to respond through an adage that I came across later in my final year—"To me, prayer is like talking to God, while meditation is listening."

The Singing Bowl

The Tibetan singing bowl possessed a magical quality in the classroom and was the material focal point of our *1-minute moment*. Once I was able to properly relegate its relevance within the ritual, the students were drawn to it. The bowl possessed an energetic component and, in itself, held the potential of creating a half-hour long conversation. I eventually gathered that students who wanted to learn more about meditation but didn't know what to ask, would 1st ask questions about the bowl. It could surely inspire a discussion about everything—from the price, to the unique sound that it made. So many wanted to hold it or strike it either for sensual stimulation, attention or just to establish some sort of recognized role in the room I imagine. The sound and the frequencies that subtly transformed the room surely did have a neurological or even metaphysical effect. It was an automatic moment of pause and observation. I remember ringing it sometimes and just seeing students pop their heads up and look around. Some began to look around, some to look within. Either way, it was a signal to take a step back and reflect on something larger at hand. I only experienced a few complaints about the actual sound of the bowl and in those cases, the individuals eventually grew fond of it after a few sessions. From the onset, some of the youth had no idea what the bowl was when I was ringing it or had never tried meditation before in their life, but they innately knew that when the bell rang, a certain sacred quality fell upon the moment. Most students respected that moment and even if they wanted to rupture the whole process, hecklers waited until the resonance of the bell was long past. No matter how loud I would raise my voice or a counselor would try to intervene and quell the chatter before class, a slight tapping of the bowl had the effect of a "call to prayer." Perhaps that's why the Muslim students responded with such consistency. Upon hearing it, students would hush one another to assume some silence and or stillness before meditation began. One time, I accidentally left the sanctified metallic piece in the room where I taught last and a student immediately brought it to the counselor for them to give to me—He wouldn't let anyone else touch it. A student illustrates the intriguing mystery that the bowl represented in a journal response below. Perhaps the bowl represented the unknown— a realm that the education system doesn't acknowledge, but students are hungry to explore.

"The bowl sends out vibrations. We can feel them and we know they're real because everyone feels good when the bowl rings...The sound is like a mystery and you can't really explain it to anyone you just have to hear it..." T.W. 2019

Who Stole the Soul?

Practicing the *1-minute moment* has reiterated for me that the education system is and has become far too secular. In an effort to quell dogma and keep religion out of schools, we have denied the influence of the spirit and the crucial knowledge that it endows us with. Public education practice has reflected such paranoia of offending religious groups so that it has whitewashed all influence of personal wellness and spiritual connectedness when learning. Just as the body, through the lens of medical science, has been reduced to a molecular /atomic working organism, the curriculum of most public schools has been reduced to another blueprint for capitalistic growth. It is merely a mundane, economically and socio-politically driven set of predictable lessons requiring predict-able outcomes. Nothing can be further from the universal truth. It is void of the magic of learning, spontaneity and the eternal promise of knowledge. It is void of recognizing the universe within. Educational theoretical perspective (for example, The Danielson framework), finds that every moment of every class period needs to be filled with a hyper-charged exchange of academic information. There is no time allotment for observation or conscious reflection. While some may say that school is not the place for these things, I would respond by asking them why then, young people are more depressed, anxious and traumatized than ever? Their place of learning and socialization, where they spend nearly most of their time, is void of any promotion of self-awareness, collective or universal consciousness or sacred ideals—such as gratitude or hope. **I challenge anyone reading this book to show me a public school system that teaches, within its curriculum, the importance of cooperation, love, compassion or collective human identity. Are these *religious* concepts only?** In a world of constant cultural and ethical debate, we have become unable to move forward in educational philosophy with the common ideals that make us human. Any such components are practically (and I would say purposefully) avoided in public education and grouped with religious ideology, when in fact, they can be quite non-religious. Some may conclude that students can't learn if they are focused on themselves. I would say that self-awareness broadens the capacity in which students can store knowledge and make learning meaningful. When they learn who they are, they cannot be indoctrinated. Additionally, when they are involving themselves and learning from each other, seeing the interconnectedness of all people, they gain a sense of family, of community and of collective responsibility. When this happens, they will become more oriented toward what is important to learn and pertinent in their lives as well as how they can achieve success and happiness by attaining all forms of knowledge. Beyond the rows of seated chairs and desks, they can involve and evolve as a whole person.

By denying our spiritual essence and emphasizing the metaverse as the ultimate reference for information, we have created a sterile world where children long for meaning and a true sense of joy with regards to being who they are. Before all, a student needs to *feel* well enough to be motivated to learn, to become responsible. How can one value and or attain information if their brain isn't working optimally with proper neural connectivity and bi-lateral channels of awareness? How can they make information meaningful if their spirit is not ignited? How can we demand that students retain information if their spirit is not moved by its relevance? How and when are they trained to embody the mental abilities of patience, focus or discipline which will help them retain knowledge? It is the spiritual wellness of a young person that can begin to provide them with the wisdom needed to deal with life's challenges and unanswered questions. They need this more than any textbook, literary piece or mathematical equation that is presented to them. Keeping our spirit or soul out of anything results in an operationalized, overly rational and robotic existence, whether the presence of God is recognized or not. Keeping our spirit out is keeping our humanity out. It seems that at this point, education is doing more harm than good for the young autodidactic who truly seeks knowledge...

◆ CHAPTER 7 ◆

GENDER

In 2017, the residential placement rate for boys was more than five times that for girls. Eighty-five percent of children in residential placement were male

During the heightened era of social change surrounding gender politics during the Obama, Trump and Biden administrations, we saw surfacing transgender awareness, the residue of a feminist awakening through the *#metoo movement* and the massive emergence of women(especially African-American) in power as political figures and beyond. Philadelphia traditionally experienced a historical blossoming of social movements, often occurring at a grass roots level with the needs and struggles of disenfranchised groups and or working people. Philadelphia neighborhoods have been a proud hub of democratic resistance to oppression—and, unfortunately, the receivers of violent backlash from authoritative regimes that reacted to them. From the brief, but revolutionary acts of the Black Panthers into the early 1970's, to the MOVE Crisis into the 1980's to the occupy movement, the women's movement, a long-standing housing movement, reparations, and in most recent times, tumultuous action against police brutality, Chinatowns' fight for survival,

Philly's rugged resilience and tendency toward resistance is clearly part of its cultural history. The African-American community has been at the crux of these movements, but one would be wrong, of course, to assume that the black community, as a whole, is in agreement about all of these issues. The politics of gender has certainly stood out as one of the divisive issues. The juxtaposition of beliefs among traditional African-American Christians and Muslims, black feminists, and LGBTQ advocates has created lines of division in the community that are reflected throughout the country across race and religion. To see how this both pressurized and created relationships in the youth center at times was quite interesting. Which identity, race or gender was most important to students, seemed to vary based on that which was under scrutiny.

Social Identity

Spiritual identity is something that, to me, is something that maybe observed on the surface by others, but ultimately is defined by an individual and their relationship with spirit or Consciousness. And so spiritual identity is both manifested inward with a relationship to a higher power and projected outward as an appearance to others. Social identity, however, literally, "happens" all around us—whether we work in a doctor's office or a youth detention center. It is the perception of how roles that we play, brother, mother, teacher, preacher define who we are. Our social identity runs as deep as we allow it in terms of its importance in our lives. Why is it important? Many would argue that it forms the basis of our perspective of the world around us. George Herbert Mead is known for his fascinating work on *The Self* and the difference between the *I* and *me*, two symbolic facets of our identity. Many in his school of thought felt that our identity was the basis for all of our interactions with others. Lately, of course, identity has been highly politicized. How we view ourselves and how others view us is at the heart of many social movements of the day. Identity, like all constructs, is real if we make it real. It certainly can influence accessibility to social status or equity on a variety of levels in our highly stratified society, especially if it refers to an ascribed role, which we have no control over, such as race. Although it can be a major part of our social reality, to me, "identity politics" provides few answers to life's profound questions and certainly does not overshadow spiritual identity in the least bit. The political arena is filled with banter and disagreement about abstract roles that we play based on the context of our surroundings. It plays into our duality—viewing two sides as opposing each other. It also plays into our sympathy if our identity enables us to feel "bad" for ourselves or someone else. **Knowing this, it is still nearly impossible to avoid the politically-charged identity discussions within our highly politicized society.** That said, gender is still defined as characteristics of a male and or female that are socially constructed. This construction is ever changing and ever demanding new ways of thinking about boys and girls, men and women. In juvenile justice based education, there was very little dialogue about it, only subtle acceptance of whoever wants to affirm their sexual orientation or identity.

The Politics of Gender

The politics of gender identity was another constant on the unit and in the classroom, but held a distinct discreteness. Unless the topic arose, it is rarely spoken about by students. I found that students didn't care or judge others overtly with regards to their sexuality, but if given a writing prompt or discussion about gender politics, many of them would have opinionated views. I saw my role as one who would try best to emulate a balance through the values of justice, responsibility and awareness. I was not there to promote the #metoo movement, transgender awareness or any other political objective, but I was someone who could speak of my own journey as a man and what I had learned as well as what being a man in 2020 meant to me and other people in my life. **While it was probably best to emphasize just being a "good human being," I saw my role as a voice of manhood and balanced masculinity in a setting where it was needed.** In an educational system that was seeing a loss of male teachers, the boys craved reliable and credible male voices who would reflect on their own path, whatever that path was like. There was also a shortage of male counselors on the DHS side and often women would have to supervise all male units. This had its advantages, but at times posed great challenges. I witnessed grown women thrown to the floor while breaking up fights between 17-year-old boys. These ladies were true warriors and also showed the tough love and care that many of the boys needed in place of their mother. Some amazing counselors and teachers contributed to the training of these young men and women, of course, and *genderization* was a large part of their socialization and education. The demand for any influential elders was greater than the supply, so it was good to just hear a positive voice in most instances—whether that voice was politically correct or in line with certain political agendas was a secondary concern, at least on the surface for most that worked with the youth. If a lady counselor began to speak to the young men about what young men need to think about, I may have disagreed with some things, but I certainly felt no right to intervene. Her intentions were well received and often she knew, more than anybody, what was needed from young men in the world she lived in..

There were observable differences in the perceptions of gender roles in both boys and girl's classes. One morning with an all-male unit, a conversation ensued between a special education teacher and counselor, both African American, concerning the issue of gender and women's' rights. The counselor, a hardened, resourceful and educated black man ridiculed the feminist movement and the lack of *feminity* in Black women, and the "false promise" of a neo-liberal education that has emasculated and criminalized young men. **He bashed LGBT rights and voiced the concern that gayness was being "pushed" upon young black men as gangsterism and drugs were. The young men on his unit revered him as a godlike figure and mentor.** He was tough on them, but took time to reveal the world to them from his perspective. He also was known to provide legitimate employment on occasion. The teacher took a defensive position and accused black men of (sic.) letting their anger and lack of acceptance inhibit their growth or opportunities through education. She also accused him of being hateful and closed minded. The conversation got very heated. I decided it was best to listen. The boys chimed in and to even out the playing field, I wrote the word "gender" on the board and defined it as a "social construct." Of course, I turned around to explain these concepts, the difference between masculinity and manhood etc.. Unfortunately, it was too late at that point and very few were in an "academic discussion" state of mind! I heard the frustrations within the black community among men and women. I reflected on the white community, the role of spirituality, the politics of identity. I agreed with some points on both sides, but eventually realized that generalizations are too difficult to support in such a dialogue and maybe it was best to keep the weatherman indoors. My responsibility was to work on myself and my job was to share my gifts with those who could benefit from them. Though tempting, I found that resisting a position in these arguments was best. In prison, everyone is pointing fingers, that is one reason why prisons exist in the first place.

Sexual Trauma

The ugly reality of sexual trauma was a major contributor of much of the TRA in the center. Whether it was with young men or women, the memories of sexual aggression, rape, incest or witnessing of any of it lay a heavy toll on many. I can say only that this trauma carried over more than many realize—from the act of using the bathroom to being involved in a quasi-related discussion. It is not a statistic that I have researched but sexual trauma in poor communities seems to be another subject swept under the rug until recently. I'm not so sure accurate statistics are even available. It is one of the more potent forms of trauma because it deals with areas of fear and sexuality, which are inextricably linked as our two greatest biological imperatives—self-preservation and repro-duction. Without these imperatives, our species would not have evolved and survived. Being that our sexuality is so intertwined with love and intimacy, it's exceptionally trauma-tizing when that part of our psyche is hurt or damaged. So, the impact of such disturbances creates devastating wounds in the emotional body and physiological systems—especially, of course, the nervous system. Our *sacral chakra*, associated with the reproductive system and glands is also our portal of creativity. It is in our sacral chakra where we spawn new ideas and emotions that reflect our deepest yearnings for pleasure. When someone, especially a child, experiences a block in that area due to trauma, it not only may inhibit them sexually or diminish an ability to experience pleasure, but it may carry over to lessen an ability to create, innovate or bring into fruition that which can essentially heal. It may block someone from being artistic, feminine, masculine, loving, playful or spontaneous.

Certainly, most cases where sexual trauma was a factor in the lives of many of these young men and women, it was not treated or addressed. It may have been discussed at some point in time with a social worker or even a psychologist, but these exchanges most likely touched upon the surface of the issue, as usual, treating only symptoms, not repairing emotional or energetic ruptures that have caused the damage. A naturopathic or holistic view of sexual trauma involves a heavy emphasis on self-nurturing and self-awareness. One technique that I used on occasion with my *one on one* group was that of the "inner smile." (see *Inner smile* Chapter 10)

The Girl Units

For a white male teacher, identity politics played out in nearly every interactive dynamic, especially within the "girl units," as they were called. Most of these young ladies were forging a battle for their identity—coping with (1) a need for safety in an unsafe world, (2) an emerging sexuality within a culture that colonized the female black body, tremendous peer pressure, as well as cultural norms and (3) expectations that posed few options for them besides fulfilling a status-oriented role as a young mother. While many of the girls couldn't articulate some of these challenges, there was certainly a subconscious awareness that they existed. With all of these factors at play, life for them in youth was one dimensional. Survive and get out. When I looked at their eyes in the morning as they sauntered into my room, I saw struggling and confused teens trying to find their own inner beauty and peace while defending their honor and identity. I saw confusion and anger. **For every girl that bubbled with a bit of enthusiasm from time to time, there were 3 who boiled with resentment.**

Undoubtedly, the imprisoned girls reflected complex and rich dynamics of gender that reflected the workings of a culture and community immersed in inner turmoil. About ⅕ of our residents identified as female and they, of course, were isolated from contact with the males, except through a distant gaze through the cafeteria or classroom window. In the evenings, it was well known that some would talk to each other through the air vents or follow up and slip notes for each other in obscure places. In a group setting amongst the boys, each individual girl was considered either physically desirable or worthless. Not surprisingly, girls who were desirable were given names by their body parts or skin tone and were all referred to in a derivative of "bitch" or "ho." One of the milder references was that of "spicey." What did I do to intervene? I took each case differently and always held a standard line of acceptability. My first "go to" was always in reference to a woman in the life of the young man who was being offensive. Would your mother like to hear you refer to a girl in that way?" Most young men could consciously make the connection to the love and respect they held for their mother to ideally carry over to their romantic interest. Unfortunately, cultural lag often got in the way. Some days it was not my place to intervene and or was a battle that I didn't have the strength for because it was so normalized. These references may strike you as offensive or generalized, but the unfortunate fact is that I rarely heard the term "girl" and or certainly "sister," "queen," or "lady." on the male unit in reference to the opposite gender. The street *trap* mentality certainly was void of the divine feminine principle and deemed that "bitches" were either "sturdy" (attractive) or "hit" (unattractive). I'm guessing that social media culture of "likes" and "dislikes" directly influenced these phenomena rather than curb them, but they began, as many of us know, far before the advent of Instagram...And we know that it exists not just in the streets of Philadelphia, but the hallways of Ivy league fraternity houses.

I had found a letter or two written to a girl from a male admirer and the tone and verbiage used was very physical and sensual, but very deferential. Individually and privately, of course, the boys expressed their desire for love with much less sensuality. This serves as a reminder that the group mentality can spell out a very different story in reference to many topics and social situations. Part of asserting the male identity in an ultra-masculine culture is being able to speak of women in ways that affirm your dominance or physical judgment over them. That's not to say that respectful or even adorational references aren't normal as well, especially with older men. Let me first elaborate on the observations of the girl unit first, now that some important information has been shared.

I found most of the girls to be intimidated, introverted and, below the surface, afraid of what they had gotten themselves into in terms of the criminal justice system. Most of them still retained many layers within their personalities, but protected themselves from the many angles of emotional or physical attack that was constantly present. In a 7-day week, a single girl could adopt a different daily mode of sweet, quiet, motivated, innocent, inspired, as well as indifferent, perturbed, resentful and hostile. They spoke of the young men in coded language and on much fewer instances than what I observed on the boys units. Their references toward the boys could be considered just as denigrating, not sexually, but socially and culturally, by referring to them "nigga's." Conjunctly, I rarely heard boys referred to as anything differently amongst their peers.

The girls conveyed to me that there was always more to

their story than met the eye. Quite a few were exploring their own sexual identity and I had two students who were in the process of changing genders form male to female. The girls seemed to accept gender-related deviance and or homosexuality from my general observation, and certainly more open to discussion about gender-related issues. **They often called each other "bro," and delighted in the thought of acting with a masculine "lean" at any given moment (making fists, rolling up their sleeves, etc...)**

Having on occasion, opened up a dialogue about perception of the girls towards themselves and each other, I found that I could only scratch the surface of layers of a fragile or damaged identity. The emotional scars and a masked existence that plagued these young teens ran deep. In many of their own minds, they had to be *bitches*—and were (at least on the surface) not so bothered that people thought of them as such. That potential to be mean, defiant, defensive or conniving equated to a certain quality of resilience. I had a student say to me in a light-hearted manner, *"Mr. B, I don't care if she call me a bitch because that's what we are, but if you call me one, Ima steal (punch) you."* As such, this single line in the sand informs us of a compromised layer of existence—one where "bitch" and "ho" were terms that were very commonplace, but if the wrong person made such a reference, it could trigger a sharp reaction. To me, it seemed like most of the young ladies were content with carrying the tools of a *bitch*, but deep down, they wanted to be regarded as an attractive, brilliant and worthy young lady who was loved by someone. **Being a *bitch* or *ho* was part of their survival personality or social identity—and it was an aspect that I experienced only a fraction of the time that I would spend with them.** Even the worst of these "criminals" was battered, afraid, lonely and confused, hoping for a miracle that would tunnel them through the life of uncertainty that awaited them. Here are a few poetic lines taken from the HD unit who created 1-line poetic quotations in September of 2021:

"My life have been tough and I know I had enough." S.B

"They call me a slut, but that's ok, I never asked them anyway." B.W

"I wanna be the inspiration I never had." R.G.

"Every night I just pray for a better heart." J.M.

Uncomfortable moments were a normal part of adapting to the versatile temperament of the girl units. As is the case for most teachers, my presence, my demeanor, my lesson plans were only a few variables that influenced a spectrum of possible outcomes held within the hour class period. I found that the girls acted more as a collective unit than a random assortment of different moods. **When a few of them were having a bad day, those having a decent day had better start having a bad day as well...** When there was hostility amongst them, one could only hope not get caught in the approaching tornado that may be on the horizon. When they were generally willing to do their work or engage in something interesting, there was a camaraderie of laughter and sisterhood that undeniably bound them together.

I found that a very reassuring and stable but non-invasive teaching style was necessary with the girls. They did not want anyone in their face motivating them or persuading them to think a certain way. They certainly were not weak-minded or naive and even the softest personalities possessed an inner *lioness* that kept a cautious watch of any encroachment or interference. There was a fierce defiance of injustice and man nor beast could curtail the will of many of these young ladies if they felt they were being treated unfairly or being manipulated. I recall one of the few black female special education teachers trying to coerce the girls to do work on a day when they were not in the mood and one of the girls threatened to take away her "Black girl card" if she didn't *fall back.*

More so than the young men, I would say that the young ladies were accustomed to general adaptation and had tremendous emotional availability. They spoke about their emotions far more freely and placed value on how they and others *felt.* I read this in their writing, heard it in their commentary and observed it in our candid conversations. They were far more complex than the "good girl" or "bad girl" dualistic labels. It was their versatility that allowed them to survive in a world that didn't understand them. Some of them would tell us how they wore hoodies over their head when they ventured out into the street to avoid harassment. Many were no strangers to serious crime and of course many were never hesitant to fight on or off the unit. Some carried knives and guns and were protectors of their homes. It was a fierce patriarchal society around them and unfortunately many of them buried their femininity into near non-existence in order to survive. They seemed to long for love but were choked by a world of sexual promiscuity and sex as an equalizer. Like many of the male students, education was not a visible priority, but attaining the skills for a career in fashion, art or public service seemed to be desirable. I know for a fact that many of them enjoyed writing and expressing themselves through music or poetry. They weren't much for hero or heroine worshiping, but strongly identified with characters that appealed to the real struggle of being black and female. As a general rule, once someone lost credibility with the girls, it was a battle to get it back. I had forgotten the name of a young lady that I had for two days in class and she never spoke to me again. In alignment with their strong sense of justice, the girls appeared to be truly genuine when it came to race or gender. If they held a prejudice, they would vocalize it, but would also usually be the first to recognize that they were wrong. If they did not recognize it, their peers or sister would certainly point it out.

An excellent work, *Pushout*, "The Criminalization of Black Girls," by Monique Morris finely relays the view from her study that Black girls have "normalized disregard of black femininity" and the misinterpreted and misunderstood demeanor of African-American girls is so often a reaction to the adapting to this disregard. They are being incarcerated at alarming rates and their experiences are validated in this book. She writes:

"Across the country, Black girls have shared narratives that reflect their own understanding of the rules that push them from school and the behaviors that have rendered them increasingly vulnerable to the use of exclusionary discipline...

So often, these girls are backed into an impossible situation and forced to acquiesce to a crime or a situation that is against their will. They are not coached in strategies of self-care or self-awareness, nor provided with training on how to make wise choices—and certainly not provided with many alternative choices within their circumstances. I had quite a few residents who were with a murderer at the scene of a crime.

In class, they responded more to conversation than meditation. As far as their response to the *1-minute moment*, most participated and some didn't. The qualitative journal responses I received are highlighted below. I gathered that the boys saw something stoically fierce in the practice of meditating while more of the girls saw it as a waste of time. Of course, a female facilitator may have certainly found different results. I learned to not pressure work on the girls or push a conversation on them. They always gave me a chance to back off if they weren't in the mood. They knew I meant well and I perhaps "deserved" such a warning. On days where the air was thick, I would just fall silent and give them 3 colored pencils, a Mandala wheel, and put on a beats playlist and softly monitor for progress. In my last days on the "girls units," I remained fatherly, supportive and in the final year or so, non-verbal. This allowed them space to take the class where they wanted it to go and therefore express themselves more freely either through writing or speaking. They produced much more and higher quality work than ever before. This is what the ivy tower of educational theory can never quite grasp—that the presentation of knowledge and information in any forceful manner results in a retraction from those who are already disenfranchised. The disenfranchised, particularly black girls, have a keen sense of the inauthenticity of public education and the invasive tactics that it utilizes. Some of the girls saw the liberating potential of the *1-minute moment*. Some saw that it was truly a time for them to claim as their own. . Here are several responses:

"Meditation helps me sit and think about what I gotta do... It's like when you are meditating, you remember what you have to do in life and ...You have to remind yourself." A.S. 2019

"Meditation is a special time of the day when we do it in class...Some people don't do it but I like it because it calms me down and I feel like I could flow...I like feeling my breath go up and down." P.M. 2019

"Meditating makes me want to write a book...I feel like I could just go off in my own world..." R.S.2019

"I feel like meditating instead of going to school some days. Mr. Biseca help us calm ourself with the meditation. Maybe some people don't like it that much but they still know it's good and they need to do it. Most of all for me, I like the breathing part. When I can breathe with myself I feel like everything will be cool..." G.G 2017

The above student, "GG," was an exceptional case who revered the *1-minute* moment. Furthermore, I would say that she authentically sought silence and peace. She one time asked if she could meditate throughout the whole class period. She would have if I let her. I knew little of her background, but she was raised by her grandmother and had aspirations of being a singer or poet. Her handwriting was immaculate. She had been brought up in Catholic schools and carried herself with a calm debonair (not that the two go hand in hand), respectful and held an innocent curiosity toward knowledge. There were some, male and female, like GG, who ended up in the prison because of pure circumstance or unfortunate isolated incidence—they bore no traits that a typical prisoner embodied. I rarely looked at charges of residents because I never wanted to allow for a bias to form in my mind. It didn't seem fair. The few times that I would go to the internal data to look it up, I was usually surprised. GG had been involved in an altercation and sprayed someone with a fire extinguisher. I learned later from asking her about it. It sounded like something out of a Saturday night live skit. She was one of a kind. I would never condone it, but in GG's case, I'm sure she had a good reason. We laughed about it a few times because quite frankly, it was absurdly comical.

Not so comical was GG's experience in the youth after a few weeks. One Monday, I received news that there was a fight on the unit over the long weekend and GG was "tipped on" (jumped). Her assailants were in my classroom two days after the incident and their punishment didn't seem to cover the bill. I was displeased greatly. That afternoon, I went up to give GG a book and some work. She was let out of her cell and sat in the plastic chair next to me in her baggy blue sweatsuit and a bandage around her right hand. Her two eyes were darkened and a little swollen and her mouth was bruised. I made light of the situation and tried to crack a joke or two because there were very few other options to initiate the conversation. She was not amused, but appreciated the effort and smiled. **Then, I noticed her tooth was chipped. She saw that I noticed and became embarrassed. Some tears began rolling down her face and I felt a deep sense of rage well up inside of me.** I asked her if she was taking some time to meditate. She responded, "I ain't got nothin' but time." I left her with a special book and reminded her that overcoming challenges is what makes life meaningful. She was here for a special purpose and it was up to her to find it. The next morning, my emotions began to escalate when her assailants, the usual hecklers in the front of the class, cracked their jokes and made their jeers during the mindful minute. I reminded them to be respectful of the minute and try their breathing, but it was hard to hide my boiling expression. It took every ounce of restraint in my being to not react instead of respond to the situation. I knew that the boastful girls that were sitting in the front of the room at that very moment—belligerent and rude on a normal basis, were the ones who hurt her. The moment of silence ended and I begrudgingly began the lesson. The defiant few ignored me and I entertained their typical displays of rudeness as the lesson continued, but within minutes, I hit my breaking point. The professional, the teacher in me decomposed and a fire inside of me lit up with rage. I turned to the group of 2-3 miscreants in the front of the room and stared at them in silence. Filtering my thoughts and words, I glared at them—one laughed nervously and taunted me and the others stared back. They knew why I was seething. I decided to call them out. "You think that you can come in here everyday and be disrespectful and that I'm going to want to teach you something?" ... And now, I see that you hurt your classmate and you show no care or remorse for what you did... You're going to get what's coming, I promise." I snatched up each of their papers, crumbled them a ball and threw them in the trash. My student—one who wanted to learn, was hurt. A blossoming young soul who tried to rise above it all, was ripped from her inspirational ascension and dragged down by the catastrophic force that seemed to plague the whole center, the city, the world. I lost my sense of tranquility and understanding. I wanted justice.

Within seconds, I found out that acting out of these emotions would trigger a reaction. One girl got up and challenged me, saying "She ain't my friend," and "I'll slap the shit out of you and her." I nodded my head and asked her to try it. The others chimed in and the room almost turned into a bad scene. Besides an incident up on the HG unit with the boys, it was the only time when I thought I would be physically attacked. Granted, fighting a bunch of high school aged girls would not be my ideal exit after all the work I had been doing, but the moment took me to a place of "whatever." The counselors intervened. I positioned myself against the wall and decided to remain silent. One of the girls approached me with a closed fist and I prepared to duck under whatever she threw, but she only postured. Something tells me that despite being offended and even threatened by me, they all knew my anger was justified. I lost my cool and almost my job that day, but worst of all, I lost my friend. GG heard about the incident and I was painted with a gray streak. It didn't help her situation. In fact, it may have made it worse. They knew GG was a favorite of the teachers and now they knew that we were friends. They didn't like it one bit. Although I showed them courtesy and respect and passion for knowledge, they found my weakness. Just as they reveled in defeating one of their own peers who may have risen above them in some way— through her wisdom, strength or character. This type of thing happened on the unit. We took a few days off from that class and came back later that week. GG had been switched to another unit and a counselor told me that they continuously harassed her. The counselor also told me to never do what I did again. It caused problems that lasted for days. Although I could have faltered much worse, I was ashamed and disappointed in myself. How could I have not known better? A Lesson learned and never forgotten. I remembered the quote, "Too much intention creates too much tension.."— Mooji.

Whereas I felt the boys needed a teacher whom they could relate to, the girls needed a teacher whom they could trust. I finally realized this at a certain point and my "female" units morphed into enjoyable classes with young ladies who did their best for their "buddy." I played a friendly and fatherly role and showed my vulnerability. The incident in GG's class was a turning point and revealed some valuable lessons. I finally found an authentic balance with the young lady residents. My new self-promise was to never show a wink of anger or frustration with them. They liked when I stayed passive and malleable. I was sure to always address them as young ladies despite their emotional tone or preconceptions about me. I found that they participated in class and meditation when I continuously spoke from the heart with them. They reciprocated it and practiced more beingness toward the end of my term in the center. They were more intrigued the more I left it alone. I didn't get a chance to use a lot of archetypal lessons with them perhaps because it wasn't my place to relate to them on that level.

Young Men and the Quest for Manhood

The "power-over" dynamic that exists in the streets of any big American city, reflects the corporate capitalist patriarchal legacy that has been intact for centuries here and around the world. One would argue that even the social movements trying to tear down this legacy still reflect its' values or at least structural makeup in some way. It seems that American culture cannot escape from its need to "hustle" and to "man up." It's a *money man's world*—and in the hood, becoming "top dog" or emulating masculinity is something that not only grown men, but women, children and young boys do to survive. With %60 of fathers unavailable to raise their children in the impoverished black communities and staggering figure for Caucasian and Hispanics/LatinX as well, *Manhood or fatherhood* could classify as something of nostalgia. Some would argue that given the circumstances, black fathers are very much present. They would cite the *criminalization* and or *de-masculinization* of the black male, which by all accounts is fueled by the prison system, leaving him with a life of fewer options for income, and, therefore, an unstable foundation for family life. Despite the social changes and gender-oriented movements bubbling to the surface on a national level, the daily grind in the largely working poor Philadelphia neighborhoods is still very much about being a "breadwinner," the earner that served as an archetypal protector and provider, among other things—that doesn't necessarily mean that men are expected as much to fulfill this role. Maybe the continuous imprisonment and homicide rates of black males in the community has created the complete opposite effect. Regardless, the pressures of gender roles were certainly found in the trauma-related events and anxiety of nearly all residents.

I later realized that it wasn't our identity, race nor our socio-economic differences that proved to be of any great barrier, but the single largest variable was that of having an active or accessible father at some point in our lives. To me, this was the most influential factor of their ability to cope with the circumstances. **The source of their anxiety, anger and hopelessness was rooted in the neurosis of desperately seeking manhood. I'll never forget after finishing a novel called *"The Fear of Becoming a Man"* by Dr. Richard Sutton, over half the class wanted to read it again— the same book!** Without admitting it, the boys seemed to unconsciously seek more admirable men. There were plenty of "success stories" shoved down their throats. Such were splattered all over the media in the sports world, and arts and entertainment. The majority of boys didn't respond to career fairs or conferences that introduced them to successful men from "the hood" in a one-day event. They wanted someone to be with them on a consistent basis. They wanted to develop a relationship of commonality and care, true mentorship, partially, I'd guess, to develop care in themselves.

I was fortunate enough to both enjoy and endure the calling of being a teacher, later learning to cherish it. **By later accepting my role and honoring what the residents taught me, I was constantly called "O.G," "unc" or "bro" or "old head," all endearing references to much needed male figures in their lives.** I and most of the teachers genuinely cared, some deeply, for the students. To most of us, it was irresponsible to do the bare minimum. For me, whether they wanted it or not, it was essential to expose and implement the practice of meditation.

Archetypes and Masculinity

I found that the young men coming into the in-take units were the most eager to meditate (or participate in any activity for that matter). The other longer-term units had experienced the drudgery of time and whether it was due to too many mind-altering pharmaceuticals or just an overriding sense of hopelessness, they were more likely to tune out. Some in their late teens or early twenties had graduated and choose not to partake in group discussion or academics in general. Life was hitting them hard as many were coming to terms with the idea of contending with the justice system into adulthood. The in-take units, however, held the younger guys who were "earning their stripes" and trying to figure out who they were. While the older were more reluctant to reveal any thoughts or experiences, the in-take units told the news of the streets. They were rambunctious and alert, always surveying their environment. I realized quickly that nearly all of them were embodying (or unconsciously attempting to embody) the archetypal path of *the warrior* (Carl Jung). That is, in some of their crime and violence ridden lives, they were developing their ability to confront, protect or defend. Granted, much of that included stealing, lying, cheating or even hurting inno-cent people, but within the cut-throat urban American land-scape, this behavior ensured survival—and it (unfortunately) mimicked the ideals of manhood. Because of the socio-economic realities unfolding in front of them, most of them choose the easiest, coldest or quickest path to money and status. **Though the concepts of the ancient artisan, shaman, joker, king or warrior were not known to most of them, they were unconsciously attempting to enact these roles.** Jungian Psychologist Robert Moore and mythologist Douglas Gilette argue that there are four archetypal male energies that serve different purposes. They can be generalized as the *king, warrior, magician* and *lover*. The authors argue that to become a complete man or embody the "divine masculine, a man must work to develop all four archetypes to serve the greater good... "The result of striving to become complete is a feeling of manly confidence and purpose." I became more interested in this philosophy after it became apparent that the boys were drawn to archetypal stories and characters. **Themes like *leadership, courage, loyalty, revenge, trickery* or *self-defense* rang a familiar chord in the hearts of these young men and they longed to explore these concepts within themselves.** Some of them, by sheer injustice, were heroes mistaken for criminals. Some were warriors and protected their homes, looking to feed their children or themselves in the battleground that was the streets. Some asserted the role of magician—wheeling and dealing in the streets with cunning and persuasion. On the high end, the idea of the king or victors were idolized—like a pro athlete or rappers "raining" one hundred dollar bills into the wind afloat expensive yachts. "You're not gonna make it if you act small or have no heart," said a former resident turned rapper. Money was associated with courage, prowess, re-sourcefulness and manhood. A chosen few saw the facade of it all, but kept their knowledge (like the wise usually do) under their cap. True self-awareness at its best. Some of our boys aspired to be rappers, others admired them and went about exploring their own talents in sports, a trade or entre-preneurial interests. Sadly, much of the trades related to carpentry, construction, electrical or other areas of craftsman-ship or related skill were taken out of school programs and technical skills (which we had a CTE program) were about the only other "trade" that remained. I found that whatever the path they were interested in, it tied directly back to one of the four archetypes.

It became important to note the different archetypes at various times in myself as well. It was most advantages for me to play the "quiet, peaceful" warrior and spoke to them as a wise man—even though my societal role was to act like a clueless Caucasian "professional." In reality, I wasn't from the ghetto, but wasn't from Disneyworld either. I knew the trials of battle as a former boxer and martial artist. Without my own warrior experiences, I would not have, undoubtedly, gained the understanding of or empathy of these young people that inspired me to write this book. When they heard my stories of growing into manhood, I was sure to remain humble and non-competitive. "You ain't never been shot" some would say. I would reply, "No, give thanks, but I know what pain and darkness are and know what it's like when death knocks at your door." Archetypal discussion was a great segue for them to reflect consciously on their experience. There were some real "jaw-droppers" of course. As with all scenarios, one facilitating such conversations had to have a super-keen and intuitive feel for what was appropriate and what could trigger a backlash. It was after real stories, real moments, that the majority would participate in any lesson presented—whether it was writing a 5-paragraph paper or analyzing a poem by Langston Hughes. Once the residents respected or identified with an adult, in any way, that respect remained. It didn't have to be anything related to violence—I witnessed a small elderly white woman tell the kids about being stuck in an airport and as they listened, they genuinely empathized with her through the feeling of loneliness. Due to their own trauma-related issues, however, they could just as easily disrespect you on a different occasion and completely disregard your feelings altogether. I tended to veer away from traditional literature (or unrelated curriculum for that matter) and focus on readings that revealed stories of responsibility, respect, self-awareness and the "divine masculine." We studied the life of Miyamoto Musashi—Japanese writer, swordsman, philosopher, and strategist. Amenhotep, builder and philosopher. Marcus Aurelius. Muhammad Ali. Fred Hampton. The boys began to see that a man could be more than one thing—he could go beyond one label and study many things to become well-rounded.

The significance of using symbolic archetypes as a healing and teaching tool has been phenomenal. It has become clear, from the response of my students, that a large majority identified with an archetype of some kind that reflected meaning in the broader sense of consciousness. These not only masculine roles, but energetic representations of consciousness that show a distinct piece of the larger picture. This is, perhaps, why students make meaning immediately with their type. They see that without winter, there is no spring, without the warrior, there is no king and without the Sun, there is no Jupiter. Once they identify with an archetype, they see not a separation from everyone else, but an interconnectedness with everyone else. **If archetypes are presented as they exist, equal entities, the young man who identifies with his *water* element does not look down upon the one who identifies with fire. They understand that both have the power to destroy and to heal etc...** This gives them a sense of integration and empathy. They began to *innerstand* the nature of consciousness when they see how all parts are linked and necessary. This is the 1st step toward the level of self-awareness that creates beingness. Beingness, our true identity.

One particular gem of a book was Paolo Coelho's *The Warrior of the Light*, a timeless and very applicable manual for inner strength and transformation. The boys would read passages aloud from this book and even the most challenged readers would flail their way through the words. They read with heart and all eyes in the room followed the text as if it bore a message directly from the Creator itself. In my mind, each passage certainly did. We would affirm and explore an archetype through, for example, the following passage, which combines the element of water and the concept of the warrior:

This was one of our favorite passages:

"The Warrior of the Light sometimes behaves like water, flowing around obstacles he encounters...Occasionally resistance may mean destruction, and so he adapts to the circumstances. He accepts, without complaint, that the stones in his path hinder his way through the mountains. Therein lies the strength of water. It cannot be touched by a hammer or ripped to shreds by a knife. The strongest of swords cannot scratch its surface. The river adapts itself to whatever route proves possible, but the river never forgets its one objective: The sea. So fragile at its source, it gradually gathers the strength of the other rivers it encounters. And, at a certain point, its power is absolute." Paulo Coelho, *Warrior of the Light*

The boys responded to this passage with revelations about the strength of water—the dynamic of its simultaneous softness and force. They were realizing the innate magic of the elements and healing power of nature and archetypal memory—it sparked something eternal in them:

"You gotta be like water or you not gonna get to the sea."
S.D 2017

"It's sayin that most of the time you have to flow like water and be adaptable. When you are adaptable you can go around the rocks...' B.W. 2017

Boys Cannot be Babied

"I do not feel bad for you...If I felt bad for you then I could not help you." I was surprised to hear these words come out of my own mouth one autumn day in 2021 as I explained the difference between empathy and sympathy. One of the major discoveries I stumbled upon along the way was the absolute distinction between the ability to see someone else's perspective (empathy) and have pity on them to the point where your emotions are saturated (sympathy). **It was critical that once I empathized with the young people that I taught, I assumed the responsibility of not sympathizing with them.** Although the circumstances were quite visible, sympathizing with them only left them with the option of assuming victimhood, ultimately playing upon my pity. Besides, if I sympathized with them, I was not only propagating their victimhood, but encouraging them to point the finger at someone else that caused their struggle. This only cultivated resentment and entitlement. We have been enculturated to think that life is about *what we deserve*. It is not. We often confuse learning and karmic debt with what we deserve. Karmic debt is the sum of what, in our soul journey of many lifetimes, we have taken and given, not what we deserve. We clear Karmic debt with compassion and coura- geous shadow work. With courage, compassion and empathy, I was able to align with them. That is, I was able to see the world how they saw it—I could learn from them, and vice versa. The small but critical difference between these two approaches is absolutely necessary to understand when working with those who are at-risk or traumatized. An adult who teaches children or helps those from this sympathetic angle is relaying to the child that it's ok to feel bad for themself; That it's ok to blame others for your predicament. Nothing can be further from the truth. Certainly, there are systems in place that create tremendous disadvantages for some and not others, but individual consciousness is the primary system that can create ones' reality. Self-efficacy and responsibility develops when empathy is in place, not sympathy.

The boys acted like infants when they were treated like infants. Especially near the beginning of my career, I was guilty of such coddling at times—feeding them candy if they did their work, compromising with them on school rules and giving in to their demands of trap videos. Every teacher faces these daily dilemmas and many times caves to the demands of a needy student population out of limited options or just plain indifference. Eventually, I found consistency of policy to be paramount. Some adults were in the center providing more of a motherly role—which was also needed. When I had the energy to passively discipline them and play the role of a somewhat father figure, they responded first with rebellion and hatred. They wanted to be treated like men so badly that when it would sometimes actually happen, they would react with aggression. Sometimes I would be the only teacher who a student had a problem with. It didn't bother me once I realized why. When I concluded one day that no matter what role I played, I would have those who did to approve, I then focused on being my authentic self. As I showed them who I was by being who I was consistently, they found my voice to be one of reliability and validity. Play a video for us real quick OG," ...When I told them "no," they knew I meant it. Even if they openly complained, I knew deep down that they found my empathy to be gratifying and my demands of them to be fair.

"Tranquility is courage in repose." Quotes like this one from Siddhartha allowed the boys to begin to associate courage with peace and discipline. One aspect of the *1-minute moment* is that it is done in a somewhat structured fashion. With many of the tough units, I would use a stern tone to convey a feeling of necessity. On my part, there was little room for error and I left no space for reactions or criticisms because I was directing each action down to counting the breath. I often received the worst reactions when I would leave moments open. I took masculinity into context in the moment because any opening in space or time would allow for interruption. I had to be direct, instructional and firm. Many people may have wondered why they heard this meditative teacher acting as a Marine lieutenant during meditation. By my 3rd year, I learned that this regimentation was what they responded to best. They did not want a man to be soft and caring. They responded best when I was a certain distance, mutual respect and deference to something greater than all of us. When I was able to create that mix, magic happened... Young guys with bullet wounds in their legs and arms would breathe consciously, then sit and write for 30 minutes, citing evidence from a novel and marking up their text like a college literature student. It all began with a simple breathing and posture exercise—the *1-minute moment.*

The Search for Balanced Masculine Identity

Like all teachers and counselors alike, I sometimes triggered a few chosen residents that would bring their anger bubbling to the surface. Sometimes, it was just asking them if they were going to do any work that day. It took me some intense reflection to come to the conclusion that I wasn't doing anything wrong by mildly probing—if so, I stand convicted. Although I was threatened from time to time, I began to realize that these threats were the boys' responses to yet another man that they may lose trust in because of false promises or ulterior motives. I came to realize that the anger wasn't with me—and it wasn't even anger; It was fear—fear of becoming a man.

Some of the boys were 2nd or 3rd generation prisoners. Their grandfathers and or fathers were in state prison as well as cousins, uncles etc... Most of the older boys had been in fist fights or serious altercations with their fathers at some point. **One boy drove a broken broomstick into his father's back after seeing his mother beaten on their porch. This retaliation from the abuse of their mother was quite common.** That said, I did find that most of the boys knew their fathers and had close contact with them at some point in their lives—some of it very positive. There is certainly a cyclical effect of fatherless children in black America that stems back to the breaking apart of families upon the arrival to America from Africa. That said, much of our views of black fatherhood are mythicized as well. Black fathers may not be in the picture as much as white fathers as a whole, but black fathers show to be more actively involved with their children than Hispanic and white fathers who are separated from their spouse. Nonetheless, children who are incarcerated, no matter their race, are less likely to have active fathers at home in their lives. This was always very apparent to me and revealed itself indirectly as much as through direct conversation. Guy Cornea says in his book, *Absent Fathers, Lost Sons,* "Lacking a father is like lacking a backbone" and a boy with a "negative father complex... lacks structure from within."

The boys held their own set of social norms with regard to gender very rigidly. Their world instilled a value of ultra-masculinity as a placeholder for manhood. There was little room for error on a teacher or counselors part as a man among them. During meditation, I learned that a reference to relaxing or softness of anything, certainly body parts, could come off as suspect and could be interpreted as perverted. They sometimes, initially, assumed that I could be gay and they needed convincing proof that I wasn't otherwise. One time, a resident sternly addressed another to stand up straight because he was "standing like a #^!$%*." I used it as an opportunity to discuss balanced manhood and the compensation that (homophobic) straight men display to assert their heterosexuality when it's unnecessary. I realized at one point that proving my heterosexuality was a form a violence, so I sometimes broke into a quick monologue about how I was once homophobic as well, but learned otherwise. The boys loved to hear stories for some reason, of bad turning good. Maybe they just liked stories, even that one. Beyond that, out of necessity, I never discussed sexual politics. Quite honestly, I would be crucified to directly preach tolerance for homo-sexuality. It was important to pose myself as not qualified to ever judge someone based on their sexual preference and that is what I did. They certainly identified with the need for respect of all people. By shear statistics, there were plenty of them who may have been gay or questioning, but they never identified themselves—conversely, I never heard of any incidences where someone was hurt because of their per-ceived sexual identity.

The boys seemed to accept a "nonjudgmental" approach and if need be, expressing what had to be said in a way that was palatable within the group setting. The few instances where they were "in their feelings" or aware of their emotions brought about an opportunity to interject the divine feminine. At that juncture, it was often shocking what the boys would reveal about the love for their mother and the need for affection. Of course, that also involved re-directions from the explicit and verbose rants dedicated toward the desire for girls. Groups that were comfortable around each other would often open up about the pain of loneliness and abandonment. They were no strangers to understanding the needs of a woman or the essence of femininity, though the hard casing of masculine cultural norms was in place in most of their social circumstances. These rare, gentle moments were found between the lines of a script written for men in the blood of their battle wounds.

The Story of "R" and "B"

The archetypal story of "R" and "B" is one that inspired me to closely examine masculinity and gender as a construct. It is a simple story, somewhat brutish and certainly masculine to the core—it took place on the HI unit in the summer of 2020. "B" came into the HI unit initially, and his mere presence screamed *Alphahood*. He was strong, tall, handsome, charismatic and streetwise. He had seen it all. He needed merely to tell someone to get up from their seat and it would be done. Do not let the intimidation fool you, "B" was good natured and smiled throughout the day. He liked to joke around, and, also liked to learn and interject into class discussion. He utilized a well-placed feminine side in his charisma. Make no mistake, however, "B" knew how to hold power. He held sway in a certain neighborhood and was regarded as an important member of a certain group there. He was the only young man I witnessed enjoying a cheeseburger during class because he told the counselors he was hungry. He would make sure people saw him doing exceptional things so that they knew that he was exceptional. I was actually glad to have him as a student and he and I got along really well. His energy was even-tempered in my presence and he took to meditation right away. He would even hush everyone before we started. He was not only great for crowd control but he carried the code of an old soul.

Shortly thereafter, "R" showed up. I had "R" a year earlier and he was one of the most challenging young people that I'd interacted with. He was also physically strong and scrappy—like a pit bull. "R" was an alpha type but had a mean streak in him. He was ill-tempered and didn't like school or classwork the least bit. When he returned to the youth a 2nd time, he was 17—we shook hands cordially and he squeezed my hand as hard as he could. I had to squeeze back just so my hand wouldn't break! He got in my face and we glared into each other's eyes like two tigers. He contorted his wide-eyed face with a demonic look and attempted to scare me. When he picked up on my unmoved stoicism, he smirked with delight. It was the only time, ever, that I saw him smile. He wanted to show me that he was now a man. One of the memorable fellows who liked to posture to see how I responded. I gave him the energy of an old warrior—one who didn't want trouble and wanted him to be at peace. When he came onto the unit, I immediately picked up on the energy between him and "B." They were cordial and cool with each other and from the onset, exchanging postures and regaling war stories. I could deduce that there had to be trouble at some point. The unit was too small for the both of them. Within days, we heard there was a "riot" upstairs and it started with HI. When I went upstairs a day or two after things calmed down, I inquired and found out that the two *alphas* went at it. And after they went at it, they led the whole unit to attack another unit. The truth is that it might well have all been prevented with an adult in contact that had an awareness of group power and masculinity. A mediation meeting with the boys, bringing them together to work on a common goal or even discussing with them their own alpha energy, would have been a great place to start. I would have told them that they may feel the need to claim the "true alpha" title for themselves through battle, but this was not the place to do it. I would have explained how these archetypal energies are inherently in us all and it's good to observe and honor them, but acting them out can be very risky. They needed to share their power and figure out how to manage a kind of "dual alpha-hood" so that each could feel legitimized. Maybe this approach would work, maybe not, but it addresses the obvious innate energies that exist amongst young men in groups and recognizes it as a determinant in how not only the aloha's function, but the whole group. It very much mirrors the wolf pack dynamics. Some have no idea how powerful a single conversation between a man and a boy can be or among boys, about masculinity. One of the traits of our justice system and culture is to punish the whole for the crimes of the few and ignore any social dynamics that could have contributed to conflict. We create blanketed policies and rules that apply to everyone the same way and expect everyone to respond uniformly. Conferring with the boys to prevent any hostility would not have given them special treatment, but would have been recognizing what unique energy they brought to the group dynamics and why that energy was important to recognize. Instead of allowing our at-risk members of society to better understand themselves and identify their role, we apply a mass system of education and juvenile justice that ignores the innate wisdom of young human beings. Applicable to both women and men, we now see a societal distrust of men, a criminalization of women and a misunderstanding of conflict in general.

The bottom line is that boys need men—not necessarily their fathers but someone that's willing to share a part of his own experience. Without it, we will see more extreme cases of imbalanced masculinity that poses dangerous outcomes for all members of our communities. We not only need more male teachers, but need to adapt the education system so that they could be paid for their time as an instructor and mentor. A single man or mentor cannot teach a young fellow everything, but he can teach him one thing—and even if that one thing is seemingly worthless, it's the act of caring that stays with the boy for his entire life. I'm sure of this because I was once a boy.

♦ CHAPTER 8 ♦

RACE RELATIONS
AND RACIAL IDENTITY

The very first week while teaching at the center, I was taken aback to come to the realization that the majority of my students weren't exactly sure who were the Native American/ Indians (as I referred to them assuming my students were given the wrong terminology from the onset instead of *The 1st nations*, which they wished to be referred to as). 'You mean them *jawns* at the gas station?" "No, not them, I replied." They are Indians from India...These were the first people to inhabit the land that we walk on everyday...They were here for tens of thousands of years in America before it was called America..." Some looked puzzled until one said, "Oh them Indians, yea with the Mohawks," one resident replied. Some recognized tribal names like *Cherokee* or *Iroquois*. Upon reading some excerpts about the "*Trail of Tears*" and documented history by Dee Brown and other authors, they slowly gained an interest. I posed fictitious survival situations and asked them to role play to them to get them thinking about food, shelter and a closer connection to nature as an alternative to a dependency on the state. This indigenous theme of self-sufficiency and one with nature stimulated their minds and some of them wrote papers on the difference between surviving in America today and surviving 500 years ago. We finished the unit by watching "*Dances With Wolves*." They're favorite scene was the Buffalo hunt. We talked about it for days. "What would it be like riding a horse at 60 mph trying to shoot down your winter food supply while not falling off the horse to be trampled upon?" Role play questions like this created raw, situational imagery for them and resulted in purposeful and colorful drawings, writings and discussions. When I brought in a snakeskin and hawk feathers, some of them refused to touch the items, but all were enamored with the feel of nature, the call of the wild. They found a great sentiment with the 1st Nations' mystique and we were all moved by descriptions of native meditation practices. During this crucial chapter in history, the residents meditated more than any other chapter and the topic of *race* was the furthest thing from their mind. The 1st nations' tribes seemed to invoke a feeling of dignity, courage and harmonious freedom. Although I reiterated the plight of these people as victims of white oppression and European imperialism, the students were not interested in that. I'm not sure why. Maybe they wanted to learn more about how the people simply lived—*as humans*.

When I arrived at PJJSC, the detention center, I looked at whiteness as a privilege. While I was there, I saw it as a curse, and when I left, I realized it was a blessing. Of course, all identities, privileges and levels of awareness within them are blessings if we use them properly. From a racially conscious perspective, my *whiteness* brought an undeniable influence upon my teaching experience, mentoring and just about any interaction at the center. Though, visibly, I could never totally separate myself from my *whiteness* and *white privilege*, I found that by focusing on my humanity and the collective human consciousness, I was able to neutralize the effects of race and racial injustice a great deal. At the risk of offending social justice warriors and those dedicated to the cause of racial injustice (as has been a theme in my own life for twenty five years), I like to offer a perspective that may seem, at times, counterintuitive even to myself. Nonetheless, I can assure you, my cherished reader, that my heart beats and bleeds for humanity, my cause is for that of humanity and I consider my identity as a divinely inspired and deeply blessed human being.

A Sacred Sociological Philosophy of Race

First, let us acknowledge the "ABC" of Sacred sociology which helps us understand the synchro-destiny of human conscious-ness. "A" is for awareness and "B" for balance and "C" for compassion. Fully embodied, these traits (as I will discuss more in my next work) define the destiny of the collective human species. When addressing the issue of race and racial injustice from the perspective of sacred sociology, we can keep these tenets or ultimate values in mind. Krishna Murti has been a tremendous influence upon the perspective and so I'd like to begin with his words:

> "Violence is not merely killing one another. It is violence when we use a sharp word, when we make a gesture to brush away a person, when we obey because there is fear...When you call yourself an Indian or a Muslim or European, you are being violent ...because you are separating yourself from mankind. When you separate yourself by belief, by nationality, by tradition, it breeds violence. So a man who is seeking to understand violence does not belong to any country, religion, political party or partial system; He is concerned with the total under-standing of mankind."

Such a poetic articulation can have the effect of utopianism for many of us. Maybe we read Murti's words and respond with, "yes, sure, in an ideal world." Maybe we deny the quote as being a liberally inspired fairy tale of "colorblindness" where people can simply "drop" their racial identity. The potential naivety of the quote when looking at the world around us can certainly be exploited, but its profound wisdom that speaks to the world within us is undeniable. It transcends naivety and begs courage and wisdom. It inspires profound questions like, when does the identity of one become the identity of all?

The identity gained through *innerstanding* collective consciousness allows for the creation of a new awareness. Creation of this awareness begins when we look within ourselves beyond external differences, be it race, skin color, class and any other social inequity that has marked our karmic past and scared our present being. This is "doing the work"—and yes, we must begin with ourselves. Murti's simple, yet profound reminder connects us with the idea of collective consciousness, of true human awareness, of oneness. From this transcendent place, we will begin to reap the fruits of universal consciousness and the dissipation of hatred or prejudice. Since the inception and provocation of the concept of the "other" or "them/dem" (i.e *demonic*)—be it other religion, other race, other party, even other gender, we have much of our extra-sensory and spiritual power as beings. As with one human body, the whole of humanity is greater than the sum of its parts. We have found plenty of categories to break ourselves into—nation, football team and in the case of many cities like Philadelphia, neighborhood block. These are all merely social constructs that have divided our communities and species, some more recently than others. Observe the way in which people separate themselves from others, it will astound you. The media and economic forces at play certainly are a large part of propagating the *profits of humanity.* Coke or Pepsi? Ford or Chevy? These are trivial examples until we look at something like race—She is black and he is white. The implicit meaning behind these simple labels has now become explosive. Truthfully speaking, a piece of paper is white. A tuxedo is black. Nobody is truly black or white. Being a longtime student of the social sciences has allowed me to truly expose these terms as "constructs," or a creation of the social order that benefited those in power. We interact in a world where the social constructs listed above are embedded into our institutions and cultural framework. The greatest reality is that in order to achieve justice or equality, we must recognize our differences, but work in solidarity to construct a new human consciousness. Indeed, we are far from such a vision and completing such a task. Perhaps achieving oneness first involves a complete divergence from it—and then creating a most unique revolution to gain it back...

The divergence from oneness as it pertains to modern race and racial injustice most certainly begins with the era and act of colonization of Africa, Asia and the America's and the enslavement of African peoples by Europeans. The very first "other" in America was "black," and then "Indian" or first nations, who ironically treated the "others" who arrived from Europe as welcomed guests (afterward, the "other" included groups like *Irish, Italians, Jews,* etc... who were able to "achieve" their *whiteness* by assimilating into white society and integrating through lighter skin color). Europeans sacrificed their culture for *whiteness* and Africans involuntarily had their culture replaced with *blackness*. Nonetheless, the enslavement of African peoples and systematic genocide of indigenous cultures brought incredible changes to societies around the world and cannot be overstated when looking at the plight of oppressed peoples throughout the globe today. It became the basis for inequality in a capitalist and Christian dominated world. The ensuing institutional systems that resulted in Eurocentric and colonial societies upheld *whiteness* "to protect and maintain privilege." Those systems, rooted in hierarchy, have reinforced racial and class dominating ideology to mold our perception of each other. The old "divide and conquer" tactics worked quite well for those few architects of power that orchestrated the most massive division of humanity that the species has ever seen. Social class was used to separate the elites from the peasantry in Europe and race was used to separate lighter skinned people from those with African blood in America. In the thoughts of Toni Morrison, race is so ingrained in our society that individuals often fail to recognize how it affects relationships. Today, we are coming to terms with much of this action. These very inhumane and intentional "methods of social control" indoctrinated *whiteness* and institutionalized the racism that we see today in our education and criminal justice systems that deny inherent bias and propagate black incarceration. Concerning academic prowess and incarceration, we can clearly see the effects of racism through the endless statistics, whether it's through studies of test scores or the influence of policy on certain drug possession sentences affiliated with racial tendencies. I need not divulge the numbers. Many would agree that addressing white supremacy is the first step in creating equality, but this addressing is a delicate matter. Those who "run" the world, yield their rule through power, not whiteness. Some may be white supremacists, Zionists or nationalists of various origins—some may be free of any such association, but they are all, undoubtedly, billionaires. They perpetuate inequality more than any other group on the planet. So, even if white supremacy was just some monster that lived out in the hills that we had to go attack, would that really solve anything? To attack it means we would have to attack whiteness itself. Is that even possible without social disruption or agitation of people who may have little to do with racism, they themselves impoverished or misguided? Being aggressive and hasty toward one group, no matter who they are will surely not produce any desirable or transformative results.

As the struggle to undo the past and present injustices stemming from racism continues, I find it necessary to approach this phenomenon through a lens of *sacred sociology*. Although Critical Race Theory (CRT) and other systems-based analysis are theoretically aligned with discussing race and racial injustice, they are merely knives that may cut through the barbed wire of racial injustice, but create yet another potential danger. I find that *CRT* falls short of solutions and is stuck in a place of congruence with mutiny, not revolution, and certainly not oneness. I will provide a brief explanation of this and beg sociologists and others to excuse my brevity and not see it as a "pass" for writing good theory or properly critiquing. This chapter is dedicated to my experience with race in PJJSC. Also, I am not here to contribute to the "racial anxiety" that permeates American society, but to offer a space where we can work from a place of commonality.

A Critical, Complimentary View of CRT

The 5 tenets of Critical Race Theory are (1) centrality of experiential knowledge over positivist research (2) the challenge to the dominant ideology (3) liberalism does not solve racial injustice (4) race and racism is codified in systems and institutions (5) race is a socio-political construct. I recognize all 5 of these tenets to be valid, progressive and well-intended. Like CRT, *sacred sociology* focuses on outcomes, not beliefs. Also, those outcomes are based on subjective experiences, which, when discussing race, is essential. Additionally,

CRT calls for direct interruption of the present systems in place, which is crucial. It's perfectly conceivable that a revolutionary ideology is needed and one that is unafraid of redressing and uprooting the white power structure. Unfortunately, CRT also calls for a challenge in ideology and critique of present institutions by working within those institutions. It is necessary, however, to realize that the white power structure is based on exactly that—*power*. Power is the basis for all Capitalist institutions, or, as Bichler puts it.. "Instead of studying the relations of capital to power we must conceptualize capital as power if we are to understand the dynamics of capitalist institutions." He goes on to refer to Capitalist institutions as "fatally flawed."

The issue we all struggle to deal with is *power*, not race. It is an innate human tendency and flaw to seek power and to abuse it. CRT seeks to pose race as the critical variable for understanding the social ills of the world, but by defeating *power* (an outgrowth of the ego) by infusing another form of power—through *race*, which is also an outgrowth of ego. This focus on *race consciousness* replaces one form of singularity for another. In this case, CRT calls for racism to be dismantled through anti-racism. Herein lies the issue of dispelling racism by replacing it with a different forced ideology. The framework of anti-racism has very totalitarian undertones. By concluding that people should inherently *work against racism* because if not, they are otherwise *propagating racism* is quite an authoritative proposition. This ideal is built on the imbalanced moral principle of: "be a good person by doing this or else you're not a good person." The effect of forcing people to be "anti-racist" or because if they not, they are upholding the racist power structure is another way of saying "if you're not with us, then you are against us." This has a divisive effect and in the long run could potentially provoke more racism than it eradicates. It is, in fact, the same propaganda tool used by the Republican party for every war they've orchestrated, especially the bombing of Iraq in 2004, where president George W. Bush said the exact words above... Iraq of course, was not against the U.S, but simply trying to coexist as a nation in a hostile region—just as most of us are trying to exist in an oppressive, totalitarian, corporate, capitalist oligarchy.

There is certainly enough ground for young students of color or "wokeness" to be critical or exclusive of whites based on past injustices—and if that is the goal, where and when does it end? Is it white people we are addressing or "whiteness?" Additionally, are my "woke" friends fit to critique the thoughts and perceptions of other human beings who are at their own level of consciousness in their own journey? This is beyond being critical of white nationalism, which is founded on specific tenets aimed to keep *whites* superior. As a reaction to white nationalism, "The founders of critical race theory identified with the black power movement more than that of integration." Power is the problem. We cannot expect to replace power through use of force. By universal law, power begets power. As such, CRT theory in education is causing quite a backlash. It presents a counter-punch attack through exclusive, counterstory-telling as a means of gaining empathy from whites or those in power. Indeed, if I get punched, and then I throw a counterpunch, *I'm still fighting.* It's best if I find a way to not punch back.

Instead of acknowledging the truth about the past and replacing the racist ideologies with one of forced tolerance, or "non-racism," we will find our children stuck in the mud with self-righteousness on one end or victimhood on the other. One who can blame others for their issues, their challenges or injustices, will not learn self-efficacy and or gain true empowerment in their lives. It seems plausible that individuals are willing to listen to someone's story if they are not forced to— and they very well may respond with empathy. As a group, I would contend, one race cannot be forced to listen to other races' "stories." This is an abstract measure that cannot take any reasonable form. Sure, it is absolutely heartwarming and healing when someone or group can learn about a different culture and gain an appreciation of that culture. Is it justifiable, however, if such an act is mandated? Is it possible to enforce racial cohesion without the backlash of creating even more racism? It is not only an impossible feat to configure on a societal level, but will have the effect of creating the backlash of authoritarianism, resulting in more divisive and competitive reactions—the two inherent qualities of "race." No race can ever be "satisfied" with how "they" are treated.

Race or any other social identity feeds the ego (remember that the ego represents the desires of the subconscious mind such as being recognized and or heard). When we are operating from the consciousness of racial identity, we are operating out of ego, and ego does not want to empathize, it wants to win. The "black" and "white" races are not two children who have gotten into a disagreement. They are now mythologized fire-breathing dragons who have wreaked havoc upon humanity, birthed by an elite few European American males, many years ago. Do we blame them or the whole of a race that looks like them? **The result of this continual upholding of racial realism has been the false pride ("white") and trauma bonding ("black") that has produced a deep sense of solidarity and common story of the past. Though formidable in their meaning, these fire breathing dragons are made of only clouds. They can vanish if we collectively dissolve them.**

So, I would ask proponents of CRT to examine their own relationship with power and their role within institutions of power. Most of the universities that propagate CRT are themselves tied to corporate and political interests that reflect historical power structures. That structure has a peculiar way of reinforcing "group think" and pitting one group against another, inciting constant disagreement. We must replace debate with collaborative healing ceremonies. We must acknowledge suffering and reward those willing to admit past injustice. Then, we can recognize forgiveness unilaterally and truly address the race problem in America. I would go so far as to say that a national formal apology by the president and congress and day of recognition of slavery and its legacy is a great ceremony to start the process. This happened in Australia with regards to the aboriginal tribes, and the results were astounding.

Whiteness in the Center

To realize what it really meant to be a "white male" teacher in *the youth* brought me to an analysis of deep and critical reflection of not only myself, but the education system, the criminal justice system and even the study of the English language as a product of colonialism. It also informed my approach to using meditation with the youth as something outside of the expected duties of an educator and a way of neutralizing the influence of *whiteness*...

Though we live in a world where someone like myself, a white American male, has benefitted from my social grouping, neutralizing my whiteness and recognizing humanity as a whole has a far more profound effect than asserting it or defending it. The success in "reaching" the residents, in truly touching some of their lives, only began to develop after I dissociated with my *whiteness*—that is any inkling of feeling superior, highly educated, and, at times even professional. It also involved shedding my guilt, which for many white teachers, played a role in their pedagogy and approach to educating inner city black and brown youth. That said, Philadelphia teachers, *black, brown, white*, and any other affiliation are some of the most tough-skinned and dedicated individuals found in America. The legacy of slavery and segregation is a complex matter and white teachers who choose to teach from a perspective grounded in that legacy are often some of the best teachers in the business. It doesn't mean they necessarily teach because of guilt, from what I would deduce. As for me, I had always possessed an ability to "un-whiten" myself in a given situation. Explaining this through the written word would be complex, but I will just say that it was developed from the time of my youth, probably from a variety of things in my background. I certainly benefited from both the versatility and the whiteness. Nonetheless, my *white privilege*, in the presence of the residents, was arguably, a non-causal, but present and *real* variable.

One instance that illustrates this was when a discussion of the "N" word came up between my students and my then, black male co-teacher. He struggled to convince the youth that the term was inherently racist and degrading. They argued back that black people have always used it and when they use it, the meaning is understood in a different context. It was, as always, a multi-layered discussion. I attempted to chime in at one point but quickly realized it was not necessary unless someone asked me. It dawned on me that my whiteness, to a certain degree, allowed me the convenience in such cases, to be apolitical. At the same time, the black teacher could have chosen the same, but instead chose to fight the battle of social justice. His own, respectable choice.

My students further confirmed for me that *race*, more than a skin color or culture, is a state of being. Although based on very real circumstances, it is a fabricated identity. At first, I was reluctant to totally shed my white identity in front of my students. That is, when I realized that my race was indeed an important aspect of my experience and their perception of me, I had to make a conscious effort to do without it. Although I had been around people of color in all capacities throughout my life, this realization crystalized during my 2nd year there. Perhaps, it was the depth of their *blackness* that caused me to examine the depth of my *whiteness*. Both of these constructs are multi-layered "states of being" associated with various circumstances, behaviors and perceptions, but we have to remember that their sole determinant, skin color, is subjective. The same person considered "white" in parts of Africa would be considered "black" in America. The same person considered white in America would be considered Irish in the British Isles, etc...

An initial contact with a resident or counselor or any other worker at the center was purely racial—oversimplified and absolute. It was only after they got to know me that I could feel their attitude change about me. I became less white as we became better friends. My own state of *whiteness,* while teaching, became defined by the fear of releasing it, a fear of losing power—the power of domain. Sometimes, I would guess, the only thing between me and 10-12 potentially volatile, incarcerated young men were the rules in place and the threat of further punishment that followed—true, institutionalized *whiteness*. This institutionalization has protected white European males for centuries and it was originally very much about skin tone. My Sicilian grandfather would have been considered black in the Jim Crow south. Ironically, in 2020, institutionalized whiteness benefits black teachers in a school district like Philadelphia by giving them the same protection with regards to students, parents and privilege. Again, whiteness is a thing of status, separation and power. It reflects one's way of seeing the world, one's behavior, one's beliefs, not so much their skin color. In this case, it was black teachers utilizing the same rules representing *whiteness* that

I was utilizing. Accessibility to whiteness or white privilege could be assumed by anyone as long as they assumed a state of whiteness as a working educator.

Maybe foolishly, I felt it necessary to purposely shed my *whiteness* in front of the residents at times to show that although these rules were in place, I would not exploit them. It doesn't mean that I acted unprofessionally or "uncivilized" or offensive, at least in my view. I was careful to "get down" with residents without losing theirs or my own respect for my role as a teacher. It was liberating to always let the young men know that they were free to find me, meet me, contact me for whatever reason—good or bad. They respected that immensely. I traveled up on the units alone and was challenged on the basis of my *whiteness* quite a few times—but it allowed me to examine my own identity and eventually shed the fabricated part of me that still partly existed...seeing myself as *white*. It was, also, the moments when I was void of whiteness, that I could finally see them. I could finally hear them. Black and brown youth know right away how you view them when they hear your words and voice. They can pick up the most subtle vibe, the most subtle fear, arrogance, sourness or bitterness. They can almost feel prejudice when it enters the room.

Roughly 80% of those incarcerated in Philly were considered black, %67 nationwide (2019). Many a day after yet another tragic incident of racist police brutality in Philadelphia or around the nation or an unfortunate story about white supremacy, I would open the door to go into the unit and think about whether I wanted to address it or let it go. There were days that I reminded the young men that although I was the face of the sometimes racist policemen or judge they encountered, I was not here to judge them or punish them. I was here to listen and to share. It was appreciated. It was better to take a risk building bridges and make friends than it was to make assumptions and stay quiet.

One day, we were watching _Harriet_ in one of the units and a particularly outspoken and critically minded student "called out" white teachers as "racist in disguise" and acting just like slave masters. The young man was outspoken on a few occasions prior and had displayed an uneasy hostility in the room. I respected his honesty and did attempt to respond to him in the classroom once or twice, but it never seemed to amount to anything. The other students didn't exactly feel the same way as he, so my co-teacher and I didn't focus on addressing the racial "elephant in the room." After we watched an intense segment from the movie, that next day, he again went on a semi-tirade. I listened and decided it was best not to respond until I could speak with him one on one. Later, I traveled up to the unit and asked to speak with him. He came out of his cell and I pulled up a chair for him. He smiled, as if to know why I was there. He sat down and asked if I brought him any snacks. We both laughed and I declined of course. I was shocked at his amiability and candidness. I directed the conversation. "I wanna talk to you about what you said in class. Cool?" "Yea," he said. I want to try to understand your feelings toward white people and maybe help you understand my feelings toward racism, does that work?" He consented, "aight." I told him a few stories about my upbringing, my background, and my philosophy. He looked into my eyes and listened, replying, "You not really white though." I responded, "Well, of course not, because white is the color of the wall... but people see me as white and so that's what I am to them...Did you see me as white when you first met me?" "No, well yea a little bit," he shrugged...I continued... "And people see you as black, but wouldn't you agree that we are both much more than a single color?" He replied quickly. "I'm black, I know _that_." I probed, "...but is that all you want people to know about you? "Are you a son, maybe a brother? And are you smart, responsible or observant?" He nodded yes. **I asked** him what he thinks of when the term "white people " comes to mind? He said "...racist, fake... always showin' off." I nodded my head with consideration and replied, "Yea, maybe sometimes that's true." I asked—"Are there black people that are like that?" He smiled and said, "Yea but it's different... Y'all started it and y'all keep making life hard for us." I looked into his eyes and said, "You could say that... There are big problems with white supremacy and racism in general even in this city...but do you see white people doing good things in the world today?" He said, "Yea, I'm not sayin' all y'all are bad...Like you cool and the lady teacher is aight... Y'all try to help us." I listened. At the next moment of silence, I honed in, "Can I ask you a favor?" He said, *yea*. I proceeded, "Can you focus on the whites that are trying to do good? And I'll focus on not acting white and remembering to help when I can...Remember that I could judge you as a criminal, but I've never asked you what you did to get in here because I would never judge you based on that...I'm here to assist you either way. Now can you do the same for me?" He said "Yea, but I want a favor too." I quizzically asked, "What's that?" In a lowered voice, he requested, "Can you bring me in some *Starburst* tomorrow?" "I'll see what I can do," I replied.

Perhaps surprisingly, many students wanted to have conversations around race. They wanted to hear from white people and white teachers about the issues of the day. They wanted us to acknowledge that the systems in place were inherently racist. They wanted to know more about where race came from and what it meant to be *white* or *black*. They wanted to know where white people came from and why they hated so much. Such conversations, when approached with authenticity and empathy, were tremendously healing. **The blessing of my *whiteness* was that it brought an ironic angle of interventive therapy that couldn't happen if I was black. It was objective and indirect.** They saw my face as the same as the white hipster in their neighborhood or police officer that found them to be insubordinate, but many times, I heard them articulate in more ways than one, that a face is only a face. Some of the boys would arrive at the conclusion that they were in prison because they were black. In this, they were partly correct, but I told them that in my view, half of the reason they were in here was because the system was racist and corrupt, but the other half is because they as an individual were not being responsible—and that's the part we needed to focus on because that's the part we could change in this moment.

Whether race is propagated as the big white elephant in the room throughout America or if it is just the elephant who won't move off the porch (for all to see), the issue takes a microform in the classroom of every white school teacher who teaches particularly African-American children. If the children are old enough to understand the basics of racism, the presence of race is always looming—even if it has nothing to do with who is black or who is white in the room. There were, of course, a trickle of white kids that came through the center and served their time. They were, for the most part, in a similar survival situation. They were similarly traumatized and also prone to violence and anxiety. I didn't validate a victim mentality with them either. They, too, benefitted from discipline, responsibility and conscious breathing. They, too, needed to heal.

The Story of "D"

"D" was one of the few cases I have ever come across that genuinely had no filter whatsoever pertaining to his choice of words. He was a pasty-skinned, blue-eyed stout young man with wild, curly hair. He held consistent with his stance on doing no school work whatsoever. I was first introduced to him on the unit and he was locked in his hut, yelling at the top of his lungs, cursing at the counselors and threatening just about everybody under the sun. As soon as I walked in, he yelled—"I'll @#$% you up too Biseca!" The counselor rolled his eyes at him and invited me to teach out in the lounge where it would be a bit more quiet. For the next few days after he returned to class. he was quiet during meditations, but interrupted on occasion. "D" used the "N" profusely and allotted it to everyone indiscriminately, including myself. His use of the word, to the residents, was conceptual and under-stood as part of his "hood" talk just as everyone else who used it at the center—except "D" was white. He was about 15 years old and had come from a difficult or non-existent family situation. His mother abandoned him at a young age and he spent most of his time in the streets of northeast Philadelphia. Quite a few times, "D" was out of control and explosive, pounding on his door window. The others on the unit were unsure how to respond to him—perhaps some were fearful of him. He challenged me again and again. I noticed that his demeanor was different with another adult on the unit, an African-American woman who worked with him, one on one. He spoke to her with respect and a degree of gentility. I soon came to the conclusion that he disliked most white people. I wavered back and forth about this until I had greater proof, but after keen observation, I was near certain. Yes, "D" was white, and, ironically, he hated white people probably more than any resident that I came across in the center. Once I realized this, I became interested. I must admit, I sought to speak with him out of wonderment and curiosity. The woman that he got along with revealed to me that she, quite frankly, believed that "D" didn't *know that he was white*... It struck me as completely true as well. We had a talk one day...

For the 1st 5 minutes in our face to face chat, "D" ignored

eye contact with me and barely spoke. He refused to try a meditation or do the 1-minute moment. He showed me no hostility or disdain, just total disregard. I desperately tried to connect with him without reacting to him—I even told him a few stories and asked him if he could relate. He put his head in his arms on the desk, so I got up and organized my stuff. As I walked away, he spoke up in rapid verbiage, muffling his words into his forearm until his head popped up—I heard something about getting beaten..."I was hidin' under a car all night with broken ribs and then they found me and threw me in the Paddy wagon. I couldn't breathe and they ain't listen.. Y'all don't care...Y'all teachers don't even know..." It was as if his voice cried out from a dark and distant place of desperation. I was stifled and the voice stopped me in my tracks. I turned back to him, "We don't know unless you tell us." He looked away, stood up, and walked back toward his room. I was saddened, surprised but somewhat satisfied all at once. We had a breakthrough. From that point on, he attempted to regulate his behavior in my class much more. Instead of lashing at me, he gave me space to speak and didn't disrespect me. He remained a non-participant in our meditations, but kept himself quiet during meditation. He still did no work nor was he courteous to anyone. And he still used the "N" word at will.

Two years later, after the pandemic, almost unrecognizably, he appeared in my HH class with 11 other 17-year-olds. His braces were gone and he had the pining's of a young man. He quietly sat against the wall near the entrance and I said nothing, but when passing our papers, delivered a subtle fist bump gesture in front of him. He returned the bump and said "*sup.*" He seemed present and his demeanor was calm. He began his assignment immediately and when he saw the rest of the class partake in the *1-minute moment*, he conceded, closing his eyes. I took note of his changed demeanor and a feeling of completion came over me. I doubt that I had anything to do with his turnaround, but, either way, he was getting back on track, serving a bench warrant and a short time in the center. He was mild mannered and respectful. I didn't hear him use the "N" word at all. I'm almost sure someone else contributed to his stopping that. He left the center quietly after a couple of weeks. He was an outlier in every way, but he seemed to be figuring things out. He was blessed with the time and space and support to somehow do so. That means he needed people to be honest with him and most importantly, to listen to him. I look back at what "D" taught me and realize that it didn't matter if he thought of himself as black or white, he was finding out who he was within, and that was making all the difference.

Race Consciousness and Becoming a Better Teacher

The *sting* of race usually hit hard for the students, counselors and myself for certain topics in history, whether it was viewing clips from the Harriet Tubman or Jack Johnson stories or discussing yet another morning report of a new police shooting of an unarmed black man somewhere in the streets of America. Academic lessons dealing with race (usually in history, but some in English) seemed to further racialize the students and as someone facilitating the lesson, could never quite dispel this phenomenon. I've compared delving into race consciousness as similar to eating meat—you may need some once in a while for grounding, but it slows you down and causes inflammation if you eat too much. That's not to say that many of the stories and voices of the past didn't inspire the students and teach them valuable lessons about the past. The countless stories of black Americans are teachings of resilience and endurance, something that all young people can benefit from. I did my best, however, to avoid a victim-based analysis and reflect on events having to do with racial injustice in a way that provided not only understanding, but healing. Sometimes, it would even involve revealing my own vulnerability by letting the students project their experiences and feelings about racism. Sometimes it would involve a more reasonable approach that required real historical inquiry, as if we were solving a mystery. For each class and every lesson, there was a side that went unplanned. This is what those who only *write* curriculum don't quite understand—that there is an aspect of a lesson that is purely intuitive. A good teacher delivers to the group what the group needs and sometimes the teacher doesn't know what they need until the moment the lesson begins. It was through a pedagogy rooted in healing and intuition that pushed me to become a better teacher.

One day during summer school, we had analyzed the documentary about the 5 teenagers sentenced to prison for the murder of a woman in central park, "*The Central Park 5*." It wasn't quite my choice to show it but it was being "suggested" by my team as something the boys could relate to. This adapting the curriculum to "something they could relate to" practice didn't always result in a great acquisition of knowledge, but it had its place on occasion. The film was good. Powerful and thought provoking. Of course, the true story was sad and unendingly unjust. As I viewed the presentation with the residents and we discussed/wrote about various themes, I began to observe their emotions. I knew it was difficult for me to watch, but then I started to sense that they truly didn't enjoy watching it either. I watched their body language and heard the tone of their responses—there was a stiffness in the air. I felt like they were unwilling to individually emerge and voice discontent. The film certainly didn't provide them with any fresh way of dealing with a system that was inherently cruel, racist and ugly—which they knew first-hand. I finally probed further and after a discussion, I found that they wanted to see the outcome of the story, but watching the film was not enjoyable. I realized that day and was able to relay it to a couple of teachers— incarcerated kids dealing with trauma don't want to necessarily see something that they relate to first-hand. I could only speculate as to why. Maybe the familiarity makes some topics interesting to them, but for them to respond emotionally to anything involves a dose of frustration, no matter the topic. Certainly the lack of integrity of this terrible system is something that made them feel better about having ended up there. They had something to blame other than themselves. Yet, it triggered thoughts and emotions that they were desperately trying to get away from. It conjured a certain hostility toward me, who they usually treated with respect and amiability for the most part. They became spiteful and even refused to hand back their pencils at one point. Something was off. So the day after the film, I decided to take matters into my own hands.

The central park 5 story made me feel so badly that I was willing to try anything different, but I knew it had to be something that both redirected and inspired us all. We know that students don't gravitate toward a new concept, usually, if their teacher isn't impassioned by it as well. I had shown them "52 cards," the captivating story of Ray Lewis and his battle with childhood trauma. We had watched some videos of Erik Thomas, the revered motivational speaker and a slew of others—They were all stories of black people doing good things. I wondered, have I ever shown them a story of white people doing good things? That night I came across the story of two white west coast college kids who founded a company that made bracelets out of trash in the ocean—you may have heard of it—*4oceans*. It was completely different from what we had watched the day before, not only because the kids were white and came from a privileged background, but because the story was about environmental justice. I was transparent. I wanted to see how they responded. I decided to begin the class by saying, "I have some good news!" I was ecstatic. "The world is an amazing place and you will soon be back in it!" They laughed and reciprocated my mood right away. I continued in animated fashion, "Good things are happening!" I shouted... The world sucks but it's getting better because people are deciding that they want to fix things." I was out of my mind. They had no idea what I was getting at, but they were watching my every move. I cranked on the smartboard and began the brief clip of the surfers and their "clean up the ocean and make money doing it" idea. The whole time, I was staying boldly positive, feigning my uncertainty. **How would they handle it? Would they say "turn this %^&* off" or "we don't give &^%* about these dudes," or would they endure it? Could they possibly embrace it?**

We finished the video and I posed the question: "Do you think it's possible to make big money through doing something that makes the world a better place? A few hands flew into the air, "Yea!" they replied. I pressed on. "Ok, how did these guys do it?" One fellow responded quickly with a summary of the story. My hands opened into the air and I squatted in a salutation as I exclaimed, "This is what the future will be all about...The world is going to get better, and it's up to your generation to change it...I'm too old but you, YOU have your whole life to do good and make money as well." They were enthralled. They didn't have any idea what I was getting at, but my excitement brought them beyond a level of mild curiosity. "What if you could solve a problem with your company's products? That's what these guys are doing." The boys followed intently as we began reading a short explanation of *4oceans* and its mission. I asked them some follow up questions and then they wanted to see the video, of course. Our next task was to come up with some problems that we wanted to see fixed—and think of products that could be made that could help fix them. By the end of the lesson, the guys had come up with the idea of melting down all of the guns in their neighborhood (with the exception of some of their own) to make hand railings for the elderly. It was a tremendous idea. They had drawings, they worked cooperatively, they were inspired. That day I walked out of the youth wondering how to follow up on such a project. I'm still wondering. The point was that we changed the paradigm that day. Instead of drudging them through victimhood and self-defeat and fueling their anger toward police or systematic problems that they experienced everyday, they virtually stepped out of the entanglements of racial oppression and became inspired by two guys that had little in common with them. A story that was so far away from their world, that it presented a novel possibility. It got them to see the future differently—in a world that had abundance, value and goodness. That day, I didn't worry about analyzing their test scores or monitoring their paragraph writing progress. I also didn't shove the racial narrative down their throats so that they could continue "choosing sides" and justifying or resenting their incarceration. For a moment, it didn't matter that they were incarcerated, all that matters is that they were soon getting out. On the way out of the room, one gentleman counselor who I'll never forget, with the only short spurt of enthusiasm he could muster said to me, "You ain't too old Biseca...Get to it..." This, to me, is defeating trauma through activating emotional intelligence and highlighting responsible behavior. This is healing. Solving a problem is intrinsically motivating and brings self-efficacy, it brings the one thing that we all need more than anything—hope.

◆

A Non-Participatory Strategy

To address the countless institutional pinnings of racism and a race-conscious society (in education, criminal justice), we must engage these institutions with non-participation. We must take steps to claim our sovereignty through learning legalese and fighting in the courts to demand our sovereign citizenship as not black, white, this nation or that nation, but solely a member of the cosmic human family. We may need to begin by truly observing the institutions that we rely on, partake in and financial support everyday. How are they contributing to uphold the power structure? By shutting off the television (where daily news and advertising agendas racialize and propagate division to an obsession), we will begin to see that our neighbors and people in our communities want the same things as we do—peace, prosperity, equity... If our education systems do not feed our soul, then why should we validate that education as a priority? When the teacher tests us, we better serve ourselves and humanity to respond to such violence with inner peace. Why are we concerned about failing the test if it has no basis for our worth? Let the media, public health and education system be concerned with *evolution* or race relations while we individuals, friends and families explore *involution and the creation of our own communities*. If our criminal justice system or any other force preys upon us, we must prepare ourselves by becoming vigilant in our deeds and actions. We must hold fast to a practice of transformative self-awareness. Let our unjust systems die from our lack of participation in them. When they demand our attention, we must turn our attention inward. When they speak to us, we must speak a different language, the language of consciousness.

The only permanent truth is that of change. In addition, the willingness to change is a mark of courage, of maturity, of patience. That said, revolution reflects natural processes. As the seasons change, a full rotation around the medicine wheel represents one revolution, with each passing into springtime as the time of rebirth. In human history, it is the era of springtime. Krishna Murti takes a critical look at what a revolution truly embodies—an altogether different consciousness:

"To revolt within society to make it a little better, to bring about certain reforms, is like the revolt of prisoners to improve their life within the prison walls; And such a revolt is not revolt at all. It is just mutiny. Do you see the difference? Revolt within society is like the mutiny of prisoners who want better food, better treatment within the prison. But a revolt born of understanding is an individual breaking away from society—and that is creative revolution."

Murti clearly draws a distinction between true revolution and societal "revolt" which becomes of crucial importance when examining institutionalized racism in education and criminal justice as well as the concepts of *whiteness, white privilege* or *blackness* for the matter. So, our first assertion when approaching the ever-changing paradigm of racial relations and institutions in America, is that if we want true revolution, we must not base it on the need for equal access and equal rights within the same institutions that denigrate human consciousness at their core. Racial injustice is an undeniable factor in the social world around us and certainly within the criminal justice system and education system. It is and always has been a (global) state apparatus. It is learned and reinforced in our schools and falsely propagated as something that determines who we are. It is not. We are much more—each a spectrum of eternal colors, textures, landscapes yet to be imagined. Race consciousness exists as we, the enactors of it, allow it to exist and society need not create our identity. When the pressures of acting out or conforming to the norms are erased, we will realize how deeply the false darkness penetrates our light.

◆ CHAPTER 9 ◆

FINAL REFLECTIONS:
EDUCATION AND WELLNESS FOR ALL

What is the *1-Minute Moment* and Why Use It?

The *1-minute moment* can be administered to a group of traumatized youth and can be manipulated to fit the needs of any group. If 30-seconds suffices as a starting point, then so be it. Any group can begin slowly and make progress by utilizing the following process: (1) Hold the singing bowl in front of you with a straight posture, and, prepare to speak firmly but not loud or forcefully, as to create anticipation for the ringing of the bowl. Wait until the class responds with a general hush. Begin speaking: *"When you are ready, please straighten the spine and let's take a slow deep breath down to our belly so that it expands slightly. Close the mouth and begin.....Inhale ....and exhale"*. Continue firmly and clearly, reminding participants to quiet the breath and follow it down to the belly. *"At the sound of the bowl, I will begin counting as you inhale 5 seconds, then hold for 5, then exhale for 5 then hold, etc... Remember to bring the breath slowly from nose to navel and let go of any tension to the body...Become the breath, which is slow, deep and quiet."* Ring the bowl and begin counting... *"Inhale, 5,4,3,2,1, hold, 5,4,3,2,1, etc..."* A facilitator can add any additional inspiration or intention or added information such as "for better sleep at night" or "to calm the nerves" etc... I would also remind (and challenge) the students to keep their breath quiet so that nobody could hear it. A simple 5-5 breath is used to create hormonal balance and decrease anxiety through activating the Parasympathetic nervous system. Finish the exercise by ringing the bowl again and turning the pestle stick around to let the sound emanate if you choose. Depending on how far you want to take this, I have seen that the kids really look forward to that part. I would not attempt it if you cannot do it with effectiveness. End the turning gradually and say something quick and conclusive at the end—even if it's "*good job* or *well done.*" There are few reminders that can help the students attach value and meaning to the breathing. You can bring up (for especially the young ladies) that a woman cannot have a baby if she does not become aware of her breath while giving birth. By the same token, the boys are usually interested to hear that the first thing a boxer learns is how to breathe when coordinating his punches and footwork. If one is present during a boxing match, they'll hear the rapid short exhales of a boxer giving and taking punches. I also remind the students that within the air that we breathe is more than just oxygen, but strength and healing. The breath contains all 5 elements, beginning with fire, becomes earth, becomes metal, becomes water, becomes air—which is then contained within it, all of existence. Therefore, within the breath is our food, our water, our blood, bones and heartbeat. In it is our home, our relatives, our ancestors, our *spirit guides* and *angels*...being aware of the breath means never to be alone.

◆

The Variations and their Effects

A 5-5-5 breath, involving a hold after each inhale and each exhale, can be done before a challenging lesson or activity that takes focus. Similarly, a 4-7-8 or 7-11 breath (for 1—minute) is used because it challenges students to "keep up" with the breath and it requires their total focus. Ultimately, these 3 counts have been proven to decrease anxiety because they consist of a longer exhale, which, as stated earlier, activates the parasympathetic nervous system (and "pressurized" Prana and oxygen into the cells) and stimulates production of neurotransmitters, including serotonin. These controlled breaths not only begin working immediately (on blood flow, oxygen to the brain and releasing of optimum hormones), but they cover a broad range of long-term health benefits. Additionally, during exhalation, the vagus nerve secretes a transmitter substance (ACh)[1] which improves Heart Rate Variability (HRV). All of these breaths stimulate the vagus nerve (which is the motherboard of the nervous system) and counteract "flight or fight" stress. In an important study in 2018, Roderik Gerritsen[2] and Guido Band[3] of Leiden University in the Netherlands published a detailed theoretical review, "Breath of Life: The Respiratory Vagal Stimulation Model of Contemplative Activity," [4] in the journal *Frontiers in Human Neuroscience*. This review presents a wide range of studies that illustrate how slower respiration rates and longer exhalations physically and tonically stimulate the vagus nerve. Using diaphragmatic breathing techniques to kickstart the calming "rest and digest" influence of the parasympathetic nervous system is referred to as respiratory vagus nerve

---

[1] https://www.britannica.com/science/acetylcholine

[2] https://www.universiteitleiden.nl/en/staffmembers/roderik-gerritsen

[3] https://www.universiteitleiden.nl/en/staffmembers/guido-band#tab-1

[4] https://www.ncbi.nlm.nih.gov/pmc/articles/PMC6189422/

stimulation (rVNS).

"Breathing is massively practical," says Belisa Vranich, ... "It's meditation for people who can't meditate." says Dr. Richard Brown, Professor of Psychiatry at Columbia University calls even breathing "coherent breathing" and goes on to say that... "When you take slow, steady breaths, your brain gets the message that all is well and activates the parasympathetic response."

Compared to silent meditation, visual meditation, guided meditation, the *1-minute moment* allows for the only sound in the room to be the voice of the facilitator guiding the breath. I found that it becomes much more unlikely to be interrupted while counting than while talking. Hence, I ring the bowl and immediately say "and inhale, 5-4-3-2-1 etc...). Questions and further explanation can be addressed afterward. Be sure that you are counting loud enough with a somewhat authoritative confidence. *Own* this exercise and be passionate about it and the students will probably buy in. If it's for a group of 14 year old boys, tell them it makes their muscles stronger (which it does by fusing oxygen into the blood and mitochondria of cells), if it's a group of 16-year-old girls, tell them it produces optimum smooth skin, healthy nails and shiny hair(which it does by activating the parasympathetic nervous system that boosts the production of new cells and stimulates the endocrine system, allowing for absorption of vitamins and minerals while better ridding the body and skin of toxins). Any motive can be used, depending on the values of the group, which speaks of just how beneficial these breathing exercises are. The *1-minute moment* produced more results and was better received than any other technique. 1 minute is a standard unit of time and long enough to where the mental process can be regulated, but not too long for attention issues to set in.

The Effects of the *1-Minute Moment* Within a Group Setting

The immune system is very much influenced, and, in fact, mirrors the workings of our social world. As the immune system relies upon a vast array of working parts and integral relationships between related entities, our family or community serves to do the same. B-cells "tag" foreign invaders and T-cells create antibodies to eradicate those bacterial bodies not working toward the good of the whole. At the same time, the skin, the nasal passage and other innate parts of our immune defense, work together to support cellular vitality and cohesion. Such is the work of the institutions (ideally) in our communities and families. The group setting in the detention center was not a community oriented toward working as a whole, but a group of isolated cases of individuals who were trying to follow the rules and adhere to social norms to their own level of comfort. The collective group mentality, however, did take form at the start of a conscious breathing exercise. The *1-minute moment* breathing in unison triggered an automatic context of "groupthink" and community. Like the immune system, each individual entity was called upon to play a role important furthering the harmony of the communal setting. Succinctly, the benefits of conscious breathing with regards to the immune system tied into this phenomenon quite well. I would guess that there is a correlation with better immunity and feeling closely connected to a family and healthy community. Studies of effects of conscious breathing are abundant and it is clear that the mere act for even less than 1 minute can bring a parasympathetic response to the body and trigger numerous healing or calming actions in the body— and in time, creating greater immunity.

Breathing together consciously, as a class, however, can create an immediate unifying effect on a group. By engaging in such an exercise and empathetic component to the class-room, we are providing a platform for relationships, positive communication and understanding within the group—despite any predispositions that were brought into the room. This platform can set a precedent for classroom culture and serve as a precedent for behavior that can extend throughout the whole class period. Breathing in unison is more than drawing students together to partake in a collective task. This act is innately powerful, sacred and subtle. Sometimes the word *ritual* has a bad connotation in our society but Malidome Some argues that a community that does not have ritual cannot exist." He goes on to say that "A true community begins in the hearts of the people involved. It is not a place of distraction, but a place of *being*. In the moments of synchronized breath-ing, students are bound together by a centrifugal force that actually begins with the ringing of the bowl and metaphys-ically invites a collective consciousness. The sound of the bowl speaks directly to the subconscious. It is sometimes the first or only time of the day when they don't have to *act* together, but just *be* together. Conscious breathing together allows them to be an accepted part of a unified effort without worrying about producing or competing. They become open, for that moment, together.

Witnessing the tremendous shift in the culture and climate of my classroom after fully implementing the *1-minute mo-ment* was nothing less than shocking. There was an obvious current of ease that brought about more congeniality and cohesiveness in the classroom—despite lack of good relations among certain students. By starting class with a challenge or a problem, teachers sometimes create an imbalanced, compe-titive environment and this results in angst, which then dominates the mood of the classroom. By first authentically acknowledging something greater than the class lesson, greater than one individual or one subject, as a group, an element of harmony guides the remaining time period in the classroom. When the *1-minute moment* was fully integrated into a class routine, students on the periphery of the room, engaged in alternative talk or idling, were invited to join into a circle or group and most of the time, choose to partake. This left a definitive moment of time and space between those committed to be "in class" or "not in class" with the majority choosing to join the group. As a team gathers into a huddle or a prayer, group circles and joins hands, meditation before class brings routine, ritual, community and deference to something greater—all elements of a cohesive effort toward harmony. It took me over 3 years to mold the method, but allowed me to enjoy my final years teaching in public school because I knew that the tool of collective consciousness through breathing and the 1 minute moment was at my disposal.

The Inner Smile

The "inner smile" is a meditative exercise not coined by myself, but is a fabulous exercise to create self-awareness. It involves consciously guiding students to become aware of and breathe "through" some of their major organs, which not only brings them a tool for creating ease and healing in their life, but also maps for them, where certain organs are located.

"Begin with bringing the breath down to the belly and slowing the breath as you notice how it calms your body... There is no tension in the muscles, only upright posture and a straight spine. Become aware of how the breath makes you feel. Bring the inhale slowly down to your kidneys, the two small organs that filter your body located on both sides of your lower back. Breath blue into those areas and smile at your kidneys. Allow them to smile back at you. Release any guilt you feel.

Now breathe down to your navel and picture your intestines becoming lighter and more relaxed. Smile at your intestines and let them rest. Release any anxiousness. Breath into the top left of your belly, the pancreas, help you break down your food, picture it golden yellow. Release anything you are angry about. Smile and allow it to smile back at you. Breathe into your liver, the top right, picture it green. Smile and allow it to relax, for it detoxes your system and cleans your blood. Finally, come up to the heart and breathe into it. Smile at the heart, your true self. Allow your heart to smile back at you. Make that real connection. Take a deep slow breath and feel how good it is to love yourself. Look up at the third eye and smile at it. Take a few final breaths of gratitude. Slowly open your eyes..."

Education and Wellness, the Big Picture

School is not a place typically associated with *wellness*. We are entering an era, however, where self-care has become an essential part of both of our ability to thrive. And so many of our children need healing in so many ways. With the possibility of more pandemics on the horizon, climate catastrophes, toxins in our food, air and water and more stress related anxiety in a fast-paced technocratic world, time taken to regulate our minds and bodily systems is becoming a necessity for people of all ages and backgrounds—especially young people. Do we expect young people to "pick up" self-care on their own or while they're mindlessly tunneling through social media portals? Alarming rates of people under 40 are being diagnosed with diabetes, various forms of cancer, autoimmune disease, mental disorders, and yes, various forms of anxiety. *Psychology Today* reported 2021 that the average high school student today has the same level of anxiety as the average psychiatric patient in the early 1950's. In a world obsessed with safety and precautions, one that tracks people and information 24 hours a day, added layers of anxiety paired with past traumatic events are sure to worsen the situation. The result of a rapidly changing and unpredictable political economy is another taxing of the Adrenal-Pituitary cortex of every individual who must navigate the terrain of the social world. How can school-aged children learn to better prevent the health concerns that are becoming more prevalent at a younger age if they are in an institution all day that is not exposing them to techniques or practices of self-care? Is it really fair to rely on parents to add self-care teachings into the remaining small window of time and energy that they have with their children at home? If parenting should involve teaching self-care then schooling should at least involve reinforcing it. Such conditions are begging the essential questions, are schools really serving our young people? Is education keeping up with the true applicability of knowledge to thrive in the 2020's and beyond? Are we cultivating the ability of our young people to feel "present" enough to learn?

Public education has neglected wisdom-based lessons or self-awareness related teachings in its curriculum whether through a *de-emphasizing of* poetry in English (of which I witnessed), a lack of philosophy or emphasis on the interconnectedness of life in science, as well as an ignoring of the eras of intellectual awakening in world history such as Daoism in China and transcendentalism in the U.S. and obsessively drives home the importance of attaining trivial information as the key to success and the only pathway to learning. Fittingly, the ancient Chinese book of wisdom, the *Tao Te Ching* reminds us that "schooling that does not involve the soul (*Tao*) is poisonous to the mind." In that case, we must address the toxicity of the education system. I can attest to teachers spending more time analyzing, assessing, tracking, documenting, standardizing and aligning their lessons to meet state standards than thinking of ways to uplift and inspire their students. Additionally, there are more parameters, regulations and rules that now stifle making meaningful social and emotional connections with students because of the replacement of human interaction with technology. Public education has become a totalitarian big brother, indoctrinating more than educating. Students continue to learn about outdated and insignificant concepts in all subjects while the world changes rapidly. As we move with uncertainty into an era of needed sustainability (with polluted oceans and waterways), the science curriculum focuses on Chemistry equations and a sterile and objectified study of Biology. Marine biologists are still "studying" life under the seas while wild plant and animal life disappears. Let's hope the goal of their efforts is to promote life. Have we not realized that chemicals will not save life on earth and digital technology is distracting us from what is important?

As the need of understanding crucial patterns of time and form in the universe is upon us, we continue to drive home the education "program" and observe our children putting thousands of hours toward quantitative math problems that rarely provide insight into solving the world's geo-social and climatic problems. In social studies, war and politics are discussed at length in the classroom while the elite transnational corporate entities grow rich from pillaging the earth and exhausting natural resources. Finally, of course, health classes, which are considered electives of lesser value, provide a baseline understanding of the human body, emotions and disease or illness while the world faces a collectively compromised immune system, skyrocketing anxiety in teens and general crisis in the rise in cancers and other chronic illnesses. In that health class, you will find very little, if anything, that teaches our young people how to take care of themselves. No holistic techniques, few self-care practices and virtually nothing in the way of finding self-awareness... By not tuning into the needs of young people in post pandemic times, our school system will soon become one large juvenile detention center complex.

Whether it is called *mindfulness* or *inner reflection time*, no progressive educational institution can call itself *student oriented* if, at this point, it is not incorporating a specific time for student wellness beyond health class or lunch/recess time. If health class is the place for this, then we need a more interventive health curriculum—one that teaches self-care and holistic wellness. A child's wellness carries over to not only how well they take care of and understand themselves, but how they treat their elders, their classmates, friends, teachers... How they perceive the world around them. What educational curriculum can be more urgent at this hour? As teachers become introduced to ways of incorporating mindfulness, conscious breathing or even beingness into their classrooms, they must be permitted and encouraged to incorporate it into their curriculum, its delivery and their own daily practice so that students can model what they see.

Teaching in the 21st Century

27% of teachers at various levels reported that they are considering quitting the profession due to reasons other than Covid-19 in 2021. This mass exodus from teaching has begun and will continue until teachers are granted the support and respect that they need to be effective. I can speak from my own experience and say that of all the perks of the job, it has become dehumanizing. An excessive amount of students in the classroom and the amount of attention that each one needs to succeed along with a host of administrative and communi-cative demands creates insurmountable stress for todays' teachers. I have seen teachers humiliated and even physically assaulted by both students and parents in a system where distrust for educators because of the actions of a few, again, has led to a disregard for their well-being. Can we not hold teachers accountable while at the same time making sure that they are at %100 capacity to manage one of the most crucial roles in our society? Instead of supporting teachers, the state and corporate ivy league education-based practices have required them to be technocratic facilitators of digital learning. They are expected to navigate their way through an ever-changing technological landscape in their field while presenting information to youth in a tech-savvy fashion. Students don't need information. They can find that on the internet. They need human connections, they need mentor-ship. Ironically, many of my own students were tech savvy and jumped at the prospect of helping me figure out technological glitches. They thought nothing less of me when I didn't produce the technological "intelligence" to entertain a concept. They, instead, looked to me for "human" wisdom. We must not forget the difference. How can a teacher be a role model or trusted adult when they are mired with anxiety and "performance" pressure? If we want schools to invest any faith in their teachers or education, we must allow teachers to be more creative and train them in the arts related to conscious experience. Only when they can adopt their own style and present knowledge in a way that they seem fit will they be the care person that we need them to be in the classroom. Teachers too, are in need of more self-care than ever.

A Final Call to Action

Young people want to be ready for the future, not falsely promised that the world will be better and certain things will happen no matter what. Let's show them how to act responsibly and courageously. Let's teach them that their wellness and happiness is just as important as any social or political issue that arises and that if they prioritize their well-being, the other areas of their life will fall into place. Let's share with them the true benefits of becoming not just an educated person, but a complete person. The message we send by ignoring their well-being is one of pure neglect. If the CARES Act can include trauma-informed educational training that is %100 online, it can include funds to train individuals to lead meditative and self-care sessions either online or in person. Whether it's teachers that can embark on this venture or an added classroom assistant, the need for self-care has to be addressed in our schools. This generation craves the discipline and responsibility that go with creating a new and better world. The next generations of children can become tremendously resourceful if we implement programs for them as youngsters.

Equally as urgent is the need to revolutionize our restorative justice system for juveniles and their educational experience. It is clear from this research that young people from the disenfranchised populations of our society have been "criminalized" through generational and disruptive forms of trauma brought about by socio-economic conditions and historically oppressive forces. The politically aligned agendas are failing our schools and communities and violence continues to increase amongst young people—especially in our urban streets. The shift toward trauma-informed, responsible education through emotionally intelligent lessons deter trauma-based anxiety that leads to violence. Let's redirect the focus on assessing the minds of the youth and documenting their every move and instead focus on honing their skills through responsibility, empathy and self-care. Let's introduce them to the magic of existence and the realm of collective consciousness, where they can gain an authentic identity. The self-awareness that they acquire through collective and conscious breathing and other forms of meditation can and is rewiring their minds and impact their way of being. If these techniques are incorporated at a young age, the next generation will learn more, communicate more effectively, have less health problems and have more energy because they will know to take the time to activate their Hypo-pituitary axis through meditation and conscious breathing... They will *respond* to their world around them with peace and courage, rather than *react* with fear and aggression. They will initiate the change by becoming change. *Beingness* will be their salvation. The solutions are, indeed, at the tip of our noses—in the air that we breathe.

Trauma-Sensitive Lessons for Young Men

The following are a few theme-based lessons taken from my personal curriculum, "Beingness: Teachings in respect, self-awareness (identity), empathy, consciousness and spiritual responsibility." in simple format, that can be applied to all age-groups and school settings. They are grounded in the philosophy of beingness and promoting spiritual responsibility with our young people. Of course, they are to be applied with adaptability and discretion. The amount of time allotted for each concept is up to the teacher. Any creative instructor can build from them and utilize the concepts to create more activities. The foundation of course I suggest following them in order so that initial concepts.

◆

THEMES:

RESPECT/EMPATHY, RESPONSIBILITY, IDENTITY

THEME 1: RESPECT, EMPATHY and SYMPATHY

Objective: Students will demonstrate their understanding of the terms respect, empathy and sympathy through interpreting a Martin Luther King quote and creating a mock "respect" T-shirt (3-4 hours)

Respect: What is it and how can we use it?

Do Now: *Have you ever felt disrespected? What does it mean? What does getting respect look like to you?*

Define ***Respect (Use Frayer model)—definition: "Acknowledging the significance, abilities and or potential of something or someone."*** Teacher provides a breakdown of (definition acknowledge **significance and potential/someone or something***)

- Teacher provides example in Frayer "example" box: check for understanding of words acknowledge and potential.

  "Someone throwing their trash in the trash can instead of on the street"

  What or who is being acknowledged and how?

"Who more has the potential to be an actress in 15 years, an elderly woman or young girl?"

Video: Erik Thomas, "Respect"— *How does Erik Thomas define Respect? What examples does he provide?*

Worksheet: Respecting self: 3 major questions:

1. What does respecting myself look like? (Words and Actions)

2. What does respecting my family look like? (Actions and Demeanor/Energy)

3. What does respecting others in my community look like? (Actions and Non-actions)

Exit Ticket: If you were to teach your child about respect, would you begin with self-respect or respect for others? Justify your explanation by citing the definition(s) of respect

Respect: Sympathy or Empathy?

Teacher uses a Venn diagram with two words defined. Students have to fill in the middle aspect. What do the two words commonly represent ("How we relate to others")

> **Empathy**—comes first (understanding someone's experience or perspective because you experienced something similar)
>
> **Sympathy**—an emotional result of over-empathizing that causes us to feel bad for someone)

Worksheet: *Fill in the following situations with either EMPATHY or SYMPATHY*

1._____ John passes a man who is stuck with a flat tire on the side of the road and pulls over to help him because he remembers when the same thing happened to him.

2._____ Lena feels bad for the homeless man on the bench and gives him 5 dollars.

3._____ When Ali adopted his dog, the dog was under-fed. Now, Ali overfeeds the dog and spoils her because he still thinks about the day he found her.

4._____ A teacher teaches his students how to meditate because he knows how difficult it could be to deal with trauma or anxiety at a young age.

5._____ A Russian-American sponsors a Russian immigrant trying to gain American citizenship.

Exit Ticket: *Which Martin Luther King quote best shows that he was empathic? Explain how so using the definition of empathy in your answer.*

Discussion Questions: *How could we teach someone to be empathetic but not be too sympathetic? Which word, empathy or sympathy, is most common with respect? How so?*

Essay: *In what ways are empathy and respect related? Provide two examples in your response and be sure to refer to the definition of both words.*

PROJECT: Respect T-shirt:

Design a T-shirt (in google slides using Stop motion etc) that uses the word respect on the front. **"Respect" something or someone.** On the back they must write **"because..."** which must reflect the significance of the thing or person being acknowledged. They can of course add an image. They must explain their T-shirt in a paragraph that describes their ideal audience and the inspiration behind their message.

> <u>example</u>
> front: **"Respect motherhood"**
> back: **"because it's a full time job."**

THEME 2: RESPONSIBILITY

Objective: Students will analyze the term responsibility in terms of self-awareness and self-efficacy in order to make inferences into their own lives and actions through 2 inventories

Anticipatory Set: Begin by tossing a nerf or harmless plastic ball at someone to see if they catch it. Throw it to another, etc... ask *"What is the difference between reacting and responding?"*

Create Venn diagram with "react and respond"

> **Reacting:** impulsive, emotions are not filtered
> **Responding:** controlled, emotions are put aside

Responsibility is the ability to respond, reacting is acting or behaving without the use of mind. Ask what is the common element of the two ("ways that we interact with the world)

Video Clip: Show clip of Jackie Chan in *Karate Kid* "Everything is Kung Fu"
[https://www.youtube.com/watch?v=G6fOw5BRasw]

Is Jaden Smith responding or reacting? How so? How did his teacher show him responsibility?

Examples: Teacher Provides several everyday scenarios of people reacting and responding.

Roleplay: Create a roleplay where students react and respond to each other. Have them write a script for each.

Responsibility

Do Now: Inventory #1. Now that they understand the term "responsibility, Students will fill out an inventory that asks them where their top responsibilities are and rank them. The list includes:

-my family	-my mom
-my spirituality	-my partner
-my friends	-my school
-my community	-my planet
-my job	-my country

Identify the top 3 and explain why they feel most responsible to this and 2 actions that demonstrate responsibly toward the entity

Students could write a 3 paragraph paper on their top 3 choices or create a poster depicting their role

Inventory #2: Identify the list of statements with either "Always" "Sometimes" or "Never"— worth 3, 2, and 1 points

I take a moment to think about the situation in front of me before I act

I picture myself doing something that is important before I do it

I sometimes become aware of my breath and try to slow it down

I don't always say what I'm feeling or thinking

I like to spend time by myself when the world gets to be too much

When I'm mad, I like to get away from people

I work well under pressure

If someone is bothering me with the things they say, I usually don't let it get to me

Add up points and give them score:
20-24: Highly Responsible
15-19: Somewhat responsible
15 and below: need work

Responsibility and Courage

Anticipatory Set: *What is your favorite example of someone being courageous? Is courage usually present due to action or non-action?*

After the discussion, we identify words associated with courage and write about a time when we were given the choice to act on courage or fear. Let the students tell or read their examples/stories. *Where does our courage come from? (supposedly the heart). This is also the place that love comes from. Is there a connection? etc...*

Where would you say the core or most important part of a

human being is located? (the heart)—this is where we get the word "courage."

"We are going to understand responsibility through watching an amazing example of courage. First, are there any animals associated with courage? Usually someone says lion.

Video: Entitled "Stealing meat from lions" (YouTube) depicts some Kenyan elders during a time of drought. The elders are in sandals, They are very humble and soft spoken, but they, and their tribe are hungry. A camera zooms in as they close in on a pack of 15 hungry lions devouring a kill. What happens is one of the most incredible things I've seen on film and that is that the men walk up to the lions, causing them to scatter from the kill. The men take a shank and drape it over their shoulder and walk off hastily but calmly. The irony and power of the scene usually leaves the boys enthralled. *How were the men empathetic of the lions and how did it help them? How were they courageous? How were they responsible?*

Responsibility cont'd: Role play situation

Photo: protestors facing off with police.

Anticipatory Set: *Which one of these groups do you believe is being more self-aware or cautious and why?* They record their answers and we have the option of discussing them. Usually it's a mixed cadre of responses, but most will say that the protestors have to watch that they don't say or do the wrong thing to the police. **I then ask them to play the role of the *opposite* person/group they choose.**

Documents (2, each with one of the two roles), depending on who they chose. In each, I provide a fictitious background of either the protester or the police officer and illustrate their perspective and point of view of what is happening (i.e *I am upset at what is happening and these police are threatening my right to assemble and use the 1st amendment etc..*). Under the description are 3 prompting questions: (1) I have to be responsible, however, today because...The students have to provide two answers. (2) I can show responsibility by .... (3) If I am not responsible, this is what might happen....

Share out: Students read out their answers and we conclude that it is essential that all parties involved are responsible at every moment.

Responsibility through Self-Efficacy
(*Visualizing the life you want*)

Do Now: Write down one thing you are grateful for
    Discuss the importance and power of gratitude. *Does anyone believe having what you want has to do with gratitude? Why so?*

Prepare for conscious breathing exercise: Students may have the option of closing their eyes. *Picture yourself on a warm beach with beautiful white sand and the sun shining. "Everything is glistening and you are eating a fabulous meal with some of your closest friends and family and your loving partner. You all are laughing as the sun sets over the ocean. You go back to your beautiful home that is right on the beach. You walk in the elegant and comfortable beach entrance and slide the door closed. A feeling of comfort, safety and accomplishment comes over you as you go to sit on the clean, new couch to turn on the big screen TV. You've worked hard and done the right things in life and you feel happy, satisfied and* *thankful."*

Answer the following questions in your journal:

1. *Who were the people you were with on the beach?*

2. *What work do you do/have you done to get you to this point?*

3. *What clothes are you wearing?*

4. *How do you feel about yourself? Why?*

5. *Describe your house and bedroom. How is it set up?*

6. *Write two words to describe this "dream" life.*

7. *Do you think this life is possible?*

8. *How could you make it happen?*

Have students write a plan set up in a chart format with "goals" written at the top and the 5 questions below written in the margin. Have them fill in the blocks:

"friends and family," "income/career," "homelife," or "emotional state"

GOALS	
How do I show gratitude?	
How do I set boundaries?	
How do I take care of my own business?	
How do I stay disciplined by practicing something?	

What is my vision?	

THEME 3: IDENTITY

Objective: Students will be able to identify various archetypes that they embody and express new ways to view their identity as a part of humanity's collective consciousness

Anticipatory Set: Show short identity film with masks. [https://www.youtube.com/watch?v=ikGVWEvUzNM]

What does the film remind us about people? What did the girl realize?

What categories are used to identify us? For example, religion

Tally answers as students name social groups/identities

Do any of these identities automatically give us something in common with others? (All of them bring us commonality with others, but none of them bring us commonality with everyone). Could we have a common identity with someone who we don't necessarily get along with?

Krishna Murti quote: "Violence is not merely killing one another. It is violence when we use a sharp word, when we make a gesture to brush away a person, when we obey because there is fear..When you call yourself an Indian or a Muslim or European, you are being violent ...because you are separating yourself from mankind. When you separate yourself by belief, by nationality, by tradition, it breeds violence. So a man who is seeking to understand violence does not belong to any country, religion, political party or partial system; He is concerned with the total understanding of mankind."

Do you agree or disagree?

Exploratory writing: What is our true identity if these have the effect of separating us from humanity?

Show medicine wheel circle—earth water, air, fire (elements)

What if we identified with elements rather than races? Would it be easy to tell who is who from the start? Would people still find a reason to be prejudiced?

Identity through elements (besides elements, you can use planets/zodiac, seasons, masculine or feminine archetypes, animals, metals, gemstones etc):

<u>**Document—**</u>

Archetypes: The 4 elements, seasons and social roles

Discover your power elements: Fill out the following questions:

1. What is your birth sign (zodiac wheel available)?

2. Would you describe yourself as:
   - (a) "go with the flow" (c) spontaneous
   - (b) stay the course   (d) stay in one place

3. Which do you best identify with?
   - (a) fish   (c) butterfly
   - (b) snake   (d) bear

4. Which do you like best:
   - (a) dancing   (c) biking
   - (b) training/exercise   (d) sitting at home

*Add up the scores (A's are water, B's are fire, C's are air and D's are earth) and use whatever simple matrix allows them to make a deduction

Introduce the medicine Wheel:

Find your power element and see which other archetypes besides elements you align with. Animals? Celestial bodies? Seasons? The Joker, Priest, Warrior or King?

Match up the 4 words with the four roles. Show 4 roles on the medicine wheel and associate it with *earth, air, fire* and *water* as well as *winter, spring, summer and fall.*

East-spring-fire-warrior
   Why is the east associated with fire? (the rising sun)
South-summer-water-joker
   Why may the joker connected to water? (fluidity etc)
West-fall-air-priest
   What is the link between air and fall? (fluttering leaves)
North-winter-earth-king
   Why is a king affiliated with earth element? (stability)

Create an identity tattoo: that includes one of your archetypes or your power element. Include a drawing/design and 3 adjectives to describe the connection to that archetype.

> **example**
> I choose summertime as my archetype ...
> "fun, free and scorching"

Be creative and authentic! I found this video and readings that take the element of water and illuminate its power, meaning and connection with consciousness

Video: *Becoming Water*
[https://www.youtube.com/watch?v=Au6VesDZrzk]

(Fela Kuti song "Water" with images of Africans and their salvaging of water)

> - **Response:** *How does the video remind us to be grateful* (many in sub-Saharan Africa and other places have to walk miles each day to retrieve water for the day)

> - The lyrics to the song are "water get no enemy— yet water can kill your child, water can cook your soup, water can flood your house etc.."

> - **Journal or discussion:** *What do you think Fela is trying to say about water?*

READING: Paulo Coelho *Warrior of the Light* p.33 "The Warrior acts like water"

> - **Vocab:** Versatility, fluidity, absoluteness, fragility

> - **Response:** *What are 3 things that Coelho reminds us about water?* (adaptable, strong, always flowing to the sea). *How could it help us* identify *as water?*

EXIT TICKET: Bruce Lee quote: *"Water can crash or flow, be water my friend."* *How does Bruce Lee's quote show us that he identified with water? remind us to be water?* Cite either something from the Fela Kuti video or the Paulo Coelho reading that supports your answer...

These lessons could be adapted with accompanying meditative or mindfulness activities. Undoubtedly, mindfulness captures much of what has been taught as ancient wisdom for generations in countless cultures before the advent of *mindfulness-based meditation* in America. Whether we examine the *Taoists* in China or Shinto's and Buddhists in Japan, *Capoeiristas* in Brazil or even the Knights Templar tradition of Europe, mindfulness, the act of becoming aware of the present moment through disciplined activities has been something people have practiced for millennia. Maybe this is where we can begin addressing the seemingly hyper-phenomena of global anxiety that exists nearly everywhere on our planet today. That said, these lessons truly go beyond utilizing mindfulness. **They invoke a collective archetypal memory that doesn't create a defensive ego-based identity, but inspire young people to find how they play a role in the story of humanity.** Some of these lessons ask them to think reflectively about the moments of their day and visualize what they want in their future and understand the values and mindset it takes to achieve that vision. By adding mindful activities or conscious breathing techniques, the curriculum is sure to create transformational experiences for those students experiencing trauma-related anxiety. I have undoubtedly witnessed it. My sole desire to create these lessons was to propel such students past their anxiety and self-doubt and gain greater respect for themselves from seeing how they are part of the collective consciousness. The lessons create, again, this unified recognition that we all experience anxiety, but can defeat fear, find self-awareness, courage and identity while acknowledging together, the difficulty in doing so.

This universal innate ability of all of us to emerge as liberated beings through consciousness is using sacred sociology. The lessons are built on that idea of a universal innate ability that we each possess to strive to understand ourselves and harmoniously exist with the universe. That striving comes with awareness, discipline, responsible practice and inner vision. It begins with becoming aware of the breath, aware of our emotional content. We must begin to incorporate our knowledge of ourselves as a species to show our young people the way. Recognizing duality, the divine masculine and feminine are essential.

Qualitative Data:

I was able to receive valuable feedback from my students throughout much of my time at the center. That feedback, in the form of surveys, student journal responses and my own personal daily reflections, is the basis for this section. It is, among other things, intended to illustrate actual verbiage from students about their experience meditating (or partici-pating in the 1-minute breath and other beingness-oriented lessons). Unfortunately, and perhaps, tragically, a large number of their writings were lost during the Coronavirus Pandemic after a major clean out project in the building included my stored stacks of student journals and responses from the 1st 3 years of teaching. Nonetheless, I was able to salvage some material that I had previously taken home and soon after, begin a new period of data collection in the spring of 2021. Nothing could replace, however, the material that was lost.

The Problem

It was clear from the onset that added intervention was needed at PJJSC in terms of trauma-related disorders in the resident population. As discussed and summarized below, traumatized students experience brain-altering stress that causes them to become more reactive to triggers and less likely to learn. While they possess, in many cases, great intellectual potentials and adaptive abilities, they are not in a state of being to intellectually engage within a group setting and or become academically oriented.

"*Recent neurobiological, epigenetics, and psychological studies have shown that traumatic experiences in childhood can diminish concentration, memory, and the organizational and language abilities children need to succeed in school. For some children, this can lead to problems with academic performance, inappropriate behavior in the classroom, and difficulty forming relationships. Learning about the impacts of trauma can help keep educators from misunderstanding the reasons underlying some children's difficulties with learning, behavior and relationships."*

The effects of trauma clearly include the loss of memory, the inability to complete tasks and the inability to regulate emotions. In a setting such as PJJSC, this often then manifests into violence, frustration and anxiety both in and out of school. Fortunately, restorative practices were being used in the school through PBIS (positive behavior incentives system) and counseling was available if requested. With added pressures, however, to secure housing, a job or a degree upon exiting the center, the presence of violence sometimes in the school area and certainly on the unit, a growing special education population and high rates of recidivism (27% would return within one year), there was room for further intervention. In addition to a restorative school culture and academic support, I felt the need for mindful intervention by using breathing techniques and guided meditation to instill discipline, address ongoing student stress and the effects of complex trauma.

Ethics, Validity and Reliability

The challenges to tracking and "proving" that some form of mindfulness or meditation could curtail anxiety, frustration or violence were numerous. The first of these was my role as a teacher and not a social researcher. I was not hired to do research and I would venture to say that I may have been reprimanded if the admin team had suspected it. That said, my duties as a teacher were always carried out as first priority and my duty to the confidentiality, stability and educational progress of the residents was prioritized as well.

Ethically speaking, I, undoubtedly, saw the meditation time and the study as well worth the time spent with the students—both for them and the implication of this study. None of their names were used in this report and no further information will be divulged about them by name. No student was ever asked to meditate as a requirement and they were given comfortable space to opt out in either the classroom and the one on one setting. Again, my priority was always fulfilling my role as a teacher and providing my students with a safe space to be inspired for learning. Although they did not know the extent of my practice with the students and were certainly unaware of this study, my administrators found it permissible to use meditation at the beginning of class and I had been granted authority to facilitate one on one sessions, given that schoolwork was done as well (which lasted about 2.5 months, during a lockdown period and before the quarantine era of Covid-19).

There were a few weaknesses of this study in terms of validity. The nature of "measuring" variables such as *frustration* was difficult because it was based on (a) semi-subjective answers representing students' observation of themselves (b) those observations could fluctuate at any given time for any given reason. The lack of longitudinal data also poses a hindrance to conclusive evidence, although there were instances where students were surveyed after a 4-5 week period after an initial survey. Due to the context in which I did my work, which includes my job title and my integrity as an employee (secondarily, a research scientist), measuring changes in student behavior due to meditation was best done through survey, interviewing, observation and journaling. I could not, obviously, record these interviews, but gained much from the interpretation of written entries, a small sample of which are included in this book.

Overall validity was reinforced with concise questioning that directly spoke to variables such as *anxiety* and *focus*. Students reported on their own feelings. The study sought to understand the effect of meditation on these variables, along with making inferences toward empathy and social connectedness. I was sure to use words that the young men understood and was keen on them interpreting those words that same way I did. The students were always told to be honest and that it would have no effect on their grade. In the survey, I was sure to make options clear and accessible without showing a bias toward any preferred answers, while choices of all possible ranges and outcomes were presented.

A weakness with validity was of course my presence during the survey in both settings, which was unavoidable. I tried my best to diminish this influence by sitting at my desk or performing another task while they finished their survey. In some instances, a small piece of candy was given to those who answered all the questions. A semi-experiment was done to show any possible longitudinal effects (over a 4-5 week time period) which would increase validity of the study in terms of measuring diminishing *anxiety* and increased *focus* or *discipline*. To make the experiment more reliable, I used a Likert scale and doubled the amount of questions for each of the variables, using synonyms so that each had two questions to assure a student was being consistent: The following synonyms were used: Anger/frustration, stress/ anxiety, unfocused/scattered. The experiment that demonstrated the possible effects of meditation over time with the young men was dynamic, but was, of course, unable to measure physiological changes in any of the students (brain function, heart rate, breathing rate, etc)...Additionally, the experiment could not account for moment to moment emotions or moods, or feelings toward me personally that could have underqualified some of the results. Finally, multiple classes were involved in the experiment at various points in the year to strengthen both validity and reliability. Students were encouraged to meditate on their own and although this could not be statistically accounted for, many reported doing so, with no reward involved. A 3-week time period proved to be sufficient enough to produce noticeable shifts in anxiety and or focus. All surveys were counted along with those choosing not to answer questions.

Concerning further reliability, The 1-minute moment was done the same each time for each class with no variation and all classes of all age groups (13-20) at different times of day throughout various points of the school year participated. The experimental group was a group of 16-17 year olds who may not produce the same results as groups older or younger. They were chosen as a median age group. As per the one on one sessions, they all lasted the same amount of time, 10-20 minutes, and each meditation was performed after an initial discussion.

Methods

The theoretical basis for this study was that meditation and particularly the "1 minute moment," had the ability to quell anxiety associated with trauma. This technique, which varied by breath sequence, was conceived organically during my time using meditation in the center. The experimental aspect of this study provided the only prospective quantitative. That which was gained from student journaling, short answer responses, surveys and my own notes consisted of the majority of qualitative feedback. That said, the experimental study was the only data collection done with the same students that showed an effect over a period of time. The surveys were given to all male groups and a group of 11 females, who each also responded to one writing prompt. The only formidable way to measure variables (given the context) such as *anxiety* and *focus*, was to create a simple metric based on multiple choice and short answer questions in both survey and interview formats. Sufficient writing time was given for students responding to prompts and keyword or phrase identification was used in a factor analysis that filtered the connectivity of such phrases or words to the "base" words—*stress*, *anxiety* and *focus*. Regrettably, I was not able to measure meditations' effect on recidivism, which would be a more complex process, but I would take the opportunity if supported to do so in the future. I was able to administer 2 different surveys in both a one on one setting as well 2 different surveys in a group setting to all male classes(see below). In each instance, the surveys were administered after the initial meditation/breathing exercises. There was one instance where we had to re-do the survey due to an incident in class. An analysis of the data is below.

The Experimental Groups

The 1st group (2 sets of 4 classes) was surveyed at the beginning of the term and they assessed their own "stress" level, "frustration" level and level of "focus" by using a Likert scale of 0-3 with 10 questions, 30 being the highest score (0=none, 1=sometimes, 2=often, 3=almost always). The "before" assessment was given to 88 residents, while roughly 63 of those same students completed the "after" survey administered 4 weeks later (Due to students leaving the center after a placement and a small percentage of non-compliance, there was not %100 response for the "after" portion). These students participated in both guided imagery meditation and the "1 minute moment" breathing technique at the beginning of each class, for roughly 15 consecutive classes. The "before" and "after" instructions were the same: "Circle the level that you currently feel while in the center." The following synonyms were used to tie stronger meaning to the variables: "anxiety"/"stress," "frustration"/"anger "focused"/"scattered" etc... The metric tallies were as follows:

"Stress" level— 8 students reported a decrease by 5-10 points, 31 students reported a decrease by 1-4 points, 20 reported no changes, 4 reported an increase by 1-5 points

"Frustration" level— 2 students reported a decrease by 5-10 points, 26 students reported a decrease by 1-4 points, 23 reported no change and 10 reported an increase by 1-4 points, 2 reported an increase by 5-10 points

"Able to Focus" level— 9 students reported an increase by 5-10 points, 12 reported an increase by 1-4 points, 36 reported no change and 5 reported a decrease by 1-4 points

The experiment revealed much in the way of meditations' possible effect on these three variables. A few factors could have altered the validity of experiment such as favorability toward the class, the time of day, my own presence in the room during the survey, as well as immediate circumstantial factors that were out of our control between the before and after surveys were administered, such as court appearances, medications, disdain for school, conflicts with others, or events with home life. A reliability issue would be the possibility of misinterpreting any of the questions, lying or not reading them thoroughly. I was sure that they understood that

I was referring to their feelings and perceptions during their time in the center.

Results

"Stress" levels were clearly diminished after the 4 weeks showing a strong correlation and a total of 39 students reported a decrease. "Frustration" levels decreased as well, but with less of an occurrence. There was a somewhat noticeable increase by one level in frustration, but we can possibly attribute this to daily mood or some of the other factors above. Students with complex trauma experienced complex emotions toward complex challenges in their life and those could frustrate them in many ways. I used the word "frustration" because it was most often associated with anger for students, which was different from stress. "Able to focus" levels were somewhat changed after meditation but there was an exceedingly high report of no change. Many students answered with a 3, or high level of focus at the onset and therefore, there was not a higher number to assess them for an increase. This could be that they associate "focus" with a skill or competency that they possess and would not show a lack thereof to report because of pride or need to impress. Overall, the experiment provided some strong possible evidence that mediation and the "1 minute moment" could very well be curbing the effects of trauma within a 3 week time period.

The 2nd group survey was in a slightly different format, but similar in questioning and style. It was given to 91 residents and 79 students completed the Likert scale portion with fidelity while 64 completed the additional 2 short answer questions. They had practiced the "1 minute moment" for 4 weeks and there was no before or after measurement.

The "group 2 survey" consisted of a Likert scale with 6 questions and four options (Often/a lot=3 Sometimes/somewhat=2 a little=1 none=0) and asked an additional two open ended questions. Below are the questions and the results of that surveys:

1. How much do you participate in meditation/breathing at the beginning of class?

2. How much does meditation or breathing exercises calm or relieve your anxiety?

3. How much do meditation or breathing exercises help you focus during class?

4. How much do you believe meditation or breathing is helping you deal with life in the youth?

5. How much do you believe the 1 minute moment improves discipline?

6. How much do you believe you would use meditation outside of the youth?

Open ended questions:

7. Below, please explain what you believe to be good about the 1 minute moment or breathing at the beginning of class:

8. Below, please describe what you have learned about meditation ?

Results for the Likert portion by question number:

1. 3—40 students 2—22 students 1—12 students 0—5 students

2. 3—36 students 2—20 students 1—18 students
   0—5 N/A
3. 3—43 students 2—24 students 1—12 students
   0—5 N/A
4. 3—20 students 2—25 students 1—28 students
   0—5 N/A
5. 3—45 students 2—13 students 1—13 students
   0—8 students
6. 3—16 students 2—18 students 1—15 students
   0—23 students

The above data reveals much in the way of possible correlations with meditation/breathing exercises and student favorability, which could reflect a positive influence on their well-being and overall school/residential experience. A few factors could have altered the validity of experiment such as favorability toward me, personally, favorability toward the class, the time of day, my own presence in the room during the survey, as well as immediate circumstantial factors that were out of our control between the before and after surveys were administered, such as court appearances, medications, disdain for school, conflicts with others, or events with home life. A general reliability issue would be the possibility of misinterpreting any of the questions, lying or not reading them thoroughly. The 1st question was asked to assess the level of participation, which was an indicator of favorability. This showed a strong indication of participation either because of group behavior and peer pressure or individual favorability. 5 students reported not participating and their responses were nullified with the exception of question numbers 5 and 6. With about half the students reporting that they partake often at the beginning of class. There may be a validity issue with associating such a response with a grade in the class, even though it was stated that it would not be. The

2nd question, like in the 1st experiment, reveals a strong possible tendency that the mediation could be relieving the stress associated with trauma. The 3rd question demonstrates that there could also be a strong positive influence of meditation on class participation. I have observed this and had made such conclusions, but this data certainly ascertains it— inferring a great possibility. Question four was somewhat showing a possibility that meditation could be helping with their overall experience in the youth. The numbers are a bit high, however, on the "little" difference side. Surprisingly, over half of the students associated mediation with discipline. This illustrates that meditation could not only be affiliated with therapy, but with behavior and discipline. The result included those who reported not participating. Such an overwhelming response shows the possibility of few other phenomena related to discipline regarding specifically the 1 minute moment. It reveals, perhaps, the need for concentration during the exercise and the revelation that "I don't do anything in my life (currently) with such precision." It could also reveal that the students associate a challenge with discipline and or me being a male and the act of counting for or controlling the group to act in unison. Finally, it may show that the boys, in some aspect of their consciousness, crave discipline and respond favorably to anything that elicits a response in reference to it. The final question reveals that most students did not plan to use the techniques outside of school, but a reasonable number of students (16) reported that they would. <u>If every 16/88 students who leave the youth practice meditation or the "1 minute moment," I would venture to say that recidivism would decrease significantly.</u>

◆

Open-Ended Questions

The purpose of this 1st question was to allow students to identify the positive effects from the meditation by using their own words and description. The question was purposefully posed with a bias towards students who found it favorably so that they would elaborate on the answer. The results for the 1st were judged as favorable or not favorable and a list of keywords or phrases was compiled referring to response (below):

Out of the 64 responses, 28 made two references of positivity and 36 made one reference to a positive result. Words/phrases used were as follows:

Words used associated with stress/anxiety:

"Stay calm" or "calming"— 9
"Relax"— 5
"Chill"— 2
"Fall back"— 1
"De-stress"— 2
"be/stay cool"— 2

Words used associated with negative emotions:

"Deal with ..." (the youth, anger, my situation, school, frustration, emotions, my life)—14
"Calm my anger"— 2
"Smooth"— 1
"Cope with ..."— 2
"Nice"— 13
"Control/manage my emotions" or "keep my emotions in check"— 6

<u>Words used dealing with focus:</u>

"Helps me focus"— 23
"concentrate/concentration"—16

<u>The results show strong expressions of the 1 minute moment helping with anxiety/stress, negative emotions and helping with focus.</u> Students overwhelmingly elaborate, also, on meditation positivity influencing their ability to focus or concentrate. This could be due to the natural need to focus while partaking in the "1 minute moment" or it could be their Regardless, such a response warrants further investigation of their academic progress and class behavior over time. This initial look, however, is convincing enough to determine that meditation is a viable and favorable intervention.

The "One on One" Setting

The one on one setting provided a different context for using both guided meditation and the "1 minute moment." The students who sat with me in these sessions were offered, at their own choice, through the words of their counselor, to "sit with Mr. Biseca, meditate and discuss any personal issues." They were residing on the *in-take* units, which were the units allotted to residents transitioning directly from court or recent arrest. Often, these young men were wounded, physically and emotionally. They had come in directly from the streets and most of the time were willing to talk to anyone or try anything to alleviate the pain. I documented 124 conversations/ mediations and several cases of the same students repeating 2-3 sessions. 116 of them involved meditation (either guided or 1 minute moment, depending on what I felt would benefit most. Usually with more emotionally charged or angry cases,

I used the 1 minute moment) after we discussed their situation and how they felt. The discussions usually lasted 10-15 minutes and I would offer them a perspective while mildly coaching them into a mindful way of handling what they were dealing with. For those who were angry or showing anxiety, I would give them the option of facing the wall or door so that they did not feel like I was staring at them. In those cases, I would usually guide them through the "1 minute moment." In most cases, the residents were in a calm state after our conversation and would more than willingly partake in a short guided meditation in which they learned conscious breathing to the diaphragm. If they were injured, I would guide them through a more healing-based protocol which specialized on their area of hurt.

At the end of each session, they would fill out one of two surveys, depending on if they did the "1 minute moment" or guided meditation. Some possible validity issues include the skewing of answers reflecting a willingness to conform (Hawthorne Effect) with me being present. Reliability may have been affected with any sense of hurry during the answering of the questions or any questions answered with the various situations present that were mentioned above. The 1st part of these (voluntary) survey questions asked them to circle any of the following that they were experiencing (*anxiety, anger, confusion, keeping focused, physical injury, depression/sadness, safety, addiction*). The next question asked them to comment on any specific information that they wanted to share or discuss related to the options above. I usually paused after this section and looked at their answers for indication of any immediate discussion. The final three(3) questions were:

1. Do you feel it was worth sitting with Mr. Biseca today?

2. Do you believe that mediation is helping you deal with any of the above challenges?

3. Circle all that apply: For me, meditation ("relieves stress, calms emotions, adds focus, brings bad emotions, creates chaos, adds stress)

1 minute moment
(total 54 students)

Guided meditation
(total 62 students)

1 minute moment (total 54 students)	Guided meditation (total 62 students)
52 Yes | 2 No	58 Yes | 4 No | 2 no answer
51 Yes | 2 No | 2 no answer	53 Yes | 2 No | 1 no answer
number of times circled: "Relieves stress" 49 "Calms emotions" 38 "Adds focus" 33 "Brings bad emotions" 2 "Creates Chaos" 0 "Adds stress" 2	number of times circled: "Relieves stress" 55 "Calms emotions" 41 "Adds focus" 21 "Brings bad emotions" 5 "Creates Chaos" 1 "Adds stress" 1

Analysis

The results above indicate a few possible interesting statistics and support a few possible trends. It is clear, first, that both the guided mediation and the "1 minute moment" according to the residents, is helping them cope with emotional or stress related issues and it is worthwhile to partake in the exercises. A slightly higher percentage shows this for the "1 minute moment." 90% of students doing the "1 minute" reported a relief in "stress" from the technique while slightly less reported it for the guided meditation. The numbers were similar for "calming emotions," which could be interpreted as the same effect. "Adding focus" revealed noteworthy differences between the two techniques. The 1 minute moment was reported by 61% of residents to add focus while the guided mediation only saw a %33 effect from the same category. Also, the 1 minute moment saw far less negative effects than that of the guided meditation, which still only revealed a few instances. <u>This data supports the trend of the "1 minute moment" being an effective tool for anxiety and relieving stress as well as enhancing focus.</u>

Qualitative responses: A sample of student responses below where specific references were made to meditation being beneficial and those references were described

"Write about the hardest part of being in PJJSC: Do you believe mediation can help?":

Student response: "GF" age 17
"The hardest part about being in the youth is not being home with my mom and brothers and sisters. I been doing some meditation and I can say it works. My mom needs to do some when I get home. I'm feeling bad about what I did and I know she is mad at me, but I know she still loves me. She gets mad at mostly my brother and he been acting crazy since I'm not home. When I get home I'm gonna show them how to meditate...I think that it's what everybody needs. These times is stressful and I know my mom would like meditation and it would calm her thoughts..."

Student response: "ZJ" age 18"

Being in the youth is tough because these #$%^&
in here drawin and I got better things to think
about. I got a daughter and they need me at home.
I been trying to keep myself together so I been
doing the meditations a lot at night and I try to
finish my work so I graduate and get a job. I think
the meditation helps me stay focused and it helps
me (pass) the time..."

"Please create a description of how to do the breathing for meditation using a step by step process":

Student response: "LS" age 15
First, you have to steady yourself and sit up
straight and start your breathing through your
nose. Next, you can count to 5 for inhaling and 5 for
exhaling. Make sure you don't breathe too fast...
Then you wait until the bowl rings."

Student response: "PW" age 16
"First, you sit up with your back straight but not
too tense. Then you can start breathing 5 seconds
in and out. Make sure you breathing through your
nose. You don't need to think too much just follow
your breath. Next when the bowl rings, you open
your eyes and you good."

"Please describe 2-3 reasons why people might want to try meditation. With those 2-3 reasons, describe how it could benefit them":

Student response: "MG" age 18
"People should try meditation for many reasons. It
is calming for anxiety and it helps keep you on

track. If you are breathing in a steady way your mind stays focused on your breath... and you don't think about things worrying you. The second reason is that meditation makes you discipline yourself. If you pick a time you can do it everyday... and stick to it...Discipline benefits you for your life and no matter what you always have discipline.."

Student response: "TK" age 16
It benefits them because when I started meditating it made me calm. I keep my breathing regulation And after I feel nice and calm. Also you would like to have a bowl because when you ring it it makes a chill sound ...and you feel like meditating..."

Conclusion

The data presented above It is clear that both the guided meditations and the 1-minute moment are effective to address anxiety and stress with young men who are incarcerated. The group setting provides an effective domain for the "1-minute moment" and despite group dynamics, it was received by nearly all students present and the vast majority of students participated. The positive results are expressed through student short answer responses and survey results as indicated by the percentages above. In the group setting, students choose to participate amongst their peers during the "1 minute moment" and in their reflections, they expand on the many benefits of the exercise. In their own words, they write that it helps them "deal with" issues, "calm anger," "cope with" and "control" or "manage" emotions. In the journal responses, they also use phrases such as "nice and calm," "staying focused," etc...Based on my own 3 year experience, guided meditations are not effective in a group setting and can lead to hostility or ongoing distraction. Guided meditations, however, did prove to be effective in the one on one setting as demonstrated in the above statistics. One on one sessions prove to be the ideal setting for gaining feedback about mindful meditation, most likely due to social factors, but those sessions are not conclusive as far as being more relevant in therapeutic value. In the group experiment, the groups showed promising results that revealed an effect of meditation over time (on focus, anger and anxiety) and student voice showed unquestionable favor toward both forms of meditation.

A CULTURAL GLOSSARY

bolh—another male

chichi—a meal made from some type of chips/Cheetos/hot fries crushed up with noodles

pickled—locked up

niz—no

oowops—rolling two Philly blunts into one

squader—old car

throwin' shade—devaluing something or somebody

the cuts—homeless people

caught a body—killed somebody

I don't want no smoke—I don't want trouble

sliz—slick or crafty

gliz—gun or firearm

nut—someone who is corny or crazy

bussin—talking

slide—to leave

scat—run, being afraid

blown—angry

knot—a wad of money

jam—robbery, to be stuck or trapped

joe—not cool

gettin greasy— getting nasty, low-down or dirty

cheekin—not swallowing meds and reselling or trading them

in his biscuit—in his face

real rap—truth or agreeance

fall back—back off

on his bumper—tailing his ass, watching

in his bag—emotional/pissed

ten toes—ready/solid

outta pocket—crazy

thurl—good, dependable or admirable

sturdy—strong/durable

rubber room—lock down room

slime—buddy, bro, dude

trenches— the hood, north Philly

da bottom—neighborhood in west/southwest Philly

from the rip—from the beginning

brickin—staring at someone

knucklin/lockin up/drinkin/rumblin—fist fighting

keep it a bean—be honest

skinny—fast, good runner

da plat—area of Fairmont park near Belmont Ave

stringy—tough, a fighter

I'm fried—I'm too high/out of it, to follow this

smoked—killed by gunfire

parked—layed out, shot or knocked out

no cap—I'm not kidding

real rap—that/they speak the truth

tip on you—jump you

drawn'—getting upset or acting out; (drawing to shoot)

OG/Old head—cool older dude

yungbohl—younger male

sachio—kingpin or pimp

mugga—money

kenso—a poor white person from Kensington

bleo—hollowed out Philly blunt

dime jawn—pipe for smoking

K & A—Kensington and Allegheny Ave

B'jawn—any person, place or thing in the universe

JUVENILE JUSTICE STATS

On a given day, 53,000 youth are held as a result of a crime. Furthermore, a study in 2011 showed that facilities do not reduce offending levels, but raise them.
[prisonpolicy.org/reports/youth2018]

Trauma stats
[www.recognizetrauma.org]

60% of adults report experiencing abuse or other difficult family circumstances during childhood.

26% of children in the United States will witness or experience a traumatic event before they turn four. (1)

Four of every 10 children in American say they experienced a physical assault during the past year, with one in 10 receiving an assault-related injury. (2)

2% of all children experienced sexual assault or sexual abuse during the past year, with the rate at nearly 11% for girls aged 14 to 17. (2)

Nearly **14%** of children repeatedly experienced maltreatment by a caregiver, including nearly 4% who experienced physical abuse. (2)

1 in 4 children was the victim of robbery, vandalism or theft during the previous year. (2)

More than **13%** of children reported being physically bullied, while more than 1 in 3 said they had been emotionally bullied. (2)

1 in 5 children witnessed violence in their family or the neighborhood during the previous year. (2)

In one year, **39%** of children between the ages of 12 and 17 reported witnessing violence, 17% reported being a victim of physical assault and **8%** reported being the victim of sexual assault. (3)

More than 60% of youth age 17 and younger have been exposed to crime, violence and abuse either directly or indirectly. (4)

More than 10% of youth age 17 and younger reported five or more exposures to violence. (4)

About 10% of children suffered from child maltreatment, were injured in an assault, or witnessed a family member assault another family member. (4)

About 25% of youth age 17 and younger were victims of robbery or witnessed a violent act. (4)

Nearly half of children and adolescents were assaulted at least once in the past year. (4)

Among 536 elementary and middle school children surveyed in an inner city community, **30%** had witnessed a stabbing and **26%** had witnessed a shooting. (5)

Young children exposed to five or more significant adverse experiences in the first three years of childhood face a **76%** likelihood of having one or more delays in their language, emotional or brain development. (6)

As the number of traumatic events experienced during childhood increases, the risk for the following health problems in adulthood increases: depression; alcoholism; drug abuse; suicide attempts; heart and liver diseases; pregnancy problems; high stress; uncontrollable anger; and family, financial, and job problems. (6)

People who have experienced trauma are:

- **15 times** more likely to attempt suicide
- **4 times** more likely to become an alcoholic
- **4 times** more likely to develop a sexually transmitted disease
- **4 times** more likely to inject drugs
- **3 times** more likely to use antidepressant medication
- **3 times** more likely to be absent from work
- **3 times** more likely to experience depression
- **3 times** more likely to have serious job problems
- **2.5 times** more likely to smoke
- **2 times** more likely to develop chronic obstructive pulmonary disease
- **2 times** more likely to have a serious financial problem

ABOUT ATMOSPHERE PRESS

Atmosphere Press is an independent, full-service publisher for excellent books in all genres and for all audiences. Learn more about what we do at atmospherepress.com.

We encourage you to check out some of Atmosphere's latest releases, which are available at Amazon.com and via order from your local bookstore:

The Great Unfixables, by Neil Taylor

Soused at the Manor House, by Brian Crawford

Portal or Hole: Meditations on Art, Religion, Race And The Pandemic, by Pamela M. Connell

A Walk Through the Wilderness, by Dan Conger

The House at 104: Memoir of a Childhood, by Anne Hegnauer

A Short History of Newton Hall, Chester, by Chris Fozzard

Serial Love: When Happily Ever After... Isn't, by Kathy Kay

Sit-Ins, Drive-Ins and Uncle Sam, by Bill Slawter

Black Water and Tulips, by Sara Mansfield Taber

Ghosted: Dating & Other Paramoural Experiences, by Jana Eisenstein

Walking with Fay: My Mother's Uncharted Path into Dementia, by Carolyn Testa

FLAWED HOUSES of FOUR SEASONS, by James Morris

Word for New Weddings, by David Glusker and Thom Blackstone

It's Really All about Collaboration and Creativity! A Textbook and Self-Study Guide for the Instrumental Music Ensemble Conductor, by John F. Colson

A Life of Obstructions, by Rob Penfield

ABOUT THE AUTHOR

ERIC D. BISECA was raised by his loving father, a warrior and schoolteacher, and mother, an artist and healer, while surrounded by a wealth of family and friends. As a young seeker, he studied social science, spirit science, meditation, and martial arts. As a teacher and healer of nearly twenty years, he has influenced the lives of many in the areas of Pittsburgh, Philadelphia, Washington, D.C., and beyond. He has recently earned his naturopath degree from the DaVinci School of Natural medicine in Larnaca, Cyprus. Biseca has spent considerable time in Brazil, Italy/Sicily, South Africa, Cuba, Ireland, Egypt and most recently Jamaica, where he now offers services as a practitioner focusing on immuno-respiratory and anxiety related disorders. He is the proud uncle of Mia, Quinton, and Claire and brother of Dina and Thomas. A brother of all races and creeds, Dr. Biseca is committed to the struggle for sovereignty and collective healing of humanity through consciousness.

He can be contacted at **techseca23@gmail.com**.

CPSIA information can be obtained
at www.ICGtesting.com
Printed in the USA
BVHW072211310123
657545BV00002B/38